By the same author

The New Frugality: How to Consume Less, Save More, and Live Better

Unretirement

How Baby Boomers Are Changing the Way We Think About Work, Community, and the Good Life

Chris Farrell

BLOOMSBURY PRESS

NEW YORK · LONDON · NEW DELHI · SYDNEY

Published by Bloomsbury Press, New York

Bloomsbury is a trademark of Bloomsbury Publishing Plc

All papers used by Bloomsbury Press are natural, recyclable products made
from wood grown in well-managed forests. The manufacturing processes
conform to the environmental regulations of the country of origin.

LIBRARY OF CONGRESS CATALOGING-IN-PUBLICATION DATA HAS BEEN APPLIED FOR.

ISBN: 978-1-62040-157-6

First U.S. edition 2014

3   5   7   9   10   8   6   4

Typeset by Hewer Text UK Ltd, Edinburgh
Printed and bound in the U.S.A. by Thomson-Shore, Inc. Dexter, Michigan

Bloomsbury Press books may be purchased for business or promotional
use. For information on bulk purchases please contact Macmillan Corporate
and Premium Sales Department at specialmarkets@macmillan.com.

For Peter and Connor
with love, always

Contents

Preface

WHEN I WAS IN ELEMENTARY SCHOOL, three remarkable women hovered in the background of my family: Aunt Julia, Aunt Agnes, and Aunt Ella. They were nuns with the Sisters of Charity, New York, an order of educators dedicated to helping disadvantaged children, many of them abandoned. I vividly remember their voluminous black habits and black caps, Irish-tinged New York accents, and their eagerness to know what my brother and sisters and I were up to, even when we were very young. They always had a treat for us, a peppermint ball or some other hard candy. They were fun and a little mysterious. After all, they were nuns.

Aunt Ella—Sister Marie Lucille Farrell—stood out. She was kind, smart, and carried herself with authority. She had a remarkable career, including running an orphanage during the Second World War, working at New York Foundling for abandoned children, teaching at the College of Mount Saint Vincent, and establishing Catholic girls' schools on Long Island.

The last time I saw Aunt Ella was at the Convent of Mary the Queen, a home for aging nuns in Yonkers. We covered many topics while we walked the corridors. Family. Current events. Education. Poverty. What has stayed with me from the visit is when she signaled it was time to leave. "I have to go now to take care of the elderly," she said. "There's work to be done."

She was ninety-six years old.

CHAPTER 1

Work Long and Prosper

Let me see what you got
We can have a whoopin' good time
　　　　　　　　　　　—Bob Dylan

TWO TITANS OF THE NEW DEAL were Harry Hopkins and Henry Morgenthau Jr. Hopkins was head of the Federal Emergency Relief Administration and a close confidant of President Franklin D. Roosevelt. Morgenthau was Roosevelt's longtime friend and U.S. treasury secretary.

In *History of Retirement*, historian William Graebner relays the minutes from a phone conversation between them. Hopkins was sick at home. The two New Dealers were on the committee charged by Roosevelt with designing Social Security, the landmark safety net for the elderly signed into law in 1935. At one point their conversation turns to concerns over the swelling numbers of old people in decades to come, relays Graebner.

> MORGENTHAU: Well, I've gotten a very good analysis of this thing . . . I'm simply going to point out the danger spots and it's up to somebody else to say whether they want to do it. I'm not trying to say what they should do—I want to show them the bad curves.

HOPKINS: I wish I was going to be there.
MORGENTHAU: I wish you were too.
HOPKINS: That old age thing is a bad curve.

I thought about the demographics of the "bad curve" while at the annual meeting of the Gerontological Society of America in 2012. More than thirty-six hundred researchers on old age from more than thirty countries had gathered in San Diego to share their findings. I wandered in and out of sessions and talked to participants during breaks. I sat in on talks titled "Older Adult Functions: Risks, Impairments, and Interventions," "Managing Chronic Disease," "Transportation and Mobility: Avoiding Withdrawal and Isolation," "Caring for Persons with Dementia," and "Adult Protection and Elder Abuse."

Dementia. Loneliness. Abuse. Talk about a bad curve! After three days of presentations I couldn't stop replaying in my mind the Rolling Stones lyric, "What a drag it is getting old."

The Stones' gloomy viewpoint is widely shared in America. Since most of us are neither gerontologists nor demographers steeped in the data of aging we can't rattle off the numbers. But we know the message: The U.S. population is getting older. Americans are living longer on average and we're having fewer children. The leading edge of the baby boom generation—approximately 76 million born between 1946 and 1964—is filing for Social Security and Medicare benefits. According to Pew Research, roughly ten thousand boomers are turning sixty-five every day, a pace that will continue until 2030. The graying of America is a media staple, usually accompanied by dire headlines like DEMOGRAPHIC CRISIS and LOOMING CATASTROPHE. Academic scholars and think tank experts routinely issue alarming reports highlighting a wide range of negative economic and social effects from an aging America.

The numbers are striking. Demographers estimate that more than 20 percent of the U.S. population or nearly 81 million will be sixty-five and over in 2030. That's up from almost 42 million or 13 percent in 2012, according to the Census Bureau. The projected sixty-five-plus population in 2030 is almost equivalent to the current residents of New York,

California, and Texas combined. Imagine the Golden State, the Empire State, and the Lone Star State as nothing but giant retirement communities. You'd walk around New York City, Buffalo, and Syracuse, drive all over San Diego, Los Angeles, and San Francisco, visit Dallas, Houston, and Austin and see nothing but people sixty-five and older. Instead of the infamous "mom gangs" hogging the sidewalks with their strollers in Brooklyn's Park Slope neighborhood, maybe an "elderly mafia" would take over the sidewalks with their walkers. The bike lane on the Golden Gate Bridge could become the wheelchair lane. Bars and restaurants during South by Southwest (SXSW) in Austin would focus on promoting their early bird specials.

Demographic projections unfold over decades, and a sense of impending gloom has long informed the national conversation about an aging population. But now the country's long-anticipated date of reckoning with older boomers is here. A landmark moment came in 2008 when Kathleen Casey-Kirschling—proclaimed by the press as the nation's first boomer because she was born one second after midnight on January 1, 1946—started receiving Social Security benefits. Boomers have gone from "forever young" to "forever old," write Laurence Kotlikoff and Scott Burns in *The Coming Generational Storm*. "The aging of America isn't a temporary event," they add. "We are well into a change that is permanent, irreversible, and very long term."

The specter of an aging population haunts America. Our public discourse is along the lines of fear and loathing (paraphrasing gonzo writer and baby boom legend Hunter S. Thompson).

What's behind the sense of a demographically driven apocalypse? Why does the emerging portrait of old age in America spawn so many dire screeds? The elderly have always been with us—to state the obvious—and opinions about older Americans have varied through the ages, sometimes weighted more toward the positive and at other times slanting toward the negative. The seventeenth-century American poet Anne Bradstreet wrote about the four stages of man—childhood, youth, middle age, and old age. The last was a time of wisdom, when "al gave ear to what he had to say," she wrote in *The Tenth Muse*. If Henry David Thoreau read that line, Bradstreet's sentiment would have filled the nineteenth-century American thinker with disgust. "Practically, the old have no very important advice to give to the young, their experience has been so partial, and their lives such miserable failures for private reasons, as they must believe," he wrote in *Walden*.

"Wait a minute, Thoreau," I imagine George Dawson saying. The grandson of slaves, Dawson was born in Texas in 1889. In *Life Is So Good*, published in 2000, the 101-year-old Dawson tells of working on farms, breaking horses, building levees, raising children and grandchildren, living with racism, and learning to read at ninety-eight years old. Elementary school teacher Richard Glaubman was Dawson's scribe. Glaubman remarks to Dawson at the book's end, "You've accomplished a lot." Dawson replied, "That's right. Yet, judge me not for the deeds that I have done, but for the life I've lived. Son, people think one hundred years is a long time. Most folks just don't understand. My life hasn't been so long at all; seems short to me. It's all gone by so fast. Life is so good and it gets better every day."

What fuels widespread fears at this moment isn't aging. It's retirement, a relatively new lifestyle for elder Americans. The shared expectation that most senior citizens will withdraw from the work force in their early sixties, yet still enjoy a comfortable standard of living and a life of leisure is a post–World War II phenomenon. The catchphrase "America can't afford to grow old" that echoes from Senate hearing rooms to neighborhood conversations is really a statement that "seniors can't afford retirement, let alone a decent retirement." Rather than savor the good life during their elder years, popular discussions concentrate on how near-and-future retirees of America face the prospect of eking out an existence like a "battered kettle at the heel" in William Butler Yeats's bleak image.

The disturbing economic and social picture of an aging population hurtling toward an inevitable decline in lifestyle and comfort draws on a handful of trends. The timing of the worst downturn since the 1930s was terrible for older workers. The economy tanked when boomers should have been enjoying their peak earnings and savings years. Instead, many employed boomers (along with every other worker) struggled to get by without a raise. Those were the lucky ones. Millions were handed pink slips by their employers and millions more forced into part-time work. Retirement savings accounts for the average worker were less than flush before the downturn and the economic trauma only worsened the savings situation. The value of 401(k)s and IRAs dropped sharply during the great recession. Management at hard-pressed companies reduced employee benefits, including cutting or even eliminating the employer contribution into retirement savings. Remember morbid jokes about 201(k)s and 101(k)s?

The financial despair about long-term economic security deepened with the bursting of the housing bubble. A home is the largest asset owned by the average American and the prices plunged by more than a third nationwide, vaporizing some $8 trillion in wealth. The price collapse badly shook optimism in the future since owning a home has been a concrete expression of living the American Dream for a long time.

The popular image is that boomers are not only spendthrifts but are also living in denial about getting older, blithely ignoring the need to plan for their old age. Surveys repeatedly show that workers aren't engaged in preparing for retirement. The table of contents from a conference report by Stanford University's Center on Longevity— *Retirement Planning in the Age of Longevity*—captures the sense of how woefully unprepared experts believe average Americans are for the last stage of life.

Pitfall 1: Failing to Plan
Pitfall 2: Underestimating Expenses
Pitfall 3: Underestimating Years in Retirement
Pitfall 4: Retiring too Early
Pitfall 5: Failing to Save Enough

Ouch. Is this how the average aging American worker feels?

Yes, according to the twenty-fourth annual Retirement Confidence Survey from the Employee Benefit Research Institute. To be sure, the

Washington, D.C., think tank reports that confidence in retirement security had rebounded slightly from record survey lows of 2009 through 2013. Yet the increased optimism was exclusively among higher income households while 43 percent of workers surveyed in 2014 still had little to no confidence they'd saved enough for a decent retirement.

A common refrain among the prophets of penurious retirement is the belief that the rising number of old folks will drain the economy of its dynamism. The ranks of workers fifty-five and older are projected by the Bureau of Labor Statistics to rise from nearly 20 percent in 2010 to some 25 percent in 2020. The fear is the appetite for risk taking that fuels new products and new markets will diminish with a dramatically aging work force, victims of aching joints, bad backs, and faltering vision. Older workers are hardly considered stalwarts of entrepreneurial ambition and productive energy. They have a reputation for being set in their ways, unwilling to challenge the established order, little interested in the latest technologies and organizational innovations. They also consume less of the kinds of goods and services that propel economic growth. The money management firm Manning and Napier in the special report *Potential Macroeconomic Consequences of an Aging Population with Insufficient Savings* frets that "the aging of this [baby boom] generation will become a headwind to growth" as they move out of their prime spending years. *New York Times* columnist David Brooks is more emphatic and characteristically eloquent about the economic dangers of a graying America. "For decades, people took dynamism and economic growth for granted and saw population growth as a problem," he writes. "In the 21st century, the U.S. could be the slowly aging leader of a rapidly aging world."

A stark implication of a demographically driven slow-growth economy is that the gray tsunami of boomers will overwhelm the government's safety net for the elderly, or so we're repeatedly told. A shrinking number of younger workers are on the hook to support an increasing number of elderly, a state of affairs that will end badly for everyone. Robert Samuelson, the longtime economics columnist for the *Washington Post*, has repeatedly warned that government entitlements are unaffordable, thanks to the twin pincers of an aging baby boom generation and rising retirement costs. His frustration over policymaker inaction over the looming threat is a constant theme of his columns. "Meanwhile our resulting inaction compounds many future dangers of an aging society: higher taxes, slower economic growth, squeezed government spending for non-elderly programs and more conflict between younger taxpayers and older beneficiaries."

Samuelson expresses his concerns in reasonably measured tones. The same can't be said for a barrage of similar sentiments repeated with far greater alarm on cable television, talk radio, and op-ed pages. A common refrain is that the fiscal, economic, and social disaster of Mediterranean Europe—think Greece, Italy, and Spain—is the proverbial canary in America's entitlement coal mine. Social Security is a "Ponzi scheme," a "monstrous lie," and faces "imminent bankruptcy." The swelling ranks of the elderly will send Medicare (and Medicaid) costs spiraling out of control. The combination of entitlement programs and aging boomers is pushing the United States toward an unprecedented fiscal crisis.

The seemingly brutal math behind an aging population, a less dynamic economy, and soaring entitlement spending stokes forecasts of an inevitable and mean-spirited clash of generations over scarce resources. Remember the 1960s generation gap? Singer-songwriter Bob Dylan poetically captured the chasm between parents and their children in the sixties with songs such as "The Times They Are A-Changin'." Dylan's lyrics like "your sons and your daughters are beyond your command" and "the order is rapidly fadin'" resonated with a younger generation—and repelled many parents—during that tumultuous decade.

The once-rebellious boomers are now the parents and grandparents, and the new alleged generation gap with their children and grandchildren is much uglier than the music-soaked version from several decades ago. The *Economist* relabeled baby boomers "sponging boomers," an aging generation sucking up scarce economic resources and absorbing government spending, barely leaving scraps behind for the young. "The struggle to digest the swollen generation of aging baby-boomers threatens to strangle economic growth," opines the *Economist*. "As the nature and scale of the problem become clear, a showdown between the

generations may be inevitable." Boomers are "reactionary elders, cling-
ing to their power and perks at the literal expense of everyone younger,"
writes Paul Campos in *Salon*. *Esquire* fumes that the economic and political system is "rigged to serve the comfort and largesse of the old at the
expense of the young."

If Thomas Paine was America's original political pamphleteer with
his passionate call for American independence in *Common Sense*, then
Wall Street billionaire Peter G. Peterson, who insists that America faces a
fiscal crisis of old age, is his contemporary equivalent.

Peterson is a remarkable American success story. His Greek immigrant
father ran a diner in Kearney, Nebraska. The driven immigrant son quickly
climbed to the heights of the establishment. Peterson's resume is long and
impressive, including chief executive of the media equipment company
Bell and Howell from 1961 to 1971, secretary of commerce under President
Nixon in 1972, chairman and chief executive of Lehman Brothers from
1973 to 1984, and cofounder of the private equity behemoth Blackstone in
1985. A billionaire, he stepped down as senior chairman at Blackstone in
2008. Peterson is a courtly octogenarian. A longtime Republican, he culti-
vates an image of rational, reasonable bipartisanship.

He is best known outside of elite circles on Wall Street and in
Washington, D.C., for his public policy passion since the early 1980s:
entitlement reform. He launched his crusade in a 1982 *New York Review
of Books* article, "Social Security: The Coming Crash." The opening para-
graph captures the tone of his campaign. "Social Security's troubles are
fundamental. Its financial problems are not minor and temporary, as
most politicians, at least in election years, feel compelled to insist. Unless
the system is reorganized, these problems will become overwhelming,"
he writes. "To put the matter bluntly, Social Security is heading for a
crash. We cannot permit this to happen, because it would put the nation
itself in very serious jeopardy."

Peterson's many books since that essay reinforce the essence of his
crusade, with titles like *Will America Grow Up Before It Grows Old: How
the Coming Social Security Crisis Threatens You, Your Family, and Your
Country*; *Facing Up: Paying Our Nation's Debt and Saving Our Children's*

Future; and *On Borrowed Time: How the Growth in Entitlement Spending Threatens America's Future*. He has used his considerable fortune to push his agenda well beyond his writings, funding a vast ecosystem of fiscal reform advocacy groups, from the Concord Coalition to the Peter G. Peterson Foundation.

Debt! Deficit! Aging! Retirement crisis! Economic stagnation! Intergenerational warfare! Talk about a bad curve. Taken altogether, it appears an aging America is hurtling toward the dismal end of Shakespeare's *Seven Ages of Man*—"Sans teeth, sans eyes, sans taste, sans everything." No wonder people are fearful about their retirement.

Well, don't be depressed. The dire jeremiads aimed at an aging America are wrong and deeply misplaced. The graying of America is terrific news. Living longer is good. Embrace the realization that boomers on average are healthier and better educated than previous generations. An aging population presents an enormous opportunity for society and for aging individuals to seize and exploit. "Never before have so many people had so much experience and the time and the capacity to do something significant with it," writes Marc Freedman in *The Big Shift: Navigating the New Stage Beyond Midlife*. "That's the gift of longevity, the great potential payoff on all the progress we've made expanding lives."

The last third of life is being reimagined and reinvented into "unretirement." If the popular images of retirement are the golf course and the RV, the defining institutions of unretirement are the workplace and the entrepreneurial start-up. The unretirement movement builds on the insight that a better-educated, healthier work force can continue to earn an income well into the traditional retirement years. A series of broad, mutually reinforcing changes in the economy and society is making an aging work force more of an economic asset than ever before. "Many people aren't slowing down in their 60s and 70s," says Ross Levin, a certified financial planner and president of Accredited Investors in Edina, Minnesota. Adds Nicole Maestas, economist at the Rand Corporation, the Santa Monica, California–based think tank: "Yes, America has an aging population. The upside of that is a whole generation of people who are interested in anything but retirement."

Like your grandfather's vacuum-tube radio set, the image of an America debilitated by old age belongs to a different economy and society. Older workers and aging entrepreneurs will find plenty of opportunities for finding meaning and a paycheck. The desire to earn an income and to stay engaged is so powerful that the embrace of unretirement will sweep aside existing barriers to working longer. Employer stereotypes that view older workers as lacking creativity won't hold up to scrutiny. The prejudice that older workers aren't productive will be proven false. The competition for talented employees will push managers to abandon long-held hiring hurdles against aging workers. Seniors will recharge the nation's entrepreneurial energy.

The potential economic payoff from society tapping into the abilities and knowledge of large numbers of people in their sixties and seventies is enormous. The economy will expand, household finances will improve, and fears of a penurious retirement will fade. Living standards will climb and the feared fiscal strain from entitlement spending will ease. The theme of intergenerational warfare will disappear as the shared interests between the generations in a jobcentric economy take center stage. Of course, a tweak might have to be made to the famous Beatles song "When I'm Sixty-Four": "If I'm at work till quarter to ten, would you lock the door?" (The author of the song, Sir Paul McCartney, continues to enjoy a productive career well beyond his sixty-fourth birthday.)

Peter Drucker, the late philosopher of management, noted that every once in a while society crosses a major divide. "Within a few short decades, society rearranges itself—its worldview; its basic values; its social and political structure; its arts; its key institutions," wrote Drucker in *Post-Capitalist Society*. "Fifty years later there is a new world." The transformation of retirement into unretirement marks such a divide.

We're at the early stages of a long, difficult transition toward a different vision of the elder years. In the process, aging boomers will influence for the better how younger generations view their jobs, their careers, and their expectations about the mix of work and leisure, engagement and meaning, especially during the last third of life. The tantalizing promise of unretirement for younger generations is realizing they will have much more time to better merge their careers and the search for meaning, to pursue job flexibility and creative variety, over a lifetime. "Older workers are going to change the workforce as profoundly as women did," says Deborah E. Banda, senior adviser, AARP Education and Outreach. "The changes they are making in the work place will benefit all generations, not just older workers." Eugene Steuerle, economist at the Urban Institute in Washington, D.C., wholeheartedly agreed in an interview at his office: "Older workers are to the first half of the twenty-first century what women were to the last half of the twentieth century."

Welcome to unretirement, a revolution in the making.

The personal economics of unretirement are compelling. For one thing, staying on the job makes it practical to hold off filing for Social Security. The payoff from waiting is large. The earliest age for filing is age sixty-two, but Social Security benefits are more than 75 percent higher at age seventy. (There's no extra bonus past seventy.)

For another, earning an income allows older workers to continue setting aside some money into savings or, at a minimum, not to tap their retirement savings. It means that the low levels of retirement savings of many workers will have time to grow into more adequate sums. The impact of working longer on 401(k)s and other retirement savings plans is striking. For instance, the standard personal finance advice is to begin saving for retirement early in a career. Starting young allows savings to build up by harnessing the power of compound interest, which Albert Einstein is said to have called the "most powerful force in the universe."

The median earner with a 401(k) and IRA who starts saving at age twenty-five rather than age forty-five can reduce their annual required savings rate for an adequate retirement income by about two thirds, calculates the Center for Retirement Research at Boston College in *How Important Is Asset Allocation to Financial Security in Retirement?* (The benchmark for how much you'll need to maintain the same standard of living before retirement while you're in retirement is an income replacement rate of 80 percent. Most experts assume the typical retired household needs less than 100 percent of their preretirement income since they don't have the typical expenses associated with a job, such as work clothes and take-out meals.)

Sad to say, you can't be twenty-five again if you're in your forties, fifties, and sixties. You can't go back in time. However, if median earners delay retirement from age sixty-two to age seventy, they can also reduce their required savings rate by some two thirds. Last, holding off the day of retirement means seniors have to support themselves off their savings for a shorter period of time.

A suggestive illustration of the financial power of waiting was created by Robert Shackleton of the Congressional Budget Office in 2003. He assumed a married couple in their early sixties earning a household income of $100,000 pretax annually. They'll need nearly $66,000 a year after taxes to replace 80 percent of their preretirement income. If both retire at age sixty-two, they would have received more than $25,000 in annual total Social Security benefits. They would need a portfolio of at least $891,000 to generate the income they wanted to live in comfort for their normal life expectancy. But if the couple waited until age sixty-six to retire, their Social Security benefits go up and the time they need to live off savings shrinks. In that case, $552,000 in savings is enough to ensure their lifestyle. Retire at age seventy? A portfolio worth some $263,000 will do the trick.[1]

Earning an income—even a slim paycheck—will put a majority of boomers on a reasonable path toward a decent retirement. The Center for Retirement Research figures that fewer than half of American workers are on a savings path for a comfortable retirement if they say good-bye to their colleagues for the last time at age sixty-five. It's a sobering statistic. But if workers wait until age seventy—only five years—to leave the work force, 86 percent should be financially secure. Much better. Here's another example, this one from the blue-chip consulting firm McKinsey and Company in 2008. The consultants figure that approximately two thirds of boomers ages fifty-four to sixty-three are financially unprepared for retirement. That is, they haven't accumulated sufficient assets to maintain their lifestyle—defined as 80 percent of their preretirement spending—when they leave the work force. However, if older boomers work long enough to raise the median retirement age from its current 62.6 years to 64.1 years, by 2015 the number of unprepared households is halved—from 62 percent to 31 percent. That is a dramatic illustration of how working longer changes prospects for comfortable living standards in retirement (although I'd like to see an even lower number of the potentially unprepared). An added bonus from the McKinsey calculation in *Talkin' 'Bout My Generation: The Economic Impact of Aging US Baby Boomers*: The additional work years would boost the economy by an estimated $12 trillion over the next three decades. To put that $12 trillion figure in perspective, it's equivalent to one year of gross domestic product currently.

That said, not all senior citizens will be physically and mentally healthy. Not everyone is able to earn a living past, say, the first year they can currently file for Social Security, age sixty-two. While average life expectancy is up, not everyone is making gains at the same pace. There are some groups in society where life expectancy is stagnant or even down, such as white women who don't graduate from high school. The ranks of those who worked in low-paying jobs on construction sites, in a warehouse, and at a checkout counter without employer-sponsored retirement and health care benefits are vulnerable. The work-longer mantra isn't realistic for many of the working poor, the marginally employed, men and women burned out mentally and physically. The long-term unemployed are at risk since, perversely, employers steer clear of potential hires that haven't pulled down a paycheck for months let alone years. "It's also a well-established fact that the individuals most at risk in retirement are those who have an economically difficult working life—namely, households with very low incomes," says Steve Utkus, director of the Vanguard Center for Retirement Research.[2]

Disparities in work histories shouldn't stop the unretirement movement—quite the opposite. The difficult realities faced by low-income households should invigorate unretirement instead. The challenge is to create incentives to broaden work opportunities as much as possible for as many as possible while protecting the livelihood of those who cannot stay employed. The good news is that unretirement will unleash vast reservoirs of economic activity, enabling an increasingly affluent society to easily pay the bill (and increase the benefit) of Social Security and other critical safety nets, including incentives and subsidies keeping people attached to work. Economist Steuerle of the Urban Institute nicely captures the underlying dynamic of unretirement:

> If labor supply increases, the nation gets additional work and larger output. More output means more income for workers. More income means more revenue at any given tax rate. With more revenue, government can pay for more spending at the same tax rates, or lower tax rates. And that total spending can be made more progressive in aggregate. Increased labor would give policymakers the options sorely lacking in today's budget world.[3]

A clear majority of aging boomers will find it possible to continue working. By many measures, about half or more of the aging Woodstock generation should have sufficient resources for a decent standard of living in old age. They'll likely stay on the job because they enjoy their work, their colleagues, and their customers. Another quarter know they'll have to earn a W2 or 1099 income for a few extra years to boost their savings accounts. Most aging workers will have the capacity to be employed, notes Steuerle, with some 84 percent of forty-five- to sixty-four-year-olds reporting they have good to excellent health, according to the Centers for Disease Control. The comparable figure for the sixty-five to seventy-four group is 79 percent.

Occupation, work history, income, and education levels over the course of a lifetime are critical factors when evaluating prospects for unretirement. Nevertheless, everyone should be wary of stereotypes about frailty and infirmity among the less-well-off and less-educated aged. Manufacturing is a hard, physically demanding business. Clarence Long, an economist at Johns Hopkins, highlighted older factory workers in a section of *The Labor Force under Changing Income and Employment*, published in 1958. Long is skeptical about the common assumption that older workers are less efficient employees, noting that research demonstrates many notions about the inferiority of the older worker are "fanciful." In an intriguing footnote, he adds, "This writer observed in a General Motors plant in 1947 that older women were preferred by many supervisors as being more industrious and reliable than the 'bobby-soxers' and 'jitterbugs.' The plant employed many women in their fifties and even late sixties. One robust woman of 70 was doing a hard job polishing precision parts to close tolerances."

More recently, PBS *NewsHour* economics correspondent Paul Solman filed a delightful story in 2013 on Vita Needle in Needham, Massachusetts. The average age of workers at the eight-decade-old family-owned needle and tube manufacturer is seventy-four years. The oldest employee is Rosa Finnegan, age one hundred, followed by Bill Ferson, age ninety-four. Bob O'Mara, seventy-eight years old, is a "retired" engineer who has worked at Vita Needle for the past eleven years. "Retirement isn't death. It shouldn't be anyway," O'Mara told Solman. "You have all this investment in people's knowledge. Why throw it away?"

Why indeed? The focus should be on supporting the employment desires of disabled older workers and those simply slowed by the inevitable tolls of aging. After all, work is much more than an income. The factory, the office, the cubicle, the retail store, and other workplaces are communities with colleagues, cubicle mates, union brothers and sisters, and fellow employees. Birthdays are celebrated, divorces mourned, coffee shared. People at the workplace care that you show up and someone will worry if you don't. Conversation is the lifeblood of the office. The unretirement approach reflects a powerful insight from the 1990 Americans with Disabilities Act. "The Nation's proper goals regarding individuals with disabilities are to ensure equality of opportunity, full participation, independent living and economic self-sufficiency for such individuals." Yes, some older workers are more susceptible to the ravages of time than others. That doesn't mean they should be excluded from unretirement—far from it.

A dramatic turn toward unretirement is already taking place. The dominant trend for aging workers—especially men—for much of the post–World War II era was to leave the work force earlier and earlier. Yet the share of Americans working or looking for work has been on the upswing for every age group fifty-five and over for any education and income level and for both men and women since the mid-1980s to the early 1990s. The shift in behavior shows up in the income data. For example, 40 percent of those ages sixty-five to sixty-nine reported earning a wage income in 1990, according to Sara Rix, senior strategic policy adviser, AARP Public Policy Institute. The number had increased to 49 percent by 2010. A fascinating figure highlighted by Rix is that in 2012 some 1.3 million workers were seventy-five and older. It's a small number, less than 1 percent of an approximately 155 million labor force. Nevertheless, the rank of workers seventy-five and over is approximately triple what it was a generation ago, she notes.[4]

Among the most powerful, surprising currents with unretirement is the rise in senior entrepreneurship. Older people are starting businesses more than any other age group. The share of new business formation by the fifty-five- to sixty-four-year-old age group is up sharply over the past fifteen years—from 14.3 percent in 1996 to almost a quarter in 2013, according to figures compiled by the Kauffman Foundation. Older workers have a number of competitive advantages in the marketplace, such as experience, networks, and credibility. The Internet, mobile technologies, and small business software have lowered start-up costs. Older entrepreneurs tend to have greater financial resources to draw on than their younger peers. An added lure of self-employment is that it often allows for greater flexibility and control over hours worked. "A greater number of older workers may be self-employed in the future because the baby boomer cohort will reach retirement with considerably more wealth and education than prior cohorts," write Rand Corporation economists Nicole Maestas and Julie Zissimopoulos in *How Longer Work Lives Ease the Crunch of Population Aging*. Observes Elizabeth Isele, cofounder of the nonprofit Senior Entrepreneurship Works: "I have started a number of businesses in my life and I have never seen anything gain traction like senior entrepreneurship."

What will the unretirement future look like? We don't really know except it involves an aging workforce and elder entrepreneurs. There is no genuine shared vision, no common narrative for accurately capturing the future rhythms of unretirement. The power of stories is vastly under-estimated when it comes to understanding major economic trends. "Economists are tellers of stories and makers of poems," writes economic historian Deirdre McCloskey in *Storytelling in Economics.* (I've read many economic studies over the years and I'm convinced about the storytelling, but I can't buy the poetry part!) Of course, storytelling in economics and the other social sciences doesn't come close to the narrative power of F. Scott Fitzgerald's *The Great Gatsby* (beautifully capturing enduring doubts about the American Dream) or Francis Ford Coppola's *The Godfather* (insightful about basic economics). Still, the stories we tell each other at work and at home, at neighborhood gatherings and in popular culture end up creating a dominant picture, a compelling theme that shapes and reflects our desires and expectations, our savings strategies and spending habits. "Our lives are ceaselessly intertwined with narrative, with the stories that we tell," observed the savvy literary critic Peter Brook.

That is, until the evidence is overwhelming that the dominant cultural narrative is no longer realistic. At that point, scholars, public intellectuals, and others compete to devise another tale that holds sway over our imaginations and actions. "A lot of people don't want to retire and go home," observes Steve Poizner, head of EmpoweredU, an education venture capital–backed endeavor aimed at retraining older workers. "What causes the most distress is when people think they're not relevant anymore."

We're at the "get me a rewrite" moment when it comes to retirement. Boomers grew up with a relatively simple model of life's arc, a life cycle with a few major markers. You went to school. You worked hard. You retired, meaning you no longer worked and pursued a life of leisure instead. Mention the word "retirement" to your colleagues and neighbors and I bet most will think about saying good-bye to coworkers for the last time, maybe moving to a sunbelt community if you live in a cold state, traveling to places you never had the time to visit while employed, reading books that stacked up on the night table over the years, hitting the links in the morning, and enjoying a home-cooked meal at night. That's the vision, at least.

The unretirement plot points are very different. The central institution of the new retirement is the workplace and the entrepreneurial start-up. What does that mean in practice? Ask your friends. What do they say? You'll get a variety of answers. Many people are stumbling about, trying to forge different work paths in their older years. The efforts range from sticking with their full-time job, starting an enterprise, joining a nonprofit, embracing part-time work, signing up for short-term contracts, and finding a bridge job. The efforts aren't always rewarded, with some managing at best to pick up a task here and there in the underground economy while others feeling invisible to employers, eventually filing for Social Security to bring in at least some money every month. An aging work force is trying out a mix of activities, sometimes by choice, other times to pay the bills, and usually a mix of the two. "People tend to think of paid work as meaningful work," says Jan Hively, an octogenarian social entrepreneur. "It could be working out of the home for fewer hours, but they'll want something for it."

In other words, we're living though a period of experimentation. Far too much of the conversation about aging ignores how much grassroots innovation is directed at the challenge. In cities, suburbs, and towns around the country, stories are accumulating about the experiences of older workers, the good, the bad, and the gray area in-between. We're witnessing the birth of a new business, the unretirement industry. "People tend to learn from examples or stories handed down from previous generations—but there are few stories to navigate the new context of old age and retirement for the baby boomers," writes Joseph Coughlin, the infectiously enthusiastic head of MIT's AgeLab, a multidisciplinary center. "When there are no set rules—you make them up. The future of old age and retirement will be improvised."

The history of innovation suggests that many large-scale transformations often start small. The Google cofounders weren't out to change the world and build one of the most powerful start-up companies when they were graduate students at Stanford University. They wanted to build a better online search engine for library books. "You start small and you learn through the process," says Peter Sims, author of *Little Bets*. "This is what creativity and innovation is all about." This is what the search for redefining aging and reimagining retirement in America is all about.

The social and economic impact of the unretirement improv act will extend far beyond signs of older workers earning an income in their later years. The transformation will ripple throughout society, inspiring changes we can't even imagine. Major innovations have a way of upending expectations and creating new institutions. Consider the automobile. The car was invented in the late nineteenth and early twentieth centuries. The car directly or indirectly played a role in the spread of consumer installment credit, auto insurance, the suburbs, a national highway system, motels, drive-ins, and shopping malls. Cars swiftly became part of American culture. "Each grand change brings into being a whole new world," writes the late historian Daniel Boorstin in the essay "Two Kinds of Revolutions." "But we can't forecast the rules of any particular new world until after it has been discovered."

The same insight operated on a smaller scale at Continuum, a global design consultancy firm founded by Gianfranco Zaccai. The headquarters are in Newton, Massachusetts, outside Boston. I was shown around by Harry West, a former professor of mechanical engineering at MIT and the company's chief executive from 2009 to 2013. (West is now senior partner at Prophet, a strategic brand and marketing consultancy.) Continuum is known for developing the Reebok pump sneaker, the red plastic shopping carts at Target, and the Swiffer for Procter & Gamble.

These days, much of its business is bringing its product-based design sensibility into the service sector and information businesses. For the Spanish bank BBVA, one of the largest banks in the world, Continuum created a customer-centric bank. The floor desks and seating arrangements were rethought to have the customer and the bank adviser look at the same computer screen and information rather than the traditional manner with a staffer viewing the information and the customer staring at the back of the computer. It's a simple change. Not much at first glance. "But that change ripples through the entire bank," says West. "You have to change how you sell, your pricing structure, your information technology, and your interaction—your interface. Once you think it through you have to change pretty much everything in that world."

The rise of unretirement will call for a whole cluster of changes in how society rewards work, creates jobs, shares the wealth, and deals with old age. Unretirement will affect where Americans live in their elder years and the definition of a good community. The movement will influence the personal finance business, shifting the discussion from an emphasis on portfolio construction and asset allocation to a focus on enhancing skills and nurturing networks over a lifetime. Colleges, universities, and other educational institutions will devote greater resources and more time to teaching older workers in addition to their classic market of students ages eighteen to twenty-four.

Companies will overhaul their employee benefits to take into account an aging work force, especially the commonly expressed desire for flexibility, a change in corporate practices that should appeal to employees of all ages. Part-time work, contract work, and other flexible work practices will expand in all sectors of the economy—private, public, and nonprofit. Federal, state, and local governments will confront rising pressure to redesign the social safety net with these flexible work practices in mind while designing incentives targeted at increasing the ranks of elder workers. Younger workers will learn from their elders to embrace more transitions throughout the arc of their careers, realizing the prospect of unretirement not only allows but also encourages exploring multiple opportunities. New organizations and new markets, new financial products and health care services will emerge and evolve to cater to the growing ranks of the unretired. All this is only a hint of what is possible.

Unretirement isn't a panacea, however. The goal of paid employment for a few years past conventional expectations isn't a magical elixir that solves all of society's ills. America's system of public and private insurance for financing long-term care for the frail elderly is failing badly. Dementia is a cruel disease and the elderly are vulnerable to its ravages. Management will continue to outsource good jobs in a global economy, putting downward pressure on wages and compensation. The business cycle hasn't been repealed and the unemployment rate will jump during the next downturn. America's education system is letting down too many young students for the world of modern work. It's also distressing to know that the kinds of legislative and institutional reforms called for by unretirement will come slowly, considering the deep divisions and partisan vitriol in Washington, D.C., and the rest of the nation. Still, older workers aren't waiting. They're moving ahead.

Who are the unretired, the leading edge of the senior revolution in expectations about the last third of life? For the moment, the core age group for unretirement is somewhere between fifty-five and seventy-five years old. However, since there are enough exceptions on either side of this guideline, for the purposes of this book the age group for unretirement ranges between fifty and eighty years of age. Of course, age fifty isn't old at all, but unfortunately many laid-off workers have learned the hard way that far too often employers consider them too old to hire. So, we'll keep them in the pool. Age eighty is pushing the unretirement age envelope since these "mature seniors" typically start experiencing greater health setbacks. But the stories of those in their eighties who stay on the job are inspiring. The long-term trend suggests working well into the seventies will become increasingly routine and practical. My own guess is that the average age of retirement over the next quarter century or so will rise to seventy.

The promise of unretirement is that it creates the income, the wealth, the entrepreneurial engagement, and the workplace transformation for dealing with our most troubling economic and social issues. Forget gloomy forecasts. Aging workers are in the vanguard of change and hope. Unretirement is an opportunity to seize. "If the past has been breaking the barriers of race and gender I think the next move is breaking down the barriers of age," says Continuum's founder Zaccai. "It will have a lot of implications." Yes, unretirement will transform society—and for the better.

CHAPTER 2

A Cause for Celebration

Talkin' 'bout sweet seasons
Talkin' 'bout sweet, sweet, sweet seasons
—Carole King

AMERICANS HAVE ALWAYS ADMIRED WORK. From farmers in the early republic to nineteenth-century immigrant factory workers to information age software programmers, we look up to people who work to pay their bills and get ahead.

The American historian Gordon Wood highlighted in *The Radicalism of the American Revolution* how nineteenth-century foreign visitors like Alexis de Tocqueville and Michel Chevalier were struck by the emphasis on work in America. Only in America, writes Wood, had labor lost its traditional association with meanness and become respectable. In the twenty-first century many people still put in long hours on the job and work is admired and valued. "Work has always meant for Americans, what you do is what you are," says Carole Haber, historian of retirement and dean of the School of Liberal Arts at Tulane University in New Orleans. The poet Marge Piercy captures the sense of why work matters in "To be of use." Here are a few lines drawn from the poem.

> The work of the world is common as mud
> Botched, it smears the hands, crumbles to dust.
> But the thing worth doing well done
> has a shape that satisfies, clean and evident.

Work isn't easy. Neither is staying employed. Most of us have gone through spells of unemployment, been involuntarily pushed into working part-time, or stuck with a job we disliked because we needed the paycheck. We've watched colleagues get laid off and wondered if we were next. The late Studs Terkel in his oral history of working life from the early 1970s wonderfully describes the hardships, the humiliations, the disappointments, and the setbacks many people suffer in their daily labors. Yet Terkel also stresses the dignity and pride in work, the sense of community and connections, as well as the desire for more from work, for a measure of worth and purpose. Americans turned the workplace into a vibrant social hub. "It is about a search, too, for daily meaning as well as daily bread, for recognition as well as cash, for astonishment rather than torpor," he writes in *Working*. People want their work to offer greater meaning than "the reward of a paycheck," he adds. The emotional and psychological rewards to work have taken deep roots in our culture, especially among aging boomers. Culture is shorthand for the rhythms and discussions that shape our beliefs and customs, expectations and aspirations, sense of right and wrong. These days, the cultural message is highlighting engagement of elders. Think of the popularity of some of the musical giants. Neil Young, Bob Dylan, Bonnie Raitt, Smokey Robinson, Stevie Wonder, Los Lobos, Herbie Hancock, the Rolling Stones, and Tony Bennett are a mere handful of names that could be drawn from a much longer list.

We appreciate and celebrate aging icons who remain productive, elders still pursuing their creative ambitions. They're part of the unretirement conversation. Neil Young's 2012 *Psychedelic Pill* album (his second that year) with his longtime band Crazy Horse had eight new songs. Bruce Springsteen's recent songs showcase a powerful artist in his sixties acknowledging hardship and dark moments while still celebrating life. Bob Dylan has been a musical force for fifty-plus years and he is still writing and touring, pursuing his art and new audiences. "What has kept him in the game is his perseverance, his work ethic, his passion for doing the work, his competitiveness, and his ability to convert defeats into victories," writes Jon Friedman in *Forget About Today*, an idiosyncratic book drawing everyday life lessons about reinvention and rejuvenation from Dylan's life. "In other words, Dylan can serve as a role model in any walk of life."

So can Mick Jagger of the Rolling Stones. The band's lead singer famously remarked during a 1975 interview when he was in his early thirties that he'd "rather be dead than sing 'Satisfaction' when I'm 45." Really? Jagger is still singing "Satisfaction" in his seventies to huge audiences as the Stones fill arenas with their 50 and Counting tour. The famed rock duo of Jagger and Keith Richards have slowed down their music production, but they still occasionally release new songs.

The role models of engaged aging aren't limited to musicians. Moviemakers are producing films with the elderly at the narrative heart of the story. Bruce Willis has humorously turned his aging to his advantage with the latest installments of the *Die Hard* franchise and, along with elder costars Helen Mirren, John Malkovich, and other peers, in *Red* and *Red 2*. (Red stands for "Retired, extremely dangerous," an apt description of the retired but still lethal CIA agents.) *Stand Up Guys* stars movie legends Al Pacino, Christopher Walken, and Alan Arkin as geriatric mobsters. Other films are more nuanced and ambitious in their portrayals. *Hope Springs* pictures a longtime married couple played by Meryl Streep and Tommy Lee Jones trying to revive their marriage, including their sex lives. *Amour* is a love story between two retired teachers in their eighties. *Nebraska* stars a grizzled Bruce Dern playing an elderly, hard-drinking Midwesterner who goes on a road trip with his middle-aged son to claim a sweepstakes jackpot he falsely believes he won.

Artists are proud of their creative longevity. Their craft defines them. Comedian Jerry Seinfeld started working in clubs in 1975. His eponymous sitcom was one of the most successful television shows ever. At fifty-eight years old, despite enormous wealth, Seinfeld is still working the comedy club circuit, coming up with new material, performing about two shows a week. He intends to do stand-up comedy "into my 80s, and beyond," according to a *New York Times Magazine* profile. Bill Cosby has almost reached that marker. The seventy-six-year-old comic legend and recent social activist performs on stages and gives talks in churches around the country.

Strikingly, a strong work ethic shapes the worldview of the modern wealthy. In an earlier era, say, the Gilded Age chronicled by novelist Edith Wharton, the children of the rich played hard on estates in Newport, Long Island, and other tony enclaves. The adult children of the rich indulged in lives defined by "conspicuous consumption," in Thorstein Veblen's acerbic phrase. They partied plenty, attended the opera, indulged in long trips to Europe, and spent small fortunes flaunting the latest fashions. The pursuit of leisure and the studious avoidance of work signaled their superior status in an era when everyone else put in long hours on the job and vacations were an unaffordable luxury for the average worker.

Today, the adult children of the wealthy work, with young scions often putting in long hours in the office. Yes, the young wealthy are different from the rest of us with multiple homes, nannies, private jets, and membership in exclusive clubs. They still party hard at exclusive enclaves. But the adult children of the one percenters are mostly raised to value work and philanthropy. Work is a status symbol. For instance, Hank and Doug Meijer grew up in a wealthy household. Their father, Frederik, built Meijer into the Midwest's largest family-run grocery store chain from 1964 to 1990. Even on a penurious allowance they would never need to work a day of their lives. The sons took over the business in 1990 and continued to expand the food empire, landing at number sixty-nine on the Forbes list of wealthiest Americans with a net worth of $4.9 billion. There are plenty of Meijer-like children throughout America's 1 percent to 0.1 percent. Richard Bookstaber, a longtime Wall Street financier, captured the value of work among the wealthy and their children: "If someone gave you the advice, 'If you want to show that you are better than everyone else, then hang around obviously doing nothing productive, and even better, waste resources,' you would think they were utterly pathetic." He's right.

Many older successful people are role models for an aging America. The sexagenarian Hillary Clinton was a powerful secretary of state during the first Obama administration and her supporters harbor hopes that she'll run for the White House in 2016. The octogenarian Warren Buffett, the stock-picking Oracle of Omaha, continues his sterling investment record. Muriel Siebert, the first woman to own a seat on the New York Stock Exchange, ran her eponymous Wall Street brokerage until only a few weeks before passing away in 2013 at age eighty-four.

Equally impressive are the unretired most of us don't know unless we happen to live in their community. Even then we may never have heard of them or crossed their path. They're vital participants locally, advising entrepreneurs, investing in businesses, wielding political power, volunteering at schools, and backing worthy causes. Someone like Pat Brune of Kansas City. She retired in her late fifties in 2009 as clerk for the federal court for Western Missouri, the top administrative position. Seven days after she "retired" she was approached by the local YWCA to be interim executive director, unpaid. She agreed. Brune has subsequently served in a variety of volunteer and paid positions, including a Kansas City public library initiative aimed at taking advantage of the local Google gigabit project to link K–12 schools, public libraries, colleges, universities, and other organizations in the area digitally. She also teaches an evening class on community leadership with two other women at Donnelly College, an independent Catholic school with a mission of reaching out to underserved communities.

The average boomers' identity is wrapped up in work. Surveys by organizations such as the Employee Benefit Research Institute, the Metlife Mature Market Institute, and others routinely show a majority of those workers canvassed want and expect to stay employed during the traditional retirement years. For example, an AARP baby boomer survey from 2011 has 80 percent saying that they planned or expected to work in retirement. The participants of the 2013 Merrill Lynch Retirement Study were forty-five years and older. Seven out of ten of these preretirees responded that they would like to include some work in their retirement years.

Among the work-more-years crowd is Stephen Shepard, a longtime magazine editor and, for many years, my boss. He was editor in chief of *Businessweek* magazine (now *Bloomberg Businessweek*) from 1984 to 2005. In his recent autobiography, *Deadlines and Disruption*, Shepard tells that when it came time for him to retire, he got an intriguing job offer: Establish a new graduate school of journalism at his alma mater, City University of New York. Nice work, if you can get it. Still, he had his doubts. "If journalism is a young person's game, then surely starting a new school at age 65 seemed foolhardy," writes Shepard. "Yes, I was in good shape and had plenty of energy. But 65?"

A dinner with Leonard Nimoy changed his mind. Yes, that Leonard Nimoy, Mr. Spock of *Star Trek*. Nimoy, age seventy-four at the time, was semiretired as an actor, spending most of his time on a second career as photographer. Nimoy "got right to the heart of the matter," says Shepard.

> "How old are you?"
> "I'm 65."
> "How long would you stay in this job?"
> "Probably five or six years."
> "So," came the punch line, "you'll be younger when you finish than I am now."

Shepard took the job. (To be sure, few of us are lucky enough to get our "live long and prosper" advice from Spock, a sad realization for a longtime *Star Trek* fan.) Shepard stayed on longer than six years, too, only stepping down as dean of the Graduate School of Journalism at the City University of New York at the end of 2013 at age seventy-four—the same age as Nimoy when they had their memorable dinner. Shepard remains on the faculty at the journalism school.

Far too much of the current public discussion about retirement has an either/or quality to it. You're either working or you're retired. Work or leisure. It's one or the other. However, for most aging workers it's a false choice. Many people with full-time jobs don't suddenly hand in their key card and stop working. Instead, between 50 and 60 percent of those who leave behind a full-time career move into a "bridge" job, such as part-time and contract work, according to a 2008 study by economists Joseph Quinn of Boston College, Kevin Cahill of Analysis Group, and Michael Giandrea of the Bureau of Labor Statistics. Their research focused on workers fifty-seven to sixty-two years old in 2004, known as "war babies" since they were born between 1942 and 1947. They concluded that gradual or phased unretirement is becoming normal, with 62 percent of the war baby respondents in their database moving to a bridge job compared to 58 percent of a comparable cohort in 1998. The war babies offer a first glimpse into what they call the "do-it-yourself retirement generation"— the boomers. "Our findings further reinforce the notion that for many older Americans, retirement is a *process*, not a single event," they conclude. "Only a minority of older Americans now retire all at once, with a one-time, permanent exit from the labor force."

The same scholars looked into the role self-employment plays in the retirement process in "Self-Employment Transitions among Older American Workers with Career Jobs." They found in their database that around 20 percent of men ages fifty-one to sixty-one were self-employed in 1992. Twelve years later more than one third of the same age group was self-employed—a 50-plus percent increase. Among older women the comparable self-employment figures were 10 percent in 1992 and over 15 percent in 2004. "The rise in self employment later in life is a result of a combination of factors, including the fact that self-employed workers tend to stay in the labor force longer than wage-and-salary workers and that more wage-and-salary workers switch into self employment later in life than vice versa," they write. "Older workers exhibit a great deal of flexibility in their work decisions and appear willing to take on substantial risks later in life."

Many people find that they really didn't want to retire after all. What they wanted was a long vacation. Economist Maestas of the Rand

Corporation learned that a surprising number of people simply need to make a break with their current job before they can figure out what they want to do next. The database informing the research in *Back to Work: Expectations and Realizations of Work after Retirement* has 26 percent of retirees reversing their decision and returning to work, either full time or part time. She notes that as many as 35 percent of the youngest retirees unretired. Those joining the ranks of the unretired mostly mostly made the decision because they found retirement less satisfying—more boring?—than they had expected. "Perhaps surprisingly, unfulfilled work expectations were much more common than unfulfilled leisure expectations," she wrote.

For many people, it takes time to figure out a right mix of activities. An unretiree-to-be wants to work, but they may also be the point person in taking a frail elderly parent to doctor appointments. Older people with grandchildren are eager to spend time with them. There are items on the proverbial "bucket list" to cross out. "Work is part of the balance, but not the only thing people are dealing with," says Karen Hostetler, director of Next Chapter in Kansas City, a community-based organization for redefining the last stage of life. "I am finding all kinds of combinations of what people are doing, and that's cool."

Luanne Mullin, age sixty, is definitely cool and she's contemplating her next act. Mullin has had a varied career. Among her jobs have been marketing for a dance company, opening her own theater company in Boston, and running a recording studio in San Francisco. She has a master's in social policy and planning and another master's in clinical psychology. Mullin works as a mediator at the University of California, San Francisco, and as a project manager at the university for the past twelve years. She oversees the construction of laboratories for scientists. When we met at a university lab near the San Francisco waterfront, she was just finishing up the task of overseeing the construction of an eight-thousand-square-foot facility. "I think there's more and more of us now that at sixty are saying, 'OK, what's my next career? What do I want to do that's fulfilling?'" she says. "I'm all for what's my next big thing. I've worked all my life and I'm kind of gearing up for the next thing."

We had a wide-ranging conversation. Eventually, I asked how she was exploring the next stage. "I think it's having a lot of extracurricular activities in addition to your job so that you allow yourself the opportunity to be in other worlds while you're building laboratories for scientists, which is what I do during the day." Mullin loves her work. She gets to interact with scientists, architects, and contractors, but she yearns for something more. The recently completed lab we met at is relatively nondescript on the outside, just another remodeled warehouse in the area. Inside, however, it's a stunning facility full of light, a futuristic environment for creative inspiration. "But it's the scientist's dream, not mine," she says, looking around. "I've helped them get there, but it hasn't been necessarily my vision. So what is my vision and how do I find it?"

She's at the early stages of thinking about creating an institute, a place for people to come together and talk about what is life after fifty. Another idea may come along, of course. Meanwhile, Mullin is wrestling with the same issues many older workers confront today. "What is this aging thing? Where do we fit in? Have I found my passion?" she wonders. "Am I living fully? Is this the second half I dreamed of, or if not, how do I pull it together at this point?"

Good questions.

Transitions are far tougher on those who left their job involuntarily. Mary White works at HIRED in its dislocated worker program in St. Paul, Minnesota. She usually has about one hundred clients, many in the over-fifty age bracket. They're scared, White says. Money is tight. They need a job and they've lost their bearings without an employer and colleagues. But even for them, White points out, this moment in their lives can offer new choices. "When I am dealing with clients I've always said, 'If you're thinking about a career change at this age, think about what you want to do in retirement,'" she says. "People like it. Instead of thinking I'm never going to find a job and I'm depressed, they start thinking about the possibilities. They start thinking, 'How can I be happy in my work?'"

That's the experience of Jacqueline Hubbard, age fifty-four. She thought she would have her job until she retired. She worked for thirty years at Dan River Mills as a customer service representative processing orders. Founded in 1882 as the Riverside Cotton Mills, Dan River was at one time the largest textile firm in the South. Like most Southern textile companies, it started to lose business to foreign competition in the 1960s. Dan River went into bankruptcy in 2004, emerging a year later. The company was purchased in 2006 by Gujarat Heavy Chemicals, an Indian chemical firm that moved some eleven hundred jobs overseas. Hubbard got her pink slip in 2008, the year the company's smokestacks were taken down by implosion. "We were warned, but I always thought something would come through to save us," she recalls. "I couldn't go home and sit down. I had to help my husband to support the family. I'm a productive person, and I wanted to do something with myself."

Hubbard and her husband, Carl, have two children and an eight-year-old grandson living with them. Carl is the sole proprietor of a body shop. Hubbard loves children, so she decided to get her associate's degree in early childhood education. The thought of going back to school at her age was nerve-racking. She went anyway to nearby Danville Community College, the oldest student in her early childhood education program. "When you lose your job, you wake up and look around and think, 'What am I going to do?'" she says. "You have to do something to keep going and the only way is through education."

She went on unemployment insurance while she was going to school. She got financial assistance from Pathways for Success, a program that helps displaced workers fund their retraining. Since she was a dislocated worker from foreign competition the federal government picked up her community college tuition tab. Hubbard is now an assistant teacher in a local Head Start program. Her income is equivalent to what she earned at the mill. She's now working on her BA to become a full-fledged teacher.

Debbie Nowak didn't see the layoff coming. She worked for thirty years and three months for Evangelical Lutheran Church in America (ELCA). Nowak was in customer relations in its pensions and benefits department. She liked talking to people over the phone about their benefits. In November 2011 she was laid off. "The layoff was a total surprise," says Nowak. "I was naïve enough to think thirty years counted for something."

She was fifty-eight years old, without a job or a college diploma. When she graduated from high school Nowak got a job as a hotel maid, worked for a Christian ministry for room and board, spent two years in Canada in a ministry program, and, eventually, landed at ELCA. She has always lived frugally, a practice which allowed her to travel, including vacations to Israel and New Zealand. She let herself grieve over her lost job until the holidays were over. In the New Year, she got her severance and went on unemployment. She wondered if maybe she should embrace something completely different from her old job. "I never thought of myself as a risk taker," she says. "After thirty years, I thought I should take a risk."

A job with a more creative bent intrigued her. She had a stained-glass hobby, making windowpanes, mosaic trays, and other objects. One of her most memorable trips was a tour of stained-glass makers in France, Germany, and Switzerland. It took her awhile, but she hit on the idea of working in the wood finishing and furniture restoring business. The National Institute for Wood Finishing at Dakota County Technical College in Minnesota offers the only certificate in the craft in the country. She completed the nine-month program in 2013. Nowak took out a loan to pay for much of her certificate. The state eventually chipped in some money to help pay for her degree from its displaced workers fund. "It's a crapshoot, a risk I am willing to take," says Nowak. "This is also a way to produce additional income in retirement."

Nowak reflects on how she has learned much more than woodworking skills during her transition. She had a deep fear of making mistakes, an attitude that she believed held her back. "The class helped me break my chains, to get out of a rut and to allow myself to make mistakes, to know that things don't have to be perfect, especially the first time," she says. "The class opened up my creativity." Nowak landed a part-time job at a small furniture restoration company. "I can't tell you how happy I am to go to work every day! I am ever so grateful I took the 'leap of faith' to make these changes. It is worth it!" she says.

The commonplace assumption among economists and other social scientists is that people prefer leisure to work. It's a reasonable belief. Would you rather work or play? Duh! In the jargon of economics, work is an inferior good and leisure a superior good. The perception is that work is hard and the workplace a harsh, unforgiving environment. The only reason to get up in the morning and head for a job is a paycheck. Leisure is enjoyable. When you're not at work you can watch television, listen to a podcast, or ride a bike. (Of course, leisure is such a broad category it also includes the time you spend commuting to work, cleaning house, cooking meals, filing income taxes, and similar chores that are hardly anyone's definition of fun.) As nations like the United States became wealthier and household incomes rose, people could afford to work less. The most powerful expression of leisure as a superior good is modern retirement.

Problem is, many people get emotional, social, and intellectual rewards out of their jobs that go beyond their paycheck and what it can buy. Eugene Steuerle of the Urban Institute notes that "labor force participation can be a source of social and intellectual fulfillment, particularly if older workers have more flexibility in when and where they work." More recently, for large segments of the workforce the boundaries between leisure and work have blurred with the rise of the creative economy, from Google engineers to artisanal bakers to senior entrepreneurs. Roughly a third or more of the labor force is engaged in the so-called creative industries, estimates Richard Florida, director at the Martin Prosperity Institute at the University of Toronto's Rotman School of Management. The ranks of creative workers are expanding. "The creative individual is no longer viewed as an iconoclast," writes Florida in *The Rise of the Creative Class*. "He—or she—is the new mainstream."

The creative process is trying, but creative expression is also rewarding. It's fun. "The whole concept of leisure is flawed," says Art Rolnick, economist and codirector for the Human Capital Research Collaborative at the University of Minnesota. Sebastian Mallaby, a senior fellow at the Council on Foreign Relations, questions the assumption that leisure beats work in a *Financial Times* article, "Why I Work on My Summer Holiday." Simply put, he works because he likes it, and Mallaby believes he is far from alone. "After all, women have tried living without paid work; they do not seem to have liked it. As cultural barriers have come down, they have voted with their feet," he writes. "Jobs impart a sense of purpose, and social connections with colleagues. The financial income is certainly welcome, but the psychic income can be as valuable." The same insight holds for the rise of unretirement. Boomers are voting to stay engaged in the market economy.

The soft-spoken visionary for unretirement and encore careers is Marc Freedman, a fiftysomething social entrepreneur who heads up the San Francisco–based nonprofit Encore.org. He founded Encore.org (formerly Civic Ventures) in 1998 with a goal of encouraging aging baby boomers to tap into their accumulated life experiences and engage in second and third careers, often by seeking out jobs that deal with disturbing social problems. Freedman plans on working for a long time. The father of three elementary school kids, he has no choice, he often deadpans. By the time his youngest is through college he'll be closing in on his eightieth birthday.

A practical optimist and charming storyteller, Marc represents the anti–Pete Peterson, the anti–doom and gloomster. He's a critical counterpoint to the "America can't-afford-to-grow-old" ecology. He's fond of quoting from a 1965 speech by the legendary public servant John Gardner: "What we have before us are some breathtaking opportunities disguised as insoluble problems." Like Peterson, Freedman is the author of several books, although his titles reflect his optimism about aging. Among his books are *Encore: Finding Work that Matters in the Second Half of Life* and *The Big Shift: Navigating the New Stage Beyond Midlife.* Freedman participates on panels around the country on rethinking retirement, always stressing the opportunities. His vision is to help create a movement that changes attitudes and expectations about getting older while building institutions and practices that support and encourage a longer work life—an encore moment. "Vision isn't enough," he says. "We need to invent."

Freedman popularized the term "encore career," and his nonprofit organization promotes the idea with its annual Purpose Prize. The award honors five people over sixty who have made a difference—people like Wanjiru Kamau, who works with young African immigrants in Washington, D.C., and Lorraine Decker, who teaches financial literacy to low-income students and families in Houston. Susan Burton gives female parolees tools for rebuilding their lives after prison—housing, legal services, job training, and more—at the shelter she established in Los Angeles, A New Way of Life. Ysabel Duron is a journalist and cancer survivor who started her encore career by founding Latinas Contra Cancer (Latinas Against Cancer). Edwin Nicholson is a military veteran and former defense contractor executive who created Project Healing Waters, an organization that helps disabled soldiers and veterans heal through fly-fishing. (Have you ever sat in an audience and said to yourself, "Wow. What have I ever done with my life?" I had a moment like that at an Encore conference celebrating the Purpose Prize winners.) Obviously, the prize winners are extraordinary individuals. But they point out to the rest of us aspirations for writing a different story about the last stage of life than those suggested by the current apocalyptic bestsellers.

Freedman is a builder. For instance, the Encore Fellowship Network is designed to support experienced mid-career professionals ready for a new challenge to shift over to nonprofit organizations in need of their skills and talent. The program helped convince the Obama administration to pass legislation to create a federal fellowship program in every state for those fifty-five and older looking to make a similar change. He has worked with Intel, Hewlett-Packard, and a number of other companies to add an encore career element to their employee benefits. Visit almost any local organization around the country dealing with boomers, work, and purpose and you'll quickly learn that Freedman has offered it counsel and encouragement.

The encore approach to an aging America is democratic and egalitarian, full of hope and possibility. Freedman's talks emphasize how much worth and value aging workers bring to the economy and society. The key question is how can society take advantage of more vigorous aging to nourish "an encore stage of life characterized by purpose, contribution, and commitment, particularly to the well-being of future generations," he asks. That's a worthwhile task for individuals, communities, and society to tackle—the generational challenge at the core of the unretirement improv act.

Encore.org is part of an emerging grassroots industry that aims to turn the desire among an older generation to keep earning an income into reality. The business is composed of a diverse group, among them career coaches, financial advisers, job placement experts, nonprofit organizations, senior temp agencies, corporate consultants, and advocacy organizations. They're all trying to drum up interest, devise standards, establish credentials, develop a common vernacular, and push the movement forward. Discovering What's Next (DWN) in the greater Boston area is a clearinghouse of information and a recruitment hub for older workers to change careers or find jobs that fit their desires better. Running through various initiatives around the country, Doug Dickson, president of DWN, says, "I'd characterize them all as a series of experiments. The question is, 'Which models will emerge as having lasting values?'" The process of figuring it out is exciting.

The word "retire" stems from a French word for "withdrawing" or heading into "isolation." I find the concept of withdrawal bleak. A far better image for the elder years came during a powerful moment in the Henry Horner public housing project in Chicago. Working on a public radio documentary, a colleague and I met with a group of women who lived there. The women, along with public interest lawyers, successfully fought for the Chicago Housing Authority to give them a voice in the remodeling of their public housing complex. At one point during the interview, Crystal Palmer, a lifelong public housing resident and public housing employee, turned to us and said, "How do we connect the disconnected? That's the key to success in this community and any other community is connecting the disconnected."

In French, "connect the dots" is *relier les points*. The English word "rely" comes from *relier*, an apt term for the evolution of the new retirement. We're starting to connect the dots. You could say we're moving from "retirement" to "retie-ment."

CHAPTER 3

Practical Idealism at Work

Problems have solutions
trust and I will show
—Stevie Wonder

AT THE EMPLOYEE BENEFIT RESEARCH Institute's seventy-third annual policy forum in Washington, D.C., in late 2013, Arnold Brown was on a panel discussing "Employee Benefits: Today (2013), Tomorrow (+35), and Yesterday (-35)." Brown is chairman of Weiner, Edrich, Brown, Inc., a trend-tracking consulting firm. Brown told the story (probably apocryphal, he added) of an American general visiting the British army just before World War II.

The American general was observing British army field maneuvers. He watched as an artillery battalion drove up in its trucks. The soldiers got out of the trucks and prepared their guns for firing. The American general turned to the British officer accompanying him and said, "I'm puzzled. You have seven men in each gun crew. But six men do all the work and the seventh just stands there at attention during the whole process. What is the function of the seventh man?"

"I really don't know," the British officer replied. "We have always had seven men in a gun crew. When I get back I'll check up on the reason why. I'll let you know."

The British officer called the American general the next morning. "The reason is that the seventh man holds the horses."

The audience burst out laughing. Brown said, "We have to look at the model we have now and ask why? Why do we have it this way?"

Case in point: Social Security and the age of retirement. The personal finance discussion of Social Security often starts with the observation that retirees can first file for benefits at age sixty-two. Of course, it's a reduced benefit, which is why it pays to wait until your "full retirement" age. It's currently age sixty-six for those born in 1943 and later, slated to rise to sixty-seven for those born in 1960 and afterwards. However, the term "full retirement age" is deceptive, as Social Security benefits are at their maximum at age seventy. There are no additional benefits for waiting past age seventy. The financial gain to waiting until age seventy is compelling, however. Claiming benefits at age sixty-two instead of seventy cuts the monthly benefit almost in half, notes Alicia Munnell, director of the Center for Retirement Research at Boston College, in "Social Security's *Real* Retirement Age Is 70." She calculates that the net replacement rate of income for the median earner—taking into account Medicare, taxes, and a full retirement age of sixty-seven in 2030—is 24 percent at age sixty-two and 43 percent at age seventy—almost double.

As we've seen, the higher Social Security monthly payout is only part of the financial returns to continuing to earn a paycheck in our elder years. Aging workers can continue to bolster their savings, and they shorten the time they need to live off their accumulated assets. For example, according to Social Security, the average remaining life expectancy in 2009 at age sixty-two for men was 19.4 years and for women 23.6. At age seventy, the expected life expectancy is 14.0 for men and 16.3 for women. This doesn't mean the age of early filing should be raised. No, the dominant message from Social Security and the personal finance industry should be that seventy is the age most people should consider filing for Social Security benefits and only if necessary should people file earlier. The full retirement age (a term I would drop) is seventy, not sixty-six or eventually sixty-seven. Framing matters.

The message is slowly getting across. Older men and women on average are delaying their retirements. The decline in the employment rates for men essentially started in the 1880s and accelerated in the post–World War II era, a century-long embrace of earlier and earlier retirement. For example, Joseph Quinn, economist at Boston College, defines the average age of retirement as the age at which the male labor force participation rate declines to 50 percent. In that case, the average age of retirement fell from age seventy in 1950 to sixty-five in 1970 and sixty-two by 1985. In *Work and Retirement: How and When Older Americans Leave the Labor Force*, Quinn notes that the trend bottomed out in the mideighties to early nineties. An increasing number of older men decided to hold off leaving the job. For women the story line is different, although the conclusion remains the same. Older women in the post–World War II era also retired younger, but the effect was offset by the embrace of paid labor by married women. The trend line for female retirement never showed a steep drop like that for men. Nevertheless, the post-mideighties experience is similar to their male peers. In 2013 the annual labor force participation rate for men age sixty-five and older was up 49 percent after bottoming out in 1985. For women sixty-five and older their participation rate has doubled over the same period. The comparable increase over the same time frame for men ages sixty to sixty-four was 9 percent and for women 50 percent. "The era of earlier and earlier retirement is over and is not coming back," concludes Quinn.

What accounts for the shift in retirement expectations? A cluster of changes came together, significant enough in the aggregate to reverse a century-long trend. The modifications of the National Commission on Social Security Reform, better known as the Greenspan Commission after its chairman, in the early 1980s were critical. The bipartisan commission was charged with shoring up Social Security's deteriorating finances. Its recommendations led Congress to legislate a sharp increase in benefits for those who waited to file for Social Security from 1 percent to 3 percent initially, gradually increasing to 8 percent for those turning sixty-five in 2008. Around the same time, the private sector started turning away from the traditional defined benefit pension plan. These pensions allowed workers to retire with full benefits between ages sixty and sixty-five with no additional gain for staying with their employer longer. Instead, starting in the 1980s, companies raced to embrace defined contribution savings plans like the 401(k). These plans are much cheaper for employers to manage and run. For employees, there is no required distribution with a 401(k) retirement savings plan until age seventy and a half and even that date for beginning required minimum withdrawals can be delayed if employees stick with their current company. Mandatory retirement at age sixty-five once covered most of the U.S. work force. The age of mandatory retirement was extended to seventy in 1978 and eliminated for most jobs in 1986.

The financial penalty for early retirement increased, too. The biggest factor is that employers, for the most part, stopped offering their employees postretirement health care coverage. Health care expenses add up even when people qualify for Medicare at age sixty-five. The mutual fund company Fidelity estimates that a sixty-five-year-old couple who retired in 2012 will need $220,000 to cover their medical expenses throughout retirement. Fidelity's calculation is conservative since it doesn't take into account any costs associated with nursing homes, assisted living, and other potential long-term care bills. The average American worker also worries about outliving their savings—with good reason. Retirement savings are far from flush for the typical household. Many employers don't offer their workers a retirement savings plan. For those employees at a company with a retirement savings plan, part of the savings shortfall stems from the shift in private pensions. With the defined benefit plan, the employer bears all the investment risk and commits to a fixed payout of money, typically based on a salary and years-of-service formula. Employees get a monthly paycheck for the rest of their lives.

With the 401(k), employees bear all the risk, deciding how much to invest (depending on the legal limits) and where to invest it (depending on the menu of investment choices offered by their employer's plan). While the 401(k)-type retirement savings plan creates incentives for workers to delay retirement, a cottage industry of experts has chronicled how poor most people are at making sound long-term investment decisions. Most of us didn't grow up learning about stocks and bonds, let alone asset allocation and the efficient frontier for retirement portfolios. Behavioral economists have cataloged a long list of systemic mistakes the average investor makes, such as an ingrained tendency to rely on stereotypes; overestimating our ability to predict the future; a willingness to hold on to bad bets because we don't like to feel regret; a tendency to follow where the herd is going. "Employees like choice," said Larry Zimpleman, chairman of the Principal Financial Group and a panelist at the Employee Benefit Research Institute's seventy-third annual Policy Forum. "But we know that left to their own devices employees make bad choices."

Other factors in the economy and society came into play, many of them on the positive side of the social ledger. Jobs are less physically demanding than before. Working with computers in occupations such as financial services and medical diagnostics is much less demanding physically than manning an auto assembly line or mining for coal. The share of jobs involving high physical demands is down in an economy dominated by services and information-intensive businesses. According to the Urban Institute, between 1971 and 2007 the share of jobs involving difficult working conditions—defined as outdoor work, exposure to contaminants, and high noise level—fell from 40 percent to 30 percent (rounding off the numbers). The share of jobs requiring high cognitive ability—reasoning skills, writing ability, decision-making, and interpersonal skills—rose from one quarter to more than one third over the same time period.[1]

Perhaps most important, older workers are well educated compared to previous generations. They have the credentials to take advantage of job and entrepreneurial opportunities in an economy that values skill and education. For instance, between 1973 and 2010 the share of jobs requiring at least some college or postsecondary education more than doubled, from 28 percent to about 60 percent, according to Anthony Carnevale, director of the Georgetown University Center on Education and the Workforce. Some 30 percent of the boomer generation has four or more years of college. Older workers are wealthy in "human capital," economic jargon for knowledge, education, and on-the-job learning. "We've invested a lot in human capital and people want to be engaged," says economist Art Rolnick. Adds Milton Roye, a fifty-six-year-old entrepreneur who has left the corporate suite in the automotive industry behind: "I'm sort of an example of what a lot of people are now starting to do. They've got this skill base. It's way too early to retire. The brain is still going."

The value of learning at work shouldn't be underestimated. Education isn't just years of schooling and degrees. The importance of the job as classroom was highlighted for me in the early 1990s. I participated in a day-long seminar organized by the late Columbia University economist Jacob Mincer. A labor economist, Mincer was one of the University of Chicago–trained economists, along with such luminaries as Theodore Schultz and Gary Becker, who developed the modern theory of human capital. We met in a seminar room on campus and the focus of the meeting was on the role that education played in widening income inequality during the eighties (a trend that has continued to this day). Among the participants was Fischer Black, the legendary financier who cocreated in 1973 the main method traders use to value options—the Black-Scholes model. At the time he was a partner at Goldman Sachs, a key member of the investment bank's quantitative brain trust. The conversation kept revolving around the gap between earnings of high school–educated workers and college-educated workers. Black said nothing for a long time. Suddenly, if I remember right, he said, "Why are we talking about school so much? What you learn on the job is nine to eleven times what you learn at school. That seems a reasonable estimate to me."

The conversation paused. We all nodded in agreement. Then we went back to talking about different education levels and the implications for inequality. Reflecting back, we should have spent more time on Black's insight. Older workers bring hard-earned accumulated knowledge and insight to their firms. What's more, seniors will keep on learning, accumulating new insights as they continue to work and pursue their entrepreneurial dreams.

Another major factor supporting unretirement is that the average older worker and aging entrepreneur is not only living longer but is healthier longer. By many measures the health of those sixty-five plus has improved over the past three decades. The gains vary by education, with the better educated healthier on average than their less-educated peers. Still, healthy life expectancy on average has improved, although at a slower pace than regular life expectancy.

Many disabilities are less prevalent today than in the past. For example, Kenneth Manton, scientific director, Center for Demographic Studies at Duke University, and several colleagues looked into a number of medical datasets for the population aged sixty-five plus from 1982 through 2004 and 2005. The researchers found that the declines in disability over this period of time were "significant for both persons with less severe chronic disability" and for "persons with more serious disability." The UCLA Center for Health Policy Research reports that disability at sixty-five and over is decreasing, falling from 35 percent in 1992 to 29 percent in 2009. Most people in their late forties to early sixties say they are in good health. "Thus, the vast majority of older workers on the verge of early retirement age do not report having a work limitation–based disability," write Richard Burkhauser and Ludmila Rovbain in *Institutional Responses to Structural Lag: The Changing Patterns of Work at Older Ages.*

To be sure, there are competing crosscurrents with health, such as obesity and diabetes. Low-income workers suffer from more ailments than their well-paid peers. Still, even with these realistic cautions it's reasonable to expect that technological advances with various assistive devices and medical interventions will enable even those currently considered disabled to stay engaged at the workplace. Advances in hip- and knee-replacement surgery are already allowing many people to remain productive and active. Researchers are making remarkable strides with voice-recognition software (think Siri) that should ease computer-related tasks for elder workers and everyone else.

Intriguingly, some recent research suggests that having a job itself is a force for staying healthy which, if you think about it, makes sense. You have to use your mind and body at work. (The Irish phrase, "health and long life to you" and the Jewish expression "as long as there's health" are wise indeed. Maybe we should add, "work for health.") In *Work Longer,*

Live Healthier, Gabriel Sahlgren, director of research at the Centre for Market Reform of Education in London, found evidence of a virtuous cycle: A job and improved health fed off and reinforced the other. In other words, paid employment in old age helps ensure a healthier population. "The policy implication of this research is that policymakers should remove disincentives to continue work in old age," he writes. "This does not mean that politicians should force people to 'work until they die', but that they should entirely remove disincentives to stop working." Sahlgren is spot-on.

Taken altogether, a mix of positive and negative forces are pushing and pulling older workers away from traditional notions of retirement. Of course, even if the combination of desire and need, engagement and living expenses convince a majority of aging employees and entrepreneurs to continue earning a living, the haunting question is, will there be enough jobs for aging boomers? The supply of potential workers is there, but what about demand? How realistic is it to expect employers will contemplate hiring a sixty-three-year-old, let alone a sixty-eight-year-old applicant? Age discrimination is real. If there are jobs, will older workers be condemned to the lowest-wage work, the least satisfying tasks, such as welcoming customers walking into a big-box retailer, asking if they'd like a cart? (Although for an early 1990s *Businessweek* story we interviewed Carl G. Rowan. He was eighty-five years old at the time. He had owned and operated Gamer's Confectionery, a restaurant in Butte, Montana, for fifty-one years. Rowan sold the business in April 1993. Everyone expected Rowan to settle into a comfortable retirement, but then Kent Parsons, manager of the local Walmart, offered Rowan a job as a Walmart store greeter. Rowan worked thirty hours a week, making $5.45 an hour. He took $50 out of each paycheck to buy Walmart stock through an employee stock purchase plan, with Walmart matching 15 percent of his contribution. "It's exciting. I said [when I sold Gamer's] that this is not the end of Carl Rowan; it's the beginning," he told us. He really enjoyed the job, talking to customers and helping them out.)

The response to questions like these from a random set of conversations with colleagues, neighbors, and people I meet at conferences suggests skepticism about the job prospects of older Americans is the default assumption, especially after the high unemployment rates of recent years. A number of laid-off workers in their fifties and early sixties found they couldn't get employers to look at their resumes, let alone hire them. "I doubt the jobs will be there," says Phyllis Moen, a leading sociologist and scholar of retirement and aging at the University of Minnesota. "Companies don't like older workers." Karl Stauber, the thoughtful head of the Danville Regional Foundation in Virginia, counts himself among the doubtful. "Working longer assumes that there is work," he says.

Economists, on the other hand, sing a different tune. They may be known as practitioners of the dismal science, but when it comes to jobs for older people economists are an optimistic group. "I think the jobs will be there," says Richard Johnson, economist at the Urban Institute and a leading expert on work and generations. "I'm not worried about the number of jobs," says economist Rolnick of the University of Minnesota. "There will be jobs." Mark Zandi, chief economist of Moody's Analytics, says, "I am not at all concerned about where do the jobs come from."

Ironically, demographics is a force for optimism among many economists, since the generation immediately following the boomers is smaller. "The demographics suggest employers will have no choice but to hire older workers," says Kevin Cahill, economist at the Sloan Center on Aging and Work at Boston College.

Take these representative calculations by Barry Bluestone, dean of the School of Public Policy and Urban Affairs at Northeastern University, and Mark Melnik, deputy director for research at the Boston Redevelopment Authority. What their numbers suggest is even if overall employment growth is slow going forward the economy will create enough jobs to absorb older workers. Bluestone and Melnik in *After the Recovery: Help Needed: The Coming Labor Shortage and How People in Encore Careers Can Help Solve It* predict anemic employment growth of about 1 percent a year from 2008 through 2018. The comparable employment growth figures were a robust 1.9 percent per year from 1988 to 1998, and a slim 0.9 percent annually from 1998 to 2008. They project a future full of opportunities for older workers without stacking the deck in favor of a hiring boom.

The scholars expect that a return to healthy economic growth could mean 14.6 million additional nonfarm payroll jobs could be created between 2008 and 2018. The projection grows to 15 million if you include farmers and self-employed family members in family enterprises. They use official projections of population growth and Bureau of Labor Statistics estimates of future labor force participation rates, which assume boomers will stay on the job longer than previous generations. They also suppose that there will be no major changes to immigration policy. The results suggest that anywhere from around 3.3 million (using the nonfarm payroll measure) to about 4 million (using the broader calculation) potential jobs could be vacant. Human resource departments will face growing pressure to retain older workers and welcome gray-haired hires. The authors believe that older workers will respond to the opportunity and that the labor force participation rate of those fifty-five and over will jump significantly. However, they add an important caveat to their projection: This assumes management will create a more hospitable and engaging work environment. "These [increased labor force participation] rates are not impossible given the improved health and lowered morbidity of older Americans, but participation at these elevated rates would fundamentally change America's employment landscape," they conclude. "The big question therefore is not simply whether there will be enough jobs for older workers but whether the work will be rewarding enough, both economically and socially, to keep them in the labor force."

That's the right concern. Management hasn't exactly gone out of its way to nurture a supportive work climate in recent years. Far too many jobs come with low pay and few prospects for advancement. With jobs scarce and many employees nervous about layoffs during great recession and anemic recovery, managers focused on requiring employees to do more with fewer resources. When the economy regains its health the green-eyeshade approach to managing employees could backfire. Talented, experienced employees may well decide when jobs are more plentiful that enough is enough. "The baby boomers aren't going to retire. They won't stop working," says David Stillman, cofounder of BridgeWorks, a consulting firm. "But when the gloom lifts we could see a mass exodus of baby boomers who have kept their mouths shut but are eager to leave their employer." Many of those fleeing workers may well embrace entrepreneurship.

Certainly, the lure of owning your own business and being your own boss is strong. A survey by the San Francisco–based nonprofit Encore. org reported that some 25 million Americans between the ages of forty-four and seventy want to start their own business or create a nonprofit venture over the following five to ten years. A number of these entrepreneurs-in-waiting will follow through on their desire. "At the moment there is a large and growing talent pool and they can focus on entrepreneurship to stay productive," says William Zinke, president of the Center for Productive Longevity. Zinke is a former lawyer turned management consultant and entrepreneur. He mostly focused on talent management and work force development during his career. He founded the center at age seventy-nine in 2006 to encourage senior entrepreneurship. For others, entrepreneurship is the best option available. "A basic dividing line is age fifty," says Edward Rogoff, economist at Baruch College, City University of New York. "You lose a good job at age fifty, the chances of getting another are small, so you do something else. You start your own business."

Take the experience of Pat Snyder of Columbus, Ohio. She is sixty-seven years old. The same year that she was eligible for Medicare she received her master's degree in Applied Positive Psychology from the University of Pennsylvania. Snyder was a newspaper reporter when she was younger, a member of the newspaper guild (the journalist's union). The guild's lawyer impressed Snyder. She decided to go to law school. She practiced law for twenty-eight years. Watching her peers burn out, Snyder hit on a third career, launched in 2010: to coach lawyers seeking a career change or greater fulfillment in their profession. "It's a practical third career for me," she says. "It's flexible, it's fun, and I feel like I am making a difference."

Don Lambert told me pretty much the same thing. I met Lambert, an engineering manager, when he was sixty-seven years old after I gave a talk several years ago in Des Moines, Iowa. He was in the audience and we struck up a conversation. Lambert retired from Fisher Controls (now Emerson Process Management, a division of Emerson) in 2002. He'd spent thirty-two years with the company, half of it abroad, mostly working on projects in the Middle East and Africa. When he retired he set up a consulting firm with Fisher among his clients. He spent two years on contract with Fisher in Saudi Arabia, where the only thing he had to pay out of pocket were his "newspaper and haircuts." After moving back to the United States, he worked about two days a week on his consulting business and spent the rest of his time doing community volunteer work with Rotary International, Meals on Wheels, the Iowa Council for International Understanding, and other organizations. "I do stay very busy," he said.

The rise of the nontraditional or contingent work force should support longer work lives. The contingent work force includes freelancers, contract workers, part-time laborers, and temps. Estimates vary, but contingent workers comprise about a third of the work force. Management consultants routinely forecast that these kinds of impermanent jobs will swell in coming decades. "As independent work becomes more common, a greater share of American workers will spend at least part of their careers as Independents," predicts the 2013 MBO Partners *State of Independence in America* survey. "By 2020, roughly 50% of the private workforce will have spent time as independent workers at some point in their work lives."

American businesses value the flexibility and cost competitiveness of a just-in-time labor force. Management has turned to contract workers to keep down health care, retirement, and other benefit costs. The rise of the "disposable worker" and the "perma-temp" allow employers to swiftly adjust payrolls to changing economic conditions. However, for employees the big drawback to contingent work is it typically doesn't come with health care and retirement benefits. By definition the job is insecure, making it hard for people to plan and to save. The contingent marketplace is becoming increasingly diverse. The core of the work force for a long time was low-wage, low-skill temp jobs. Contingent employment is now geared more toward well-educated workers, including engineers, information technology specialists, health care workers, and finance professionals. The rhythm of working temporarily with one company, moving over to another, and so on in an endless chain is suited for many older workers ready to say good-bye to full-time employment but not work compared to their younger peers. Accenture consultants Yaarit Silverstone, Catherine Farley, and Susan M. Cantrell in *The Rise of the Extended Workforce* note that "many retiring baby boomers have joined the extended workforce because they want the stimulation and the income from working as well as the benefits of flexibility." My suspicion is that the Affordable Care Act and (eventually) robust state health insurance exchanges should make contingent work less risky and more practical for aging boomers, since they'll be able to get decent health coverage at a reasonable price.

Government and corporate policies should adjust to the rise of the flexible work force. Too often the discussion about the government's social safety net and employer benefits assumes the only worker that matters is the full-time employee, a deeply mistaken point of view. Work lives are far more complex, and a common theme emerging from unretirement is that flexibility and variety is critical. "Older workers value flexibility," says Richard Johnson of the Urban Institute. "They don't want to work nine to five, five days a week."

Robert Kaufman, age sixty in 2013, values flexibility at this stage in his life. Kaufman has had a varied work history. Among his jobs were heavy equipment operator, truck driver, and welder. His last job? Pastor at Rainbow Mennonite Church, in Kansas City, Kansas. "I've changed jobs about every five years and made a career change about every ten years," he chuckles.

Kaufman says that when it was time for him to stop being a pastor it was much easier to tell people he was retiring. He didn't have to explain himself. His goal is to work three days a week, keep three days for himself, and spend one day giving back to the community. "I don't consider myself retired," he says. "A lot of us are trying to figure out, 'What does it mean to be in our age bracket?'"

He is currently employed driving a van for nonemergency medical appointments for the elderly and disabled. The contract is with the Veterans Administration. The job doesn't pay well, but he enjoys meeting the people on the van and he values the flexibility offered by the job, the trade-off for low pay. He has a long list of projects of his own to accomplish. Fixing up their home. Tinkering at a rural property with ponds they own about an hour away. And he's a hard-core grandfather. Kaufman is still figuring out what to focus on for the day devoted to giving back. In the meantime, he is on the Next Chapter planning committee and on the board of the local Rosedale Development Association. The former helps aging boomers decide what their encore career might be and the latter runs a variety of youth and neighborhood initiatives in the Rosedale community. A major reason why he has been able to scale back is that his wife works full-time. She doesn't plan on cutting back until she reaches age sixty-five in five years. "We aren't thinking about just quitting work," Kaufman says. "We don't want to and we can't afford to."

That said, the transition toward a flexible lifestyle is often difficult. A common expression among laid-off workers fifty-five years and older who are struggling to find work is "you don't even exist." You cobble a job here and a job there, always marginal to management. Apply for a job you're well qualified for and you'll probably never hear back from the employer. You're invisible. Just ask Sharon Rodriguez of Kansas City. Age sixty, she had a thirty-year career in the information technology business. She got a data processing degree in 1983 and entered the computer field, working her way up to project manager. She also earned a master's degree in organizational development in information technology. Rodriguez was laid off from her last IT job in 2007. "I had experience and credentials," she says. "I laid back for awhile. Then learned it isn't a pretty picture for people in their sixties. I said to myself, 'What the heck happened?' I was so embarrassed I couldn't find a job. I would have interviews with thirtysomethings. They would say you look good on paper, but they'd hire someone younger."

Her unretirement involved several routes. She took evening classes training to become a lead-based-paint inspector. But the equipment was costly and she decided she couldn't risk spending her minimal savings on it. Her focus shifted to teaching about healthy homes and lead safety, but not that many people were interested. She kept looking. Without a steady income, she filed for Social Security benefits and she lowered her standard of living. "I was so embarrassed that I didn't know what I had in retirement and learned I didn't have what I needed to retire," she says. One time she went to a retirement seminar, the kind that comes with a free dinner. "It was so dismal," she says. "I didn't have a million dollars to invest, let alone a hundred thousand dollars."

She gradually pulled together a business that reflects several of her passions. She hasn't gone into debt to fund her business. Instead, she reinvests what she makes into the enterprise. She offers wellness and meditation training to individuals and groups. Her art business centers on photography, inspirational stories, and meditation. For example, *Rebels, Legends, and Icons* combines photographs and stories of local men and women age fifty-nine to ninety-one years old. Another photo-graph-and-stories book is *Meditation for Everyday Use*. She shows her work at local art shows with an eye to getting companies to purchase her art for their offices. "Now, I am producing a product," she says. "I have something at the end of the day that is my work and I couldn't say that when I was in a corporation."

Rodriguez says she's healthy. She regularly exercises and does yoga. She also tries to learn something new every day. Rodriguez notes that all the pieces of her work tie together. "It looks like it is all unrelated, but they are all well related," she says. "Slow down a bit. Don't buy into the media and all the chaos. I was part of that when I was corporate."

The stress of unretirement looms large for many since we're only at the early stages of figuring out the narrative. The uncertainty is often excruciating with few guideposts. The ambiguity inherent in the current unretirement saga reminds me of a panel conversation I moderated several years ago. The topic was "The Joys and Challenges of Pursuing the Work You Love." One panelist was the famed arctic explorer Ann Bancroft, the first woman to reach both the North and South Poles by dogsled, on skis, and on foot. The other panelist was Kate DiCamillo, an award-winning author and national ambassador for young people's literature through the Library of Congress. Her first published book was *Because of Winn-Dixie*, the bestseller and later movie. *The Tale of Despereaux* was another bestseller and movie. (It was one of the easiest panels I've ever moderated. All I had to do was sit back and let these two remarkable people tell their stories, feeding off each other.)

We met before our panel discussion and decided to rename the session, "The Misery and Hardship of Pursuing Your Passion." The real story behind their unusual careers was that success wasn't preordained. They took risks, and for a long time the choice came with much doubt and many setbacks. DiCamillo wanted to be an author. She worked at a minimum-wage job at a bookstore in the Twin Cities for a decade because it offered health care benefits. She says she received 470 rejection letters for *Because of Winn-Dixie* before finding a publisher. Imagine the difficulty of sticking to your writing passion while the rejection letters pile up and your wage tops out at $8.40 an hour. "I knew I wanted to write," she says. "It was six years of writing and collecting rejection letters."

In contrast to DiCamillo, who followed a single path, Ann Bancroft began one career and shifted to another. She was a special education teacher in the Twin Cities, a job she loved. She was a mountain climber in her spare time, and to supplement her income she worked part-time at a mountaineering store. One day the famed arctic explorer Will Steger walked into the store, and Bancroft heard him mention to one of her coworkers that he was looking for a woman to join his next expedition. Bancroft seized the opportunity and volunteered. "I just thought, 'I have to go for it,'" says Bancroft. Her second career began in her midthirties.

DiCamillo and Bancroft didn't complain about the pain, the misery, and the obstacles—from the psychological to the financial. They didn't minimize the price each paid to figure out how to make it all pan out, either. They both stuck with their passions even though neither knew it would work out for the best. The stress is even greater for older workers since time is precious.

When you take a step back and think about it, the evolving story about older workers and aging entrepreneurs in modern America is really a conversation about the nature of work and the good life for all generations. We don't know exactly how unretirement will shape up. We do know the price of social experimentation is that some endeavors won't pan out. The learning curve is steep. Still, the goal is worth the effort for individuals and the economy. Indeed, the unretirement push has major implications for the catchphrase of the moment: inequality. If you doubt that concerns over inequality are on the rise, just reflect on the remarkable fact that the most celebrated and controversial publication of 2014 is a six-hundred-plus-page book by a once obscure French economist, a dense tome full of charts and graphs. Yes, Thomas Piketty's. He persuasively documents the growing gap between the rich and poor in the United States and other nations.

Whatever your personal response to the growing debate over inequality and social mobility, I don't think there is any question that as a nation we must focus more on addressing long-term unemployment, especially for those job seekers with few skills and sketchy employment history. Millions of Americans are struggling to get by these days. Many were born in poverty, growing up in neighborhoods that offered few clear ways of escaping a life of struggle. Key to reviving dynamism and prosperity in America is increasing the incomes and job prospects in low-wage communities.

Unretirement is part of the effort to think boldly and practically about the job market and wages, especially for the majority of working-age Americans. The stakes are high for a society looking to be more inclusive and vibrant. Put it this way: Nearly 180 years before Piketty's book was published in the United States, another astute Frenchman wrote smartly about America—Alexis de Tocqueville. The opening sentence to his magisterial reads: "No novelty in the United States struck me more vividly during my stay than the equality of conditions." A back to the future moment lies at the heart of the unretirement movement.

Says Nobel laureate Edmund Phelps, economist at Columbia University, in "Great Catch-Ups and Fall-Backs I Have Seen: And Their Misinterpretations": "Prosperity means high job satisfaction—jobholders developing through the change and challenge of their work—and low unemployment, thus ample access to such jobs." Notice he didn't say anything about age. Phelps is seventy-nine years old.

CHAPTER 4

The Only Thing We Have to Fear Is Fearmongering

I've got a new attitude
—Patti LaBelle

WHAT ABOUT THE FISCAL NIGHTMARE, the inevitable slide toward a Mediterranean-style catastrophe? The strongest-held belief in in Washington, D.C., is that the combination of an aging population and entitlement obligations will drag down the economy and possibly even bankrupt the federal government and the country.

Political commentator David Frum captured the conventional outlook when he drew a rather wicked analogy between bad elderly drivers and an aging society. Frum notes that our driving skills erode as we get older. The odds of a car accident increase after age sixty and the probability of a crash jumps past age seventy. Yet society is wary of telling the elderly to get off the road. "It's almost always easier and safer to shift the costs of an aging society onto other groups: to force the other drivers on I-95 to veer out of the way," he writes in *Newsweek*. "And no, it's not just about driving. Whether we can ever learn to say no to the elderly is the great political question hanging over all modern societies, in Europe as much as in the U.S., as we face a 21st century of diminished economic opportunity and staggering government debt."

Whenever I get into a conversation with neighbors and colleagues about retirement and Social Security someone will always say, "Social Security won't be there when I retire. I'm not planning on it." They're far from alone in their sentiment. When the pollster Gallup asked nonretired adults, "Do you think the Social Security system will be able to pay you a benefit when you retire?" 60 percent said no. That's up from 42 percent a decade earlier.

The widely accepted assumption that Social Security and Medicare are hurtling toward disaster isn't surprising. A cottage industry of academic studies, think tank reports, media commentary, and political entrepreneurs has made the point repeatedly. In a representative article published in *Reason* magazine, editor in chief Nick Gillespie and Veronique de Rugy, senior fellow at the Mercatus Center at George Mason University, say that based on current trends Social Security and Medicare alone will account for half of all federal outlays by 2030, up from 37 percent in fiscal year 2011. "These programs, then, are the very definition of *unsustainable*," they conclude. "They pay out more than they take in and cannot exist without constant tweaks, fixes, and adjustments—all of which point toward a future of higher taxes for workers and smaller or nonexistent benefits for retirees."

A trademark issue among conservatives is the need to cut back on entitlement spending. The message is part of their political brand. But the worry over entitlements and aging spans much of the ideological spectrum. "The arithmetic simply doesn't work, unless we face the fact that entitlements are a bargain we can't afford to keep, not in full," writes Bill Keller, columnist for the *New York Times* and former executive editor of the newspaper of record. Fred Hiatt, editorial page editor for the *Washington Post*, shares his concern that unless entitlements are made less generous, America faces a bleak outlook. "That's a future in which spending on retirees crowds out spending on national parks, national defense, schools, research, and the poor. It's a future in which American prestige and power decline abroad while economic prospects dwindle at home."

Think again. The ghost of Thomas Robert Malthus and the notion that in demographics lies a grim destiny informs the arithmetic behind aging. Malthus was a key figure in the eighteenth and early nineteenth century in developing modern mainstream economics. (Darwin hit on the idea of natural selection after reading Malthus's *Essay on the Principle of Population.*) Malthus is best remembered for his bleak argument that there is a tendency from "the wretched inhabitants of Tierra del Fuego" to "the beggars of Teshoo Loomboo" for population growth to outstrip resources. The grim dynamic runs something along these lines: Growing incomes lead to increased fertility and reduced mortality. There are more mouths to feed on the same land. Growth and income fall. The process repeats itself, over and over again. Little wonder the Victorian historian Thomas Carlyle described Malthus as "dreary, stolid, dismal, without hope for this world or the next."

Yet economic predictions based on major population shifts often miss the mark and for a good reason. What really counts is innovation, technology, the organization of business, the expansion in human capital, and the animal spirits of capitalism. In other words, productivity trumps Malthusian demographics. That's reassuring news. For instance, a half century ago America had five workers for every retiree. This figure has since declined to some three to one. The demographic trend at first glance is ominous, right? Yet over that time frame the United States was the most productive large economy in the world. American living standards rose smartly, despite eleven recessions since 1948 including the great recession. The United States has become a vastly wealthier nation over the past six decades. We have larger homes, many more cars, access to vast networks of cheap high-tech communications, rich entertainment offerings, a world-class university system, a healthy social safety net, and many other signs of economic strength and vitality.

Economist Dean Baker offers an illuminating calculation to keep in mind whenever someone spins out a tale of demographic woe. Baker is the codirector at the Center for Economic and Policy Research, a small nonprofit housed on the fourth floor of an older townhouse near Dupont Circle in Washington, D.C. He calculates that between 2012 and 2035, aging alone will reduce American living standards by 8.5 percent. This decline reflects the projected drop in the ratio of workers to retirees from about three workers for every retiree in 2012 to approximately two for every retiree in 2035. Fewer workers will be supporting more retirees, a drag on the economy if there is no increase in productivity. It's the basic relationship behind the demographics of fear with an aging population.

Enter the productivity factor. Baker considers three scenarios. What if productivity growth runs at a 2.5 percent average annual rate, the pace of the first three decades following the Second World War? The cumulative gain to American living standards is almost 58 percent. He also runs the numbers with productivity expanding at 1.5 percent, the pace since 1995. The gain to living standards is some 41 percent. On his most pessimistic note, Baker simulates a productivity scenario matching the slow rate of 1 percent from 1973 to 1995. Living standards are up by about 26 percent.[1] In other words, the gains from higher productivity growth even with his bleakest projection are more than three times as large as the projected decline in living standards from the falling ratio of workers to retirees. "That's the story that matters," Baker emphasized when we met in the center's conference room. "Productivity growth."

The kicker for the purposes of unretirement: Baker says his projections are too low since his calculations don't take into account the prospect that workers will stay on the job longer.

Let's draw on another study, this one by Maestas and Zissimopoulos of Rand. In *How Longer Work Lives Ease the Crunch of Population Aging*, they note that demographic projections for 2030 are reasonably solid. The same can't be said for labor force participation rates between now and then. They use the economic dependency ratio, defined by them as the ratio of nonworkers sixteen and older to workers sixteen and older, multiplied by one hundred, to illustrate the possibilities. The economic dependency ratio implied by the Bureau of Labor Statistics forecast of labor force growth between 1990 and 2030 is sixty-two nonworkers per one hundred workers by 2030 as boomers retire. That's a sharp increase from fifty adult nonworkers per one hundred workers in 1990. Government statisticians assume in their forecast that labor force participation rates will increase through 2020 and then level off. But what if the embrace of unretirement continues and doesn't decelerate? In other words, ask Maestas and Zissimopoulos, what if the labor force participation rate continues to rise at the same pace after 2020 as before. It's a reasonable forecast. The economic dependency ratio in 2030 would be fifty-three, they calculate—a negligible change over four decades. "Demographics is destiny in the sense that the population age distribution is set decades before its impacts are realized," the Rand scholars write. "But the economic response is typically more adaptive than demographic determinism would suggest. Indeed, in the United States, a variety of economic forces is likely to push labor force participation at older ages higher even if there are no further changes in policy, including changes in pensions, longer life expectancy, delay in disability onset, and rising labor force attachment among women."

Let's look at one more study. Richard Johnson and Karen Smith of the Urban Institute attempted to model the impact on the federal budget and household incomes if the recent trend toward delaying retirement continues over the next three decades. The results are heartening and in line with other studies. First, they note from prior research that additional Social Security taxes generated by five additional years of work by nondisabled older Americans would offset more than half of the Social Security Trust Fund deficit in 2045. Put somewhat differently, they note that if we put the added federal and state income taxes generated by these years of unretirement into Social Security the safety net would remain solvent through 2045 without any benefit cuts. Secondly, the results from their model simulations suggest that "older workers will contribute to higher national output, reduce the growth of government spending, raise tax collections, and increase household incomes." Perhaps most important—and too often neglected—is that their results show that the rewards to unretirement are skewed toward the less well off. "The big gainers are workers in the bottom half of the income distribution. Net income of 65–69-year-olds is projected to increase 38 percent for those in the bottom income quintile and 20 percent for those in the second lowest quintile," write Johnson and Smith. "African-Americans,

Hispanics, and lower-educated seniors gain more than whites and better educated seniors."[2]

As you can see, economic studies like these use different assumptions, time frames, and databases. The results are suggestive, not definitive. The models reflect sophisticated attempts to capture the impact of an aging population continuing to earn a paycheck on the economy. Think of these studies as a disciplined approach to test what common sense suggests would be the outcome of longer work lives: a wealthier United States. The specifics of the studies vary, but importantly all come to the same conclusion: There is no crisis of aging in America with unretirement. We need to be proactive and reframe dour conversations about unaffordable entitlements and aging to the vast opportunities opened up by an aging work force and older entrepreneurs. The rise of unretirement is good news for the economy's vitality, the material well-being of individuals in life's third stage, and for shoring up the financial health of the social safety net.

That said, let's look at Social Security on its own terms. In essence, the nation's main retirement safety net is okay. Yes, "okay" is hardly an exuberant term, let alone a technical description. But "okay" is an appropriate word considering the dismissive language hurled at the social insurance program. Remember when Texas governor Rick Perry called Social Security a Ponzi scheme during the Republican primary in 2011? (Think Bernard Madoff. A Ponzi scheme—named after the 1920s fraudster Charles Ponzi—is an investment swindle where the promised returns are illusory, with money from new investors used to pay off earlier investors until the money runs out and the crooked scheme collapses.)

Fundamentally, Social Security is sound, although it needs some tweaks to shore up its finances for the long haul. The program has been adjusted—sometimes dramatically—since it was signed into law in 1935. Additional changes will be enacted in the future. The sweeping budget overhaul proposal sponsored by former Republican Senate Budget Committee chairman Pete Domenici and Alice Rivlin, the White House budget director under President Clinton, noted that Social Security "does not need to be fundamentally altered; rather, it needs only

modest adjustments so that it can continue to serve as a financial foundation for millions of retirees, survivors and disabled workers across the
country." They're right in their measured perspective about "modest
adjustments," a far cry from the more commonplace and misused word
crisis or worse yet, bankruptcy. Look at it this way: the projected long-
term Social Security funding gap is smaller than the increase in defense
spending from 2001 and 2011, according to Henry Aaron, economist at
the Brookings Institution.[3] "In present value terms, the gap is about one-
third the size of the tax cuts enacted under president George W. Bush,"
he writes in "Entitlements and Population Aging: Crisis, Problem, or
Opportunity?" "It is hard to see in what sense this is a crisis." Agreed.

Social Security isn't hurtling toward bankruptcy, even in the worst-
case scenario that nothing is done to shore up the system's finances.
(Don't get me wrong. Doing nothing would be an irresponsible blunder.
But some perspective is called for.) The Social Security system will pay
out its promised benefits in full until 2033, according to the latest projections. There will still be enough revenue coming into the program after
2033 to pay for about 75 percent of all benefits owed. That isn't a desirable outcome, of course. Far from it. But it also means that the financial
status of Social Security isn't doomsday, a catastrophe waiting to happen.

The sooner the shortfall is addressed the better, since Social Security
is the foundation of the American retirement system. That doesn't mean
cut benefits. Two thirds of senior households rely on Social Security for
a majority of their income. Specifically, over 65 percent of those sixty-
five and older get half or more of their income from Social Security,
which is why the option of reducing the benefit is the wrong way to go.
There are a number of alternatives for improving Social Security finances
without embracing a "we can't afford it" strategy. For example, defense
spending and Social Security each account for some 20 percent of the
federal budget. Perhaps the cuts should come out of defense? Don't like
that idea? Try this out: Raise the current ceiling on the Social Security
payroll tax from $117,000 in 2014 to $250,000. The change would extend
the date of exhausting trust fund reserves by about four decades. Get rid
of the cap altogether and Social Security is on sound financing past the

Social Security Administration's official seventy-five-year time horizon for projections.

The specific change you favor is beside the point for the moment. What matters is that closing the long-term funding gap is manageable without reducing monthly payments to beneficiaries.

The bigger, more troubling safety net issue is Medicare (and Medicaid). Total Medicare spending will grow as baby boomers file for their Medicare cards. The Congressional Budget Office estimates that enrollment in Medicare will nearly double in coming decades, reaching 80 million by 2030. The bulk of the long-term federal budget deficit concern comes from higher health care spending. Longer life expectancy doesn't necessarily lead to steeper Medicare bills, but working longer does reduce Medicare costs. Johnson and Smith of the Urban Institute estimate that the cumulative Medicare savings over thirty years is more than $400 billion under their various increased labor force participation rate scenarios for older workers.

Briefly, the main components of Medicare include premium-free Part A, which essentially pays for hospital services. Part B covers the costs of physician services, such as doctor visits and outpatient procedures. Part B comes with a monthly premium, adjusted to some degree for income. Medicare Part D is the prescription drug benefit provided by private companies. Part D can be tricky to navigate, and premiums vary by coverage. One other major choice is Medicare Advantage, a managed care option offered by a number of private insurers. You must be enrolled in Part A and Part B to join a Medicare Advantage plan and the premium is affected by the extent of coverage. (Caveat emptor: Looking at the Medicare rules, there is an exception, a nuance, an underappreciated twist to almost everything.) Although Medicare offers universal health care coverage for those sixty-five and over, there are many common medical expenses Medicare doesn't pay for, such as dental costs and long-term care.

Projections of Medicare spending are coming down. For instance, in recent years the Congressional Budget Office has lowered its forecast of cumulative Medicare spending from 2013 to 2020 by 16 percent, or one trillion dollars. A number of factors have come together to account for the slowdown, including the Affordable Care Act, or Obamacare. Despite the controversy enveloping the Affordable Care Act, thoughtful opponents keep many of its Medicare initiatives in place when proposing an alternative restructuring of the heath insurance system. The reforms have shored up Medicare's finances by raising payroll tax rates on high earners and with a new tax on their investment income. The health reform legislation is also slowing the rate of growth of payments to hospitals and some other providers. However, much more could be done and should be done without focusing on reducing benefits. For instance, the health care experts David Cutler, Ezekiel Emanuel, and Topher Spiro for the Center for American Progress in Washington, D.C., outlined a series of sensible institutional reforms that could reduce the federal budget by $100 billion or more. Among their proposals are instituting competitive bidding for durable medical equipment, electronic simplification for filing claims, and refusing to pay extra for expensive technologies with results similar to cheaper alternatives.[4]

Other market-based initiatives could also boost competitive pressures in the industry. For example, how about sweeping away barriers to international trade? U.S. physicians are paid about twice as much as their peers in Canada, Germany, and other major industrial nations. The Association of American Medical Colleges estimates that there is a nationwide shortage of doctors totaling more than thirteen thousand currently. The solution to the physician shortage lies in freer trade and lowered protectionist barriers. We should make it easy for foreign doctors who have been trained to our standards to come to the United States and practice their profession, says Dean Baker of the Center for Economic and Policy Research. His back-of-the-envelope calculation is illuminating. Baker estimates that doctor protectionism costs the United States about $80 billion in extra payments a year compared with other wealthy countries. Here's another competition-enhancing proposal: Medicare recipients should be allowed to spend their Medicare dollars anywhere in the world, which they can't do now. The competition and additional choice would put downward pressure on the overall medical price trend.[5]

That said, efforts to contain Medicare costs are really part of reforming America's overall health care system and not just programs geared toward the elderly. Medicare is a subset of the overall safety net issue. The turmoil surrounding the Affordable Care Act—including the disastrous launch of the state insurance exchanges and the rejection of Medicaid expansion by a number of states—concretely demonstrates that bringing change to some 18 percent of the U.S. economy is extremely contentious and difficult. However, the potential payoff makes the effort worthwhile. The United States pays more than twice as much per person for health care as the average for other wealthy countries. Bringing U.S. health care costs more in line with countries like Germany, Switzerland, and Canada while providing universal access will free up staggering resources for all generations. "It's all about controlling costs. It isn't about Medicare," says economist Baker. Harvard University economist and health care specialist David Cutler agrees. "One way or another, when medical costs increase, we all pay. The key is to lower total spending, not just spread it around in some different way."

Health care reform offers an enormous potential for boosting the economy's prospects. Valerie Ramey, economist at the University of California, San Diego, offers these intriguing rough calculations to give an idea of the potential payoff. "If the U.S. spent only 11 percent of GDP [on health care]—like Canada," she noted on a conference panel, "we would save $950 billion a year. That sum is about a third more than the peak in U.S. defense spending during the Iraq and Afghanistan wars," she says. "If the $950 billion went to K–12 education we could hike spending an extra $19,000 per student per year. Or we could give everyone a $3,000 tax rebate per year." In the meantime, remember that Medicare isn't an unsustainable economy crusher. There is much that can and should be done to boost Medicare efficiency and improve outcomes but, once again, crisis mongering is the wrong approach to addressing the issue. Working longer, encore careers, and unretirement are a big part of the solution with Medicare and other entitlements. Think opportunity. Not disaster.[6]

Now is a good time to deal with another major safety net issue that is often discussed as yet one more crisis: the family. There is a widespread sense that the bonds of family in modern America are badly frayed, especially compared to the past. The figures supporting the belief that an aging population can rely less on family members than before are well-known. About half of all first marriages end in divorce. Single parenthood is commonplace. Many women and men choose to be single and childless. Families are smaller. A majority of men and women work outside of the home, making it tough to find time to act as caregivers for aging parents. A strand of popular commentary is how the current generation isn't caring for its parents like an earlier generation did.

Problem is, every generation seems to believe that families cared for each other more in the past. For example, the eighteenth-century French social philosopher Alexis de Tocqueville stated that the American family was weak because in the new republic fathers exercised little authority over children. More recently, the decline in marriage rates is seen by many commentators as signs of a cultural crisis. Now, there's no question that family arrangements and family roles are changing. Yet the evidence strongly suggests the underlying bonds of family are remarkably durable. Family still matters. "Wherever it is investigated in the later twentieth century, an enduring feature of the family is its resilience and flexibility; and its emotional importance as a source of security and identity is perhaps increased in a world that seems increasingly insecure in other respects," writes Pat Thane, historian of aging, in *Old Age in English History.* "The commitment of reciprocity between generations has been continuous over time, though the forms and the needs which give rise to it have changed." The focus of her book is England but her insights apply to the United States.

Certainly, the message in the money suggests healthy family bonds. The estimated economic value of unpaid work by some 42 million family caregivers in 2009 was $450 billion, according to Susan Reinhard, senior vice-president for public policy at AARP. To put the sum in context, the former community nurse noted that total Medicare spending that year was $509 billion.[7] How about a really big figure: nearly $3 trillion, or $2,947,636,000,000 to be precise. The sum represents an estimate of the lost wages, Social Security benefits, and private pension for men and women ages fifty and over caring for their parents. According to research by the MetLife Mature Market Institute, the loss for the typical fifty-years-and-over caregiver averages $324,044 for women and $283,716 for men.

Thing is, the caring relationship often cuts the other way. Older people are often independent with fewer disabilities than before, able to stay engaged in the labor market late in life. They're just as likely to offer shelter and care to their middle-aged children, say, during a divorce or a spell of unemployment, as their adult children are to help them out when the frail years come. E-mail, social media like Facebook, tablets, and other advanced communication technologies allow for generations to stay in touch with ease. Other research emphasizes the strength of commitment among family members and relatives. For example, Naomi Gerstel of the University of Massachusetts and Natalia Sarkisian of Boston College find that compared to married couples, childless single individuals spend more time with and offer greater practical support to parents, kin, and friends.[8]

Even the family breakdown numbers aren't quite as overwhelming as they sometimes seem. Greater economic and social equality between the sexes have made families stronger. The divorce rate peaked in the late 1970s and it is as low as it has been in two generations. Many divorced couples with children have learned from the painful experiences of an earlier generation of divorce. The marriage may be over, but former partners try harder to stay in touch, sharing custody and child-rearing obligations. Men and women are spending more time with their children than in the idealized Ozzie and Harriet era of the one-income nuclear family. Women's economic independence and contributions create more resources for the family to draw on during times of crisis. The rise in same sex marriage and civil unions is also expanding family networks. According to the Census Bureau, the percentage growth in same sex couple households was 80.4 percent to 646,000 from 2000 to 2010. The numbers of married same sex couples will soar as the legal recognition of gay marriage spreads.

Other institutions are stepping in to help out, too. For example,

African American caregiving has long been defined by the extended ties of kinship, noted Peggye Dilworth-Anderson, the interim codirector at the University of North Carolina Institute on Aging, at a Gerontological Society session. She is well versed in taking care of the aged both as a scholar and from personal experience, since she and her husband were caregivers to his parents for sixteen years. She has studied African American families, especially in an area of rural North Carolina known as Out East. Forty years or so ago, she said, the typical family had four to six children. Now, it's two or three, and at least one of them has moved away from the poor region for greater opportunity. Families are smaller and African Americans are living longer. "How do you fill the gap?" she said. A partial solution in the Out East region is churches. Congregations regularly check up on their frail aging parishioners. "The need is to expand the support networks," says Dilworth-Anderson.

People will go to great lengths living up to their responsibilities. Debbie Durham is program manager at Life by Design NW in Portland, Oregon. The nonprofit is housed at Portland Community College with a mandate to help boomers redefine the last stage of life. Her current lifestyle, which she enjoys, didn't come easy. She had been living in North Carolina as executive director of a local nonprofit. Her mother, who lived in California, became ill in 2004. As the oldest daughter, Durham left her job the following year. She figured she would care for her mother for about six months. She ended up staying in a mid-sized California town on the coast for two years. The second year as a caregiver was particularly tough. She moved her mother to a residential care facility in Portland in 2006. Nine months later she moved to Portland and started her job search. She thought she would get something quickly, but she was wrong. Unemployed, she learned the hard way that two months is about as long as you can stay with relatives—even close ones. Her car became highly organized, with her trunk transformed into the equivalent of a mobile storage unit with, for example, a box for the bathroom and another for clothes. Durham finally got a part-time job at Life by Design NW, a schedule that allows her to spend time with her mother, who lives nearby. "People have to get creative," she says. "And I have no intention of retiring."

The dynamics of an aging America are complex. The real problem when it comes to an older population isn't a strained fiscal purse, an aging population, and changing family arrangements. These concerns are routinely exaggerated. No, the genuine worry should be over the ranks of those who haven't enjoyed good work opportunities and incomes over a lifetime, living on society's margins. Their life expectancy experience lags well behind that of their better-educated peers and among some groups in society is perhaps even shrinking. They haven't managed to save much if anything for their retirement. Their prospects aren't terrific for a decent job in their elder years. While the unretirement movement isn't a social and economic cure-all, unretirement goes a long way toward improving both personal financial security for the majority and boosting shared economic prosperity for all. The personal, economic, and fiscal payoff from racing toward the unretirement future is potentially huge—a game changer.

CHAPTER 5

The Vanguard of the 25/65 Revolution

Don't stop thinking about tomorrow
Don't stop, it'll soon be here
                                        —Fleetwood Mac

THE WIDELY EXPRESSED DESIRE TO stay engaged among older workers suggests a very different image for an aging work force than David Frum's accident-prone elderly drivers. Remember, the elderly weighing on society that Frum believes we need to say no to, whether it's driving or entitlements.

An alternative metaphor came during a dinner by a lake near Zeeland, Michigan. I was with Don Goeman, executive vice-president for research at Herman Miller, the innovative office design company, and Mark Schurman, the company's director of corporate communications. Goeman is a good storyteller with a deft, low-key touch. He deals with many of the world's top designers. At one point we turned to the economics of an aging work force. I explained my investigation into prospects for working longer and Goeman immediately responded, "It's a design problem."

Really? I was skeptical at first, but thinking about our conversation later on I concluded he's right. The hand-wringing about a new generation gap, the rise of intergenerational warfare, the drumbeat of young versus old is a dead end. So is the idea that older workers and aging entrepreneurs are a deadweight on the economy, a generation depriving society of creativity and innovation, the wellsprings of capitalist dynamism. I learned that a far better metaphor for grasping the relationship between the generations—especially in the workplace—lies in the story of a chair: the Aeron. The Aeron is an apt image for unretirement.

Herman Miller is based in Zeeland, not far from Grand Rapids, Michigan. Miller had published a number of thoughtful pieces about the coming demographic transformation in the workplace. I guessed the company's managers and designers would have a savvy grasp on what it takes to keep an aging work force productive.

D. J. DePree founded Herman Miller in 1923. He bought the floundering Michigan Star Furniture Company with the financial backing of his father-in-law, Herman Miller, and a small group of local businessmen. DePree focused on manufacturing traditional eighteenth- and nineteenth-century reproductions of massive, ornate furniture, the kind of furniture suited for mansions. During the Great Depression, the furniture maker nearly closed its doors when demand for large furniture sets collapsed.

The struggling company was visited in 1931 by the New York City–based industrial designer Gilbert Rohde, a modernist influenced by the spare, practical vision of the German Bauhaus movement. Rohde convinced DePree to allow the designer to create a line of furniture for ordinary homes. Rohde would get paid on commission. The bedroom line was shown at the 1933 Chicago World's Fair and it went over well with both fairgoers and reviewers. Rohde remained as design director at Herman Miller for a number of years.

The Miller business model since Rohde is to collaborate with world class designers, such as Charles and Ray Eames, George Nelson, Isamu Noguchi, and Gianfranco Zaccai. Designer Robert Propst famously developed the office cube in the late sixties for Miller. His idea was to encourage collaboration, teamwork, and health. (The thought was that you would move around more.) Companies may have tried similar language in selling cubicles to their employees, but what management really liked about the office cube was it offered a cheaper floor plan. You could pack more workers into your existing space. Employees don't really like cubicles. They lack privacy. They're noisy. The typical cubicle office is depressing, bland colors livened with colorful Post-it notes. Even Propst came to hate the "monolithic insanity" he helped create.

Walking around the offices at Herman Miller you can see an evolution in the cubicle concept. Offices are still relatively open and your desk is next to other desks. But there are lots of different space configurations for work, such as small conference rooms for meetings, "havens" for talking in private and big tables in an open space for laboring in the thick of things. Wireless, laptops, and smartphones make office mobility practical. The emphasis is on encouraging creativity rather than bland efficiency.

While visiting Miller, I learned about their earlier Metaform project, when the company was looking outside the workplace for other commercial markets. In the mid-1980s, management turned their energies toward an aging population. Was there a business opportunity for the company? Given that most Americans want to stay in their homes when elderly, Miller gathered together a number of leading designers to rethink the home for seniors, from the bathroom to the kitchen. The overall project was code-named Metaform (not to be confused with a more recent design by the same name the company has since introduced).

Among the design challenges was developing a chair better suited for the elderly than, say, the popular La-Z-Boy. Bill Stumpf, a Minnesota-based designer and Don Chadwick, a designer from Santa Monica, California, researched and rethought the chair. The designers recognized that the combination of limited mobility and sedentary lifestyle meant the elderly tend to sit for long periods of time—what the designers referred to as the elderly's more "limited universe." They looked into issues of heat buildup and pressure distribution, "trying to design the ultimate lazy boy that would allow somebody to sit comfortably and avoid all these other problems that are associated with being sedentary," says Miller's Schurman.

The code name for the chair was Sarah. The chair allowed for good air circulation, with foam cushions supported by plastic mesh. Sarah was easy to get in and out of, a boon for elderly people with weak legs and an aching back. A pneumatically controlled footrest folded under the chair when it wasn't needed. Sarah was well along in development and moving toward commercialization by 1988. Miller shelved Sarah because management couldn't figure out a profitable way to distribute the home-based products its designers had devised.

Several years later, the company started on another major project, a next-generation office chair. Miller's researchers had observed that office workers spent hours at their desks, banging away on their personal computer keyboards. The company's leaders began talking with designers, describing the sedentary, nearly immobile task-focused habits of the modern office worker. "Bill and Don remarked," says Shurman, "'They sure sound a lot like the elderly.'" The two pulled out Sarah, applied many of the Sarah concepts like pressure distribution and heat dissipation to a new work chair form, and included suppliers in the project so that they could create advances in materials. Sarah was renamed Aeron and, introduced in 1994, it became one of the bestselling office chairs in the world. The Aeron is a design badge for creative industries from high-tech start-ups in Silicon Valley to multimedia advertising agencies in the New York. The Aeron is even part of the permanent collection at the New York Museum of Modern Art and the Smithsonian.

Here's the thing: A chair designed for the elderly stands for youth, energy, and creativity. Don't worry about the generation gap, bad elderly drivers, and greedy geezers. Think the Aeron instead. The Aeron is a metaphor for the powerful ties between generations, old and young, especially on the job.

The design theme of generational bonds and shared interests runs deep. For instance, Miller has installed "universal design" elements throughout its buildings on its corporate campus. Universal design is a movement for taking into account aging in the blueprint for various products, such as door handles, lighting, and work surface heights. Products are created to be both utilitarian and aesthetically pleasing. No one wants to work in an office or live in a home reminiscent of a sterile hospital room or nursing home. The doors at Miller have levers rather than knobs. A small difference, but levers are easier on aging hands. The drawers at Miller have an easy-grip pull. Yet lighting fixtures that help older workers see better at the office, tools that require less physical strength, and other ergonomic techniques are also good for younger workers. "I would say from a product design and development standpoint, yes, we need to pay attention to those fundamentals that fall under the headline of 'universal design,'" says Gretchen Gscheidle, director of insight and exploration at Miller. "But guess what? Whether it is chronic aging or acute injury, whatever we do to accommodate those particular situations they're going to be useful for everyone."

A slight twist on her insight comes from the luxury automaker BMW. Germany's population is older than America's. The average age of BMW's plant workers is expected to hit forty-seven years of age by 2017, up from thirty-nine in 2007. In an experiment in Dingolfing, Germany, BMW modified an assembly line and staffed it with "older workers" with an average age of forty-seven. At first, the "pensioner's line" (also known as the 2017 line) was less productive than the regular BMW assembly lines. But BMW quickly improved worker performance by introducing seventy relatively small changes, such as installing wooden flooring, adding chairs to some parts of the line so workers can perform tasks sitting down, and installing larger computer screens with bigger type, large-handled gripping tools, and magnifying glasses. The total cost of the investment in the assembly line was only about $50,000. (To put that figure in context, the manufacturer's suggested retail price for BMW Series 3 sedan in 2014 was $37,995.) BMW also introduced stretching exercises and job rotation across workstations to limit time spent on the most physically demanding jobs. "What did BMW get in return? The line achieved a 7% productivity improvement in one year, equaling the productivity of lines staffed by younger workers," according to a 2010 *Harvard Business Review* article, "How BMW Is Defusing the Demographic Time Bomb." "BMW now touts the 2017 line as a model of productivity and high quality in its internal communications."

The knowledge gained from the pensioner line experiment is being adapted to the benefit of all BMW assembly-line workers—not just the older ones. (It seems we always have to relearn what we should know. Henry Curtis, a member of the State of Michigan Commission to Study Problems of Aging, wrote in 1952 in *Harper's* magazine that there had been many investigations into the attitude of workers toward retirement at age sixty-five. He had never heard of one where a great majority of the surveyed wanted to stop working. In the early 1900s, Curtis noted, "Henry Ford put his old men in a separate building and gave them a short rest period in the morning and afternoon. His report was that they did as well as the others. During World War II, in the state of New York, 340,000 workers over sixty-five were taken back into industry and again the report was the same—their work was perfectly satisfactory.")

When it comes to jobs and careers, far more unites than divides twentysomethings and sixtysomethings. Younger adults starting their careers are typically idealistic, eager to land a job with both an income and meaning. The same desire motivates many aging boomers. The older and younger generations both value flexibility, although for slightly different reasons. Young workers would like to spend more time with children and older workers with grandchildren. Older employees have gotten the unretirement message, but many seek more than an income. The big difference between the twentysomething and sixtysomething generations is a sense of time. The young believe they have plenty of time, while for older workers time is precious. "Time is running short, and many boomers want work that also offers purpose," says Marc Freedman. "They too want work that gives meaning."

Sounds like something a newly minted college graduate would say, doesn't it? The design firm Continuum has been interviewing boomers for a number of their projects. Former CEO Harry West noticed striking parallels between older and younger workers in the interviews. "I heard this resonance between going to college and retirement. Sometimes, they couldn't articulate it clearly, but there was a juxtaposition there," he says. "Because when you go to college, that is in some ways the ultimate moment of freedom. It was about choices, about what was going to be self-fulfilling for them as an individual."

There are generational differences, of course. Boomers, gen Xers, and millennials have been exposed to different technologies, educational practices, business cycles, and other world-shaping experiences. Society is increasingly diverse. Physical abilities erode with age. There are no sixty-year-old basketball players in the NBA or sixty-five-year-old women competing for gold in the hundred-meter dash in the Olympics. Many people start seeing the effects of aging on their vision sometime in their forties. Adults in their sixties and over seem to have a smaller working memory for processing information than their younger peers. Still, despite their age and experience differences, what's remarkable is how each generation essentially values many of the same things. Allen Glicksman is director of research and evaluation at Philadelphia Corporation for Aging. He's an expert on policies that transform urban environments into age-friendly communities. What's a major lesson he's learned over the years about the generations living together in communities? "What's good for old people is good for everybody and what's bad for older people is bad for everyone in the community," he says. The same insight holds for work.

The work place is also a community that allows for the generations to learn from one another. That's the experience of NextSpace. The company sells membership in collaborative offices to freelancers, contract workers, and independent entrepreneurs—the 1099 work force. NextSpace was founded in 2008 in Santa Cruz, California, by Jeremy Neuner (former economic development manager), Ryan Coonerty (former mayor), and Caleb Baskin (local attorney). It's in a number of California locations with plans for expansion. The San Francisco office space is near Union Square. The floor I was on has plenty of tables, conference rooms, easy chairs, large windows, a coffee machine—and plenty of people with laptops. Nothing fancy. Welcoming. Utilitarian.

Members are called *café members*, "because we pull them out of cafés," says Neuner. "We also think a little bit about what is the old-school version of nineteenth-century Europe. Cafés were the gathering places. Revolutions begin in cafés. So that's part of what we're trying to tap into as well, the notion that if you put people in a cool place and you give them all the free coffee they can possibly consume, that cool things will start to happen."

Among the people doing cool things is Scott McGilvray, sixty-eight years old. He had been co-owner and president of the landscape company Jensen Corporation and Jensen Landscape Services from 1982 to 2004. The company focused on big commercial landscaping jobs. Over the years he learned how wasteful Americans are with water. When he retired, McGilvray formed a consulting firm, Water Aware. He works part-time, three days a week. He has a handful of employees. The consulting firm is a way to stay engaged, discover if there is a market for smarter water management, and use his knowledge to better the environment. "I am in the black, I'm proud to say," McGilvray says. "I don't have to do the consulting business. I don't depend on it for income. I do it because it's worth the effort."

He worked out of NextSpace in Santa Cruz. "I work better around people," he says. Neuner elaborates.

> What's cool about having him at a place like NextSpace is that Scott understands what it takes to run a business. He is able to offer a little bit of sage advice to the twenty-, thirtysomethings. The flip side, the twenty-, thirtysomethings are able to help Scott program his MacBook and figure out the apps for his iPhone. I don't see generational tension. Instead, I see opportunity and collaboration in some interesting ways when it comes to the younger and the older demographic.

Many companies are making formal efforts to encourage interaction between generations. Older, experienced managers and employees have traditionally helped develop promising young workers. In an intriguing twist on mentoring—called reverse mentoring—a number of companies are asking younger workers to mentor older ones. The best-known proponent of the practice was Jack Welch, the former head of General

Electric. In 1999, he started pairing young junior employees savvy about new information technologies (at that time the Web) with senior managers who needed to quickly grasp the potential of the technology.

The financial services giant Hartford runs a reverse mentoring program. Management realized its senior executives should understand emerging social media and similar communication techniques for reaching customers. A small group of millennial employees had been holding informal meetings about information technologies, frustrated at how slow Hartford was to exploit social media. They approached senior management, and a reverse mentoring program was established matching young, technologically savvy staffers with Hartford's senior management. "The opportunities for learning and open discussion provided by reverse mentioning are fluid and countless. The new relationships formed by mentors and mentees can be inspiring and genuine," concludes a study into the Hartford reverse mentoring program by the Sloan Center on Aging and Work and the Center for Work and Family, both at Boston College. "Perhaps the most important gift of reverse mentoring, regardless of the specific business issues the strategy can be used to address, is the affirmation in all sectors of a company and across generations that the next big idea can come from anywhere."[1]

Let's get rid of one popular canard about young and old workers: the belief that older folks staying on the job means fewer employment opportunities are available for younger workers economywide. We've heard variations of the argument over the years and, at first glance, the idea that older workers are crowding out younger workers is persuasive. At the level of an individual firm and business, it's true that jobs aren't opening up to new entrants if the employer is shrinking or stagnating. Troubled companies cut budgets and hand out pink slips. Younger employees tend to leave for better opportunities or they're pushed out by management with some variation of the last-hired, first-fired approach. Older employees hang on to their positions, sometimes desperately. Little wonder the notion that the job market in the United States is a similar zero-sum game—more jobs for one group translates to fewer jobs for another group—is deeply ingrained. That doesn't mean the belief is right, looking at the overall economy. "They aren't taking jobs from younger workers," says economist Rolnick. "They may be creating jobs for them."

Case in point: the rise of the women's movement in the seventies, eighties, and nineties. At the time, more women joining the labor market and competing for well-paying jobs sparked plenty of commentary in the office and on opinion pages that gains for women meant job losses for men. Instead, increasing numbers of women in the workplace has been a boon for the economy and overall job creation. Between 1970 and 2009, women went from holding 37 percent of all jobs to almost 48 percent. Without the nearly 38 million increase in women over that time frame the economy would be some 25 percent smaller, "an amount equal to the combined GDP of Illinois, California and New York," calculate Joanna Barsh and Lareina Yee of McKinsey and Company in *Unlocking the Full Potential of Women in the US Economy*. At the same time, the increase of women into the paid market economy didn't translate into declining opportunities for men. Another common zero-sum labor market fear is that immigrants take away jobs from American workers. Yet a cottage industry of economic research persuasively demonstrates that the job impact of immigrants on native-born Americans locally and nationally doesn't drift too far from zero, either positively or negatively. "Data show that, on net, immigrants expand the U.S. economy's productive capacity, stimulate investment, and promote specialization that in the long run boosts productivity," writes Giovanni Peri, economist at the University of California, Davis.[2] "Consistent with previous research, there is no evidence that these effects take place at the expense of jobs for workers born in the United States."

These insights from the experience of women and immigrants in the job market translate well into older workers. The economy is not a fixed pie or the competition for work a zero-sum game for society at large, after adjusting for the business cycle. The economy is much more dynamic than that, with new jobs and new businesses created all the time even as many older jobs and industries fade. (It's surprising how many jobs don't completely disappear. We don't ride horses to get around town and work the fields anymore, yet there are more than twenty-five thousand farriers caring for horse hooves in the United States. Massachusetts-based Westfield Whip Manufacturing, founded in 1884, is still making leather horse whips.)

Economists call the belief that there are only so many jobs over the course of a business cycle the "lump of labor fallacy." Research by the Pew Economic Mobility Project found good reasons for doubting the generational employment pessimists. From 1977 to 2011, a one percentage point increase in the employment rate of older workers was associated with a decline in youth unemployment, an increase in youth employment, and a hike in hours worked. "The fact that the lump-of-labor theory does not hold is powerful information for both policy makers and employers, given the state of the U.S. retirement system and the need for people to work longer in order to have a secure retirement," the Pew Study concludes. "Retaining older workers does not hurt the job prospects of younger ones, meaning that protecting Boomers from downward mobility goes hand in hand with promoting the upward mobility of youth."[3] Alicia Munnell, of the Center for Retirement Research at Boston College, sliced and diced the data in a number of nuanced ways. Her succinct conclusion in *Are Aging Baby Boomers Squeezing Young Workers Out of Jobs?* echoes Pew. "This horse has been beaten to death," she writes. "An exhaustive search found no evidence to support the lump of labor theory in the United States. In fact, the evidence suggests that greater employment for older persons leads to better outcomes for the young—reduced unemployment, increased employment, and a higher wage. The patterns are consistent for both men and women and for groups with different levels of education."

While we're at it, let's also bury the conventional wisdom that younger workers and older workers are vastly different in their ability to create and innovate. Good employers typically value older workers for their experience, the knowledge they've built up over the years, their proven ability to solve problems. Stumped colleagues will turn to someone with gray hair for advice. But even far-sighted employers don't associate gray hair with creativity. That's reserved for youth.

Paul Dirac, the 1933 Nobel laureate in physics, captured popular sentiment in a poem, although he's specifically addressing his profession.

> Age is, of course, a fever chill
> That every physicist must fear.
> He's better dead than living still
> When once he's past his thirtieth year.[4]

Einstein and Dirac made major contributions around age twenty-six
(although recent research suggests the age of scientific breakthroughs is
occurring at later ages). On the other hand, many poets rebel against the
notion that putting the words "creativity" and "elder" together is an
oxymoron. "Sophocles completed his *Oedipus* trilogy at ninety. Titian
painted the magnificent *Christ of Pity* at ninety-nine," wrote poet Roy
Addison Helton in 1939. "At seventy Franklin began the task of gaining
for our struggling colonies the alliance of France. At eighty Thomas
Edison was deep in research as to the possibility of producing rubber
from native American plants." Henry Wadsworth Longfellow wrote a
poem for the fiftieth anniversary of the class of 1825 at Bowdoin College.
He ran through a list of older giants, like Cato who learned Greek at
eighty, Chaucer penning *The Canterbury Tales* at sixty, and Goethe finishing *Faust* when "80 years were past." He exhorted his Bowdoin classmates
to not lie down and fade. No, "something remains for us to do or dare."

> For age is opportunity no less
> Than youth itself, though in another dress,
> And as the evening twilight fades away
> The sky is filled with stars, invisible by day.

More recently, *Skyfall*, the twenty-third James Bond movie, issued on the
fiftieth anniversary of the franchise, has some fun with stereotypes
between generations. An aging, battered James Bond meets the new Q—
the high-tech wizard for MI6—in a museum. Q is young, not long out of
graduate school. Bond and Q are staring at a painting.

Q: 007, I'm your new quartermaster.

BOND: You must be joking.

Q: Why, because I'm not wearing a lab coat?

BOND: Because you still have spots.

Q: My complexion is hardly relevant.

BOND: Your competence is.

Q: Age is no guarantee of efficiency.

BOND: And youth is no guarantee of innovation.

More serious, scholarly research is demolishing the notion that older workers are less effective workers, a spent force on the job, a waste of employer money. Older workers are still learning decades into their careers. A study into air traffic controllers suggests that thirty-year-olds had better memories than their older workmates. The researchers also learned that sixty-year-old air traffic controllers did just as well in an emergency situation as their thirty-year-old peers—a reassuring result for anyone who flies. "There is no observable decrease in older workers' overall performance, because what they lack in cognitive abilities they compensate for with an increase in job knowledge, skills and various coping strategies," says Sara Czaja, codirector of the University of Miami's Center on Aging.[5] Science is moving away "from the dismal characterization of aging as an inevitable process of brain damage and decline," write Patricia A. Reuter-Lorenz and Cindy Lustig, of the University of Toronto and the University of Michigan, respectively. "Instead, the emerging story from cognitive neuroscience is that aging can be successful, associated with gains and losses. It is not necessarily a unidirectional process but rather a complex phenomenon characterized by reorganization, optimization and enduring functional plasticity that can enable the maintenance of a productive—and happy—life."[6]

More important, the assumption that creativity and aging are anathema to one another is yet one more false stereotype. Perhaps the most significant research is by University of Chicago economist David Galenson. He is looking into the relationship between aging and innovation, with an initial focus on artists. We all consciously or subconsciously associate artistic breakthroughs with youth. The young are cool. They're bold. They aren't bound by the past. Galenson notes that some famous artists burst on the scene with a major innovation when they were young. But, he adds, others do their genuinely innovative work in their sixties, seventies, and even eighties. "Every time we see a young person do something extraordinary, we say, 'That's a genius,'" he said in an interview for Encore.org. "Every time we see an old person do something extraordinary we say, 'Isn't that remarkable?' Nobody had noticed how many of those old exceptions there are and how much they have in common."

Galenson illustrates his thesis by highlighting the career of nineteenth-century painter Paul Cézanne (1839–1906). Cézanne died at age sixty-seven and did his best work toward the end of his life, says Galenson. Cézanne struggled with his art throughout his life, always experimenting, always pushing to the edge of the possible. He was never satisfied, but the paintings of his last few years "would come to be considered his greatest contribution and would directly influence every important artistic development of the next generation," writes Galenson in *Old Masters and Young Geniuses: The Two Life Cycles of Artistic Creativity*. "As Cézanne grew older, his paintings could increasingly be understood as visual representations of the uncertainty of perception, for the more he worked, the more acutely he became aware of the difficulty and complexity of his chosen task."

Galenson contrasts Cézanne with Pablo Picasso (1881–1973). His genius burned brightest when he was young. Picasso's stellar, revolutionary accomplishment came when he was in his midtwenties with the 1907 painting *Les Demoiselles d'Avignon*, argues Galenson. *Les Demoiselles* is a large, dramatic, disjointed painting of five prostitutes, a seminal moment in cubism and modern art. "The painting was a brutal departure from the lyrical works of the rose period that immediately preceded it, and its arrival jolted Paris' advanced art world," he writes. Artist Peter Plagens wrote about the painting on its hundredth anniversary in *Newsweek* in 2007, calling it "the most important work of art of the last 100 years."

Age isn't the key distinction with innovation. What seems to count much more is approach. Experimental innovators gradually build their skills over a lifetime. (Think Cézanne.) Conceptual innovators focus on boldly communicating specific ideas or emotions. (Think Picasso.) There is also choice, the decision to remain creatively engaged. (Think Bob Dylan.) Galenson's perspective is that experimental and conceptual innovators exist in every field and workplace. The insight isn't limited to a handful of traditionally creative endeavors like poetry, painting, and music. No, the same holds for professionals like lawyers and doctors, managers and entrepreneurs, factory workers and cubicle dwellers. In the Encore.org interview, Galenson called Wilma Melville, a 2007 Purpose Prize winner, an experimental innovator. Her encore career is training search and rescue dogs after the Oklahoma City bombing tragedy of 1995. "Here's a retired gym teacher who has a trained search dog. She comes back from this searing experience in Oklahoma City. All of a sudden all of the things in her life came together. And these were things that she had never thought were connected," Galenson explains. "She said, 'I could write a curriculum because I had been a teacher. I knew how to teach young men, fire fighters, because I'd raised four sons. I knew how to train dogs because I had. And all of a sudden I saw a thing I could do using all of those skills.' You see the opportunity and then you say, 'Wow.'"[7]

I think the significance of Galenson's insights tells us something essential about the evolving nature of work—for the better. In a long, discursive essay published in 1956, the late sociologist Daniel Bell investigated the relationship between factory work and perceptions of everyday life. He noted that Smokestack America's high-speed assembly lines were ruled by the clock, by management's relentless drive for efficiency and standardization, by the breakdown of tasks into minute rhythms that didn't require thought from men (they were mostly men at the time) on the factory floor. "The image of tens of thousands of workers streaming from the sprawling factories marks indelibly the picture of industrial America, as much as the fringed buckskin and rifle marked the nineteenth century frontier, or the peruke and lace that of Colonial

Virginia," wrote Bell in *Work and Its Discontents: The Cult of Efficiency in America*. (A peruke is a wig.) "The majority of Americans may not work in factories, as the majority of Americans never were on the frontier, or never lived in Georgian houses; yet the distinctive ethos of each time lies in these archetypes."

The factory is no longer the dominant symbol of everyday work in America. A painful decline in American manufacturing took hold about two decades after Bell wrote his essay. Corporate rivals from Europe and Asia competed with American manufacturing for jobs and markets at home and abroad. Membership in private industrial unions plunged as American manufacturers overhauled their operations and outsourced production to cheaper markets such as China. America remains a global manufacturing powerhouse, but the industry employs a relatively small share of the overall labor force. The era of young adults graduating from high school, joining a union, and making a good living at a factory—working class on the job and middle class at home—has largely disappeared.

Our sense of the modern workplace is now shaped by the creative industries. The defining tools of creative businesses are computers, the Internet, mobile devices, and quicksilver network connections. The common images of work in present-day America draw heavily on employees and entrepreneurs from industries like biotech, information technologies, multimedia production, and graphic design. Their ranks range from option-laden programming engineers at Google to chefs opening their own restaurants and indie musicians making a part-time living playing the local clubs. Some creative-industry workers make a lot of money (read Silicon Valley stock options) and others struggle to get by (like most indie rockers).

The Walker Art Center in Minneapolis is a monument to modern experimental art. Years ago the museum had a special exhibit about Joseph Beuys. A contemporary of Andy Warhol, Beuys was a prolific German artist and political activist with heady ambitions to transform the world. The exhibit didn't do much for me at first. A bunch of yellow erasers. A giant, ugly felt suit hanging on a wall. A large clear water bottle with green water. A hare on a sugar packet. (Yes, a hare. He really liked hares.) What did grab my attention was a poster with the words CREATIVITY EQUALS CAPITAL in bright red letters. "The words 'creativity equals capital' were kind of a slogan for him," said Joan Rothfuss, at the time an associate curator at the Walker. "He also used 'art equals capital' quite often. He meant to suggest that the new monetary instrument could be human creativity rather than money."

Beuys hit on a fundamental transformation in the economy. The twin pincers of technological advances and globalization, two of the most powerful economic forces of our age, puts companies under enormous pressure to come up with new products and new ways of doing business. Since creativity is money, management and the wider culture have become obsessed with finding ways to encourage innovation. Hence the business-speak slogans to break down command-and-control management hierarchies, tear apart bureaucratic walls, and encourage teamwork. These and other organizational initiatives are all pursued with an eye toward getting their employees to devise better products and new services. Similarly, indie capitalists are artisans starting their own companies, many of them urban based. Bruce Nussbaum in his book *Creative Intelligence* defines the foundational principle of indie capitalism: "Creativity drives capitalism. Creativity is the source of economic value. Creativity transforms what money can't buy into what money can buy." Beuys would approve of Nussbaum's perspective.

"I think Beuys was talking about a way of living and a way of working. He often talked about creativity as being something that could be produced by anybody in any profession," says Rothfuss. "He really wanted to take it away from the realm of artists and give it back to everyone else, whether they were engineers, or doctors, or housewives, or whatever they were doing." That sums up the creative economy manifesto.

The urban studies theorist Richard Florida estimates that creative workers are more than a third of the U.S. work force, up from roughly 5 percent to 10 percent at the turn of the twentieth century.[8] That's a larger share of the workforce than were factory workers when manufacturing defined the economy. The creative work force is also growing and it will continue to expand as more jobs are tied to the creative economy infrastructure, with the most significant change the rise of start-up businesses. For our purposes, it's important to emphasize that creative work doesn't exclude older workers—quite the opposite. Many older workers are productive, educated, and healthy, just like their younger peers. Research into the founders of technology companies reveals more than twice as many founders older than age fifty as those twenty-five years and younger. "Many, in fact, were in their sixties when they founded their startups," note scholars Richard Freeman, Ben Rissing, and Vivek Wadhwa.[9] Says Marc Freedman: "New ideas need old people."

Yes, the Aeron chair is the right metaphor for the generations feeding off each other in an economy that thrives on creativity and innovation. Tom Agon, cofounder and managing partner of Rivia, a brand consulting firm, put it nicely in a *New York Times* column. "If an organization wants innovation to flourish, the conversation needs to change from severance packages to retention bonuses."

Karl Marx would approve. Marx grasped the deadening effect of the factory, those "dark satanic mills" of the nineteenth century. For Marx and other nineteenth-century classical economists the only way to produce more goods for sale was to work employees harder and longer and to pay them less. This perspective was behind Marx's famous proclamation that workers faced a future of relative "immiseration," or impoverishment, a judgment widely shared at the time even among those opposed to unorthodox economic arrangements like communism and socialism. Less appreciated, writes Bell, is how Marx also saw an alternative solution to a bleak future of immiseration: variety. Work should sustain the mind, the spirit, and the body.

> It becomes a question of life and death, for society . . . to replace the detail worker of today crippled by life-long repetition of one and the same trivial operation, and thus reduced to a mere fragment of a man, by the fully developed individual, fit for a variety of labors, ready to face any change in production, and to whom the different social functions he performs are but so many modes of giving free scope to his own natural and acquired powers.[10]

Sounds like something a Silicon Valley chief executive would say. (I've sat through many CEO talks along those lines.)

Marx believed one society of his era showed the variety promise: America. He liked what a Frenchman wrote about his experiences in San Francisco:

> I was firmly convinced that I was fit for nothing but letterpress printing. Once in the midst of this world of adventurers who change their occupation so often as they do their shirt, egad, I did as the others. As mining did not turn out remunerative enough, I left for the town where in succession I became a typographer, slater, plumber, etc. In consequences of thus finding out that I am fit for any sort of work I feel less like a mollusk and more of a man.[11]

Paul Revere was no mollusk. The Boston silversmith is best known for his celebrated ride to Lexington and Concord warning the colonial militia that British forces were coming. His business career resembles that of Marx's Frenchman in San Francisco. This "enterprising mechanic," notes historian Daniel Boorstin, was a silversmith who also learned copper plating and the art of dentistry. He designed frontispieces for singing books and works of history. Revere founded a mill for rolling sheet copper and a foundry for manufacturing bolts and spikes. He built church bells. "The eighty-three years of Paul Revere's life brought him from an era of colonial craftsmen into the early modern industrial New England," writes Boorstin in his essay, "The Transforming of Paul Revere." "He was alert to the new local opportunities in the new age."

The career and job experiences of Marx's Frenchman and Paul Revere are reminiscent of the current encore and unretirement movement. Instead of doing one task and one job all your life, many more people will try multiple careers. Most people will tap into the skills and knowledge they've accumulated over the years, but exercise their creativity in different industries and entrepreneurial ventures. For example, you might practice law, but shift from earning a paycheck at a private law firm to spending a few years on legal matters at a nonprofit organization. A stint in a government agency might follow and perhaps, when the time is right, a return to the private sector. A mechanic might focus on repairing and maintaining cars, and at other times build a business with boats, motorcycles, and trucks. Serial entrepreneurs create one company after another, sometimes in the same business, sometimes in an entirely unrelated area, but always tapping into the start-up insights they've accumulated over the years.

Ellie Giles, for example. We met at her second-floor open office housed in an old hardware store remodeled with a high-tech sensibility in Rockville, Maryland. (She shares the office space with young biotech engineers working on their business plans.) Giles was an educator for thirty-six years in the Montgomery County, Maryland, school system. She focused on special education, an area just getting off the ground when she started teaching in 1977. She held a number of education jobs, including administrator. She also stayed on top of the latest research, since the relatively new field of special education kept evolving. She got her doctorate from the University of Phoenix in education in 2010. Giles says she loved what she did, especially the special education. But around the time she got her doctorate she realized it was time to try something different. Montgomery County was setting up an economic development group with a board comprising local CEOs. Through a connection, she was asked if she would volunteer to help advance the project. She agreed to volunteer for six months, twenty hours a week, to help set up the economic-development initiative. Well, the job went so well that she is now director of operations for the Montgomery County Business Development Corporation. "I realized I had a skill set. I just needed to reframe it," she says. "I was a CEO. They called it principal. I knew how to address stakeholders. I knew how to write a mission statement. I knew how to follow up on the mission statement." She is clearly having a blast.

Nicholas Ribush, age seventy-two, embraced a more dramatic change. An Australian, he graduated from Melbourne University Medical School in 1964 and practiced medicine for seven years. He loved it, but he was also overworked and restless. He decided to travel the world in 1971. It was time to have some fun, Ribush recalls. The following year he was in Thailand and he discovered Buddhism, an encounter that changed his life course. Ribush was drawn to Buddhism and, wanting to learn more, he made his way to the Kopan Monastery in Nepal. He became a student of Lama Yeshe and Lama Zopa Rinpoche. He worked for their Foundation for the Preservation of the Mahayana Tradition and became one of the first Westerners ordained as a monk in the Tibetan Buddhist tradition. He helped Lama Yeshe found Wisdom Publications in 1975. He lived in Nepal, India, and England publishing Buddhist texts and, in 1989, moved to the United States. The director of the Lama Yeshe Wisdom Archive in Lincoln, Massachusetts, he translates and edits Buddhist teachings. The publishing house is a small operation, some $350,000 in annual revenue. Most of the books are given away and no one is paid much, more like a stipend. He plans to keep at his work as long as he can. "I love my job," he says.

The current conversation over the pursuit of encore careers and the unretirement improv act is dominated by the experiments, the desires, and the struggles of aging baby boomers. But the biggest impact of unretirement will be on the younger generation of workers. They will learn from the mistakes and the successes of unretirement to shape and reshape the trajectory of their careers. They will learn the practicalities of how to feel less like a mollusk. Variety and flexibility will become the catchphrases of lifelong transitions and careers. Variety could mean shifting to part-time work for a time or stepping off a career track temporarily to pursue a passion, followed by throwing yourself deep into a project on the job or starting your own company. Flexibility can mean taking your skills and applying them to a different department in the organization, another industry, or an alternative sector of economy.

Thing is, the financial penalty of variety and doing more of the things you love is much less than you might think if you include the unretirement variable into the calculation. Remember, the key is earning a paycheck well into the traditional retirement years. In that case, your standard of living will probably be the same if you work less but earn an income into your seventies compared to earning more and retiring early.

Laurence Kotlikoff, economist at Boston University and founder of ESPlanner, the online financial planning firm, ran this simulation illustrating the trade-off between a high salary and retiring early and a lower salary and working longer for a *Businessweek* story I wrote.

The hypothetical Janet is a fifty-five-year-old heart surgeon earning $250,000 a year. She is burned out. Her hypothetical husband, Jack, is also fifty-five. He is unemployed at the moment and he has a modest earnings history. Their sixteen-year-old son will head off to college in three years. Kotlikoff built many assumptions into his model, from college costs to property taxes. Among the more critical figures are $500,000 in a 401(k), another $500,000 in assets, and $100,000 left on a mortgage. They'll take Social Security at age seventy. He assumes a 3 percent inflation rate, a 6 percent return on retirement assets, and a 5 percent return on taxable assets.

Here's how the numbers could work: Janet quits her high-powered job for one that pays $65,300 a year. It's work that she loves. She offsets the big drop in income by tapping into the family's taxable savings. Janet continues to save some money in a 401(k) through work. She stays on the payroll until she's seventy-five. Her family's standard of living would stay the same as if she had remained at her $250,000 job and retired at age sixty. If she decides to kick back at seventy, a salary of $73,250 would maintain her family's standard of living. If Janet chooses to retire at sixty-five, the same story holds at $113,555. These salary figures could easily be too high, assuming that they learn to focus their spending on what they value and less on what society says the average person or household should spend their money on.

The experience of Sally Peters supports the message of the simulation. Peters went to work at the Pillsbury test kitchens as an intern in 1976 while a student at the University of Minnesota. She worked at Pillsbury until she was laid off in 2000 (along with some 750 other middle managers), about a year before the iconic food company was acquired by its crosstown rival, General Mills. During her career at Pillsbury, Peters worked on the company's famed Grand National Recipe and Baking Contest (an annual contest from 1949 to 1978, biannual since then). She eventually became the contest's project director. She also headed up Pillsbury's cookbook and magazine business. Right before she left Pillsbury had sold 100 million copies of the cookbook. About two weeks before she got her layoff notice she had been praised by the company's president for the most recent Bake-Off contest. "I was stunned, mostly because we were still performing very well, just published around 100 million copies," she says.

Peters recalls that she was exhausted. She had worked hard, raised three kids, had a wonderful husband, and also volunteered at her Lutheran church. In her forties, it was time to figure out the next stage of life, a transition eased in her case with a good severance package. "I had an opportunity," she says. "I knew I wanted to get out of the corporate world. I wanted to do something with more meaning and purpose."

She took the summer off. In the fall of 2000 she met with the new head of lifelong learning at Luther Seminary, the largest of the Evangelical Lutheran Church in America seminaries. The focus of the lifelong learning program was to break down the traditional disconnect between people's work lives and their church time. "I thought, 'I have to work here. This is me,'" she says. She started out a few hours a week and by 2003 she was a full-time employee earning 75 percent less than she did at Pillsbury. Even after becoming director of the program in 2007, she makes less than half her previous income.

But she loves the work. With a few slight tweaks, Peters's standard of living hasn't changed from Pillsbury to Luther. They stick to a budget during the holiday season, something they didn't have to do when the kids were younger. The car loans and house mortgage are paid off. Their children are out of college with no college loans and good jobs. Her husband still works. "You lose some resiliency as you get older," she says. "But you do get smarter."

The idealism motivating unretirement is practical. Rather than give credence to screeds about how America can't afford to grow old, listen to W. Andrew Achenbaum instead. Age sixty-five, Achenbaum is a professor of history and social work at the University of Houston. His books and articles on the history of aging, especially in America, are delightful reads. He gave a charming talk on "The Changing Meaning of Time to an Aging Gerontologist" at an annual meeting of the Gerontological Society of America. Does he want a retirement party? No. Has life been easy? Not really. Is he still productive? Yes. What's more, toward the end of his talk he marveled at finding love later in life, quoting from Virgil, "Seize the day. Gather ye rosebuds while ye may." Good advice for individuals and a nation.

CHAPTER 6

The Movement Against Old Age Stereotypes

You can bend but never break me
—Helen Reddy

THE BARRIERS TO UNRETIREMENT ARE formidable and change won't come overnight. Far too many employers are hostile to the idea of hiring someone with gray hair. Negative stereotypes are rampant, cutting older workers out of new projects and corporate initiatives. You know the prejudices. Older workers can't keep up in a 24-7 business environment. Older workers are conservative. Older workers are set in their ways. Older worker skills are obsolete. They're counting down the days to retirement. "The past seven years, age discrimination became really apparent, watching folks suffer and their age a large barrier for them getting another job," says Harry Melander, president of the Saint Paul Building and Construction Trades Council in Minnesota. "Age bias is prevalent in many industries," says Tim Driver, head of Massachusetts-based RetirementJobs.com.

In 2005 Driver cofounded RetirementJobs, an employment agency for seniors headquartered in Waltham. He had previously worked at Salary.com and AOL. He got the idea for the business after watching older family members and friends face unfair obstacles to employment because of their age. "The company is very much a cause as well as a business," he says. "We will be successful if we convince employers to hire older workers out of a competitive need. It can't be an act of charity. We have to be providing a business resource."

To be sure, age is an advantage in some lines of work. Cathy Fyock, currently an independent adviser to authors, was a human resources consultant in Louisville, Kentucky, for more than a quarter century. She notes that the consulting industry values older talent. "You want some-one with skills and experience," she says. "But with a traditional employment opportunity it's a lot harder to get in the front door."

Like fast food. Fyock was in human resources at Kentucky Fried Chicken in the mideighties. Traditionally, fast-food restaurants have relied on a young work force. The common perception among managers in the fast-food business back then was older workers couldn't keep pace with the demand for speed, she recalls. But the company learned that older workers are productive workers, although they do things differ-ently. Not a bad thing, she adds. Yes, older workers don't run around the restaurant like younger workers, but they don't slip and fall as much. Older workers file fewer worker compensation claims and miss fewer workdays. "Older workers can do the work," Fyock says. "It's all about perception."

Driver of RetirementJobs believes retailers will look more favorably at an aging work force in coming years. Retailers would like to reduce the high cost of rapid employee turnover and the evidence suggests that older workers leave their jobs at one third the rate of their younger peers. Absenteeism is lower and interpersonal skills are often better. Research indicates that older employees are well suited to dealing with customers on the floor of the store, an increasingly valued skill when brick-and-mortar establishments are fighting for sales with Internet-based competitors. "The hiring managers still see themselves going out on a limb hiring an older person if the job could go to a younger person," says Driver. "That will change. We'll look past age and look at other qualifications."

The list of employer misconceptions is long. We've already seen how older-worker stereotypes about creativity, engagement, and productivity are untrue. Similarly, the widespread notion that older worker health care costs are higher than their younger peers isn't right. Health care costs are actually less, argues Peter Cappelli, head of Wharton's Center for Human Resources. The reason: Most older workers no longer have dependent children on their health care plan and, at age sixty-five, they go on Medicare, further reducing their employers' cost. In an interview with Knowledge@Wharton, the school's online business journal, Cappelli confirmed Fyock's and Driver's perspective. "When it comes to job performance, older workers frequently outdo their younger colleagues," says Cappelli. "Basically, older workers perform better on just about everything." The bottom line: Age discrimination is morally wrong and it isn't economically rational.[1]

Of course, discriminating against someone on the basis of age is against the law. In 1967, Congress passed the Age Discrimination in Employment Act (ADEA), which protects workers over the age of forty from discrimination in hiring, firing, and other conditions of employment. Congress strengthened the ADEA in 1979 to cover all firms with twenty or more workers. Still, the Equal Employment Opportunity Commission reports that age discrimination charges totaled 22,857 in 2012, up from 16,548 in 2006—a 38 percent increase in five years. (The peak year was fiscal 2008 at 24,582 charges.) These are only claims filed, the proverbial tip of the iceberg. Most men and women workers don't bother to protest if they believe they're victims of age discrimination, figuring it isn't worth the time or expense to litigate. Sad to say they're usually right. Time for them to move on.

Age discrimination is also difficult to prove. Very few employers, especially large ones, engage in overt discrimination anymore. The written note, the e-mail, and violent verbal public outbursts trashing workers because of their age rarely exist. Older workers must rely on indirect evidence to prove that an employer discriminated against them. Yet even if an employee seems to tell a story that supports a valid claim (you and I would find it credible and wrong), employers have learned they can usually escape liability by offering a business reason for an employment action. A 2009 decision from the United States Supreme Court—Gross v. FBL Financial Services, Inc.—made it even tougher to prove age discrimination. The supremes ruled that employees have to satisfy a more demanding burden of proof under the federal ADEA than with other antidiscrimination laws.

Age discrimination may be difficult to prove in court, but older workers certainly believe the prejudice against them is pervasive. A 2005 survey of eight hundred adults looking for work found that 71 percent of job seekers believed older workers were more likely to be laid off. Two thirds of workers in a 2002 survey of employees forty-five to seventy-four years old said they believed older workers face discrimination on the job, according to the AARP. During the great recession the median duration of unemployment for workers fifty-five and over was thirty-five weeks compared to twenty-six weeks for younger job seekers. In 2011, more than one third of all unemployed older workers had been unemployed for more than a year. "Focus group participants told us they believed employer reluctance to hire older workers was their primary reemployment challenge, and several cited job interview experiences that convinced them age discrimination was limiting their ability to find a new job," according to a 2012 U.S. Government Accountability Office report, *Unemployed Older Workers*. "Moreover, many experts, one-stop career center staff, and other work force professionals we interviewed said that some employers are reluctant to hire older workers. Because of legal prohibitions against age discrimination, employers are unlikely to explicitly express a lack of interest in hiring older workers; however, one work force professional told us that local employers had asked her to screen out all applicants over the age of 40."

In a fascinating experiment, Joanna Lahey, economist at Texas A&M University, sent out resumes to almost four thousand firms in the Boston, Massachusetts, area and St. Petersburg, Florida. The 2002 and 2003 labor market experiment focused on women with work histories of ten years or less applying for entry-level positions. The only difference in the resumes were ages, which ranged from thirty-five to sixty-two. She compared the employer responses for younger and older workers. Applicants under the age of fifty were 40 percent more likely to be called back for an interview than were those over age fifty, according to Lahey in "Age, Women, and Hiring: An Experimental Study." The extent of discrimination against older workers is similar to that of discrimination against women and black workers, she adds. Older workers are right to be suspicious about age discrimination.

The settled age discrimination cases published by the Equal Employment Opportunity Commission (EEOC) make for a depressing read. Here are a few cases resolved in 2012 taken verbatim from the EEOC's website[2]:

> Hawaii Healthcare Professionals, Inc.: (D. Haw.) resolved 7/19/12 by Los Angeles District Office—The Commission alleged that charging party, a then-54-year-old office coordinator, was terminated based on age after Defendant's owner ordered a manager to fire charging party because she "looks old, sounds old on the telephone," and is "like a bag of bones." Case settled for $193,236 in monetary relief and injunctive relief.

> Advance Components: (N.D. Tex.) resolved 5/18/12 by Dallas District Office—The Commission alleged that charging party, a 64-year-old national sales manager with 20 years of experience with the company, was subjected to ageist comments by Defendant's executive vice president and general manager. Defendant's management repeatedly expressed his preference to hire younger salesmen and referred to charging party as "old fashioned." A day after defendant fired charging party, it hired a man in his 30s. Case settled for $201,000 in monetary damages and injunctive relief.

> Star Tex Gasoline and Oil Distributors: (S.D. Tex.) resolved 5/16/12 by Dallas District Office—The Commission alleged that charging party, a former fire chief with extensive relevant

work experience, was not hired for a truck driver position with Defendant because of his age. Defendant's hiring official focused entirely on charging party's age rather than qualifications and experience during the interview. Case settled for $10,000 in monetary relief and injunctive relief.

Central Freight Lines: (N.D. Tex.) resolved 5/10/12 by Dallas District Office—The Commission alleged that a class of employees was discriminated against based on age. The EEOC alleges that Defendant used a reduction-in-force as a ruse to fire eight dockworkers, some of whom had worked at the company for 20 or more years and were approximately 50 years old and older. Defendant subjected this class of workers to names like "grandpa," "old farts" and "old bastards." Eventually, the company replaced the class of workers with younger hires. Case settled for $400,000 in monetary relief and injunctive relief.

Age discrimination laws may have had an unintended consequence. At first, the law improved the job prospects of older workers, especially since the legislation was accompanied by a number of other reforms, such as ending mandatory retirement. With time, however, Lahey thinks age discrimination laws became a factor in why older workers are less likely than younger workers to find a new job after a layoff. "I wouldn't go back. You don't want to go back to a world where employers will only hire twenty-five- to thirty-five-year-olds. Social norms have changed," says Lahey. "But the easiest way for everyone to avoid the age discrimination problem is don't hire older workers. They can see that older workers are under age discrimination laws, and younger workers aren't."

Society's values are continuing to evolve, with aging boomers fighting for respect and a place at the job table. But the age movement has much more to do to change everyday values and employer attitudes. The civil rights movement, the women's rights movement, and the gay rights movement show that grassroots pressure breaks down stereotypes and overcomes prejudice. This isn't to say that blacks, women, and gays don't have further to go. But in all three cases it isn't the 1980s anymore, let alone the 1960s. Considerable progress has been made. The same promise holds with unretirement.

The women's movement in particular offers a number of intriguing parallels. In the fifties and sixties women were mostly excluded from good jobs—careers that came with responsibility and decent pay. Low-income women have always had to make a living and, at the time, they were usually limited to hotel-room cleaner, beautician, and laundress. Educated middle-class women got jobs as secretaries, teachers, and assistants with the expectation that they would stop working when they found a husband and started a family.

Phyllis Richman's story captures the era. She applied to Harvard University's graduate program in city and regional planning in 1961. While her application was pending, Richman received a letter from Harvard professor William Doebele that read, in part: "However—to speak directly—our experience, even with brilliant students has been that married women find it difficult to carry out worthwhile careers in planning and hence tend to have some feeling of waste about the time and effort spent in professional education," he wrote. "Therefore, for your own benefit and to aid us in coming to a final decision, could you kindly write us at your earliest convenience indicating specifically how you might plan to combine a professional life in city planning with your responsibilities to your husband and possible future family?" Discouraged, Richman doesn't think she ever completed the application.

Two years later, feminist pioneer Betty Friedan wrote in *The Feminine Mystique* about a housewife: "As she made the beds, shopped for groceries, matched slipcover material, ate peanut butter sandwiches with children, chauffeured Cub Scouts and Brownies, lay beside her husband at night—she was afraid to even ask of herself the silent question—'Is this all?'"

No, it wasn't. The rise of women in the workplace and career-oriented jobs was a long struggle. A classic moment came in the early 1970s when a band of well-educated, talented women at *Newsweek* challenged the common magazine practice of hiring men to write stories and women as researchers and secretaries. Lynn Povich was a leader among a band of women who fought ingrained gender discrimination at *Newsweek*. She has retold the story of their successful lawsuit in *The Good Girls Revolt: How the Women of* Newsweek *Sued Their Bosses and Changed the Workplace*. Povich later became the first female senior editor at *Newsweek* in 1975, editor in chief for *Working Woman*, and managing editor/senior executive producer for MSNBC.com. "In 1970, we challenged the system and changed the conversation in the news media. For women who participated in the lawsuits, the struggle rerouted our lives, emboldened us, and gave many of us opportunities we never would have had," she writes.

Reporters Catherine Winter and Stephanie Hemphill tell the story of another epic battle for women's rights in *No Place for a Woman*, an American RadioWorks public radio documentary. Far from New York City and its media industry is the Mesabi Iron Range, a hundred-mile stretch of northern Minnesota rich in iron ore. No women worked in the mines in 1970, but by the midseventies women were starting to operate mine machinery and trucks. The women were routinely harassed, threatened, groped, and punched in the mines. The documentary notes:

> Many women in Minnesota's iron mines endured the hard work and dirt and abuse from coworkers because there wasn't really another choice. A job in the mine meant escape. An escape from poverty. An escape from a husband with a violent temper. When men tried to shove them out of the mines, the women were forced into an ugly fight that many of them didn't want.

Eventually, twenty-one women at the Eveleth Mines sued in 1988. Eleven long years later—with many disheartening twists and turns—the women won and the case was settled. Life at the mine is much better these days. University of Colorado Law School professor Melissa Hart notes that the company-wide harassment commonplace in the mines and other establishments in the seventies are far less frequent in the oos. "I think there's been a sort of a settling down to a place where a lot of workplaces, most of the time, most employees live without sexual harassment," she says. "At the same time, it's still out there, and still out there so much more regularly than you wish it would be. But I definitely think things are wildly better than they were 30 years ago in 1975."

As for Richman, she had three children, divorced, remarried, managed an active career, and found herself "specializing in multitasking." She had a good run as a journalist, rocky at times, often a struggle, but definitely a highly successful career. In an open letter to Professor Doebele more than a half century later, she eloquently describes the steps she took to manage a family and career, as well the sexism that dogged her.

Among her accomplishments is coauthoring *Washingtonian* magazine's restaurant guidebook. Of course, she had been promised that she would replace the magazine's food critic when he retired. Instead, the editor chose a man without experience. Still, the next year the *Washington Post* hired her as its restaurant critic. "I was the first woman to hold that job at the newspaper, and one of only a handful in newspapers and magazines around the country," she writes. "Even in the field of food writing, I found a gender split. When food served home and family, it was considered the realm of women. When it involved sophistication and money, men were the writers. Women wrote about cooks; men wrote about chefs."

The traditional gender splits in journalism that Richman observed in her twenty-three-year career at the *Washington Post* are fading. Lynn Rosetto Kasper talks to plenty of chefs—male and female—in her public radio program *The Splendid Table*. Ruth Reichl was editor in chief of *Gourmet* magazine for ten years until its closing in 2009. "This is not a letter that I would write today," Professor Doebele recently responded to Richman. "While far from perfect, conditions for women working in the profession of city planning are, I believe, far more accommodating than in 1961."

That's for sure. Women comprise about half the labor force. Women surpass men in both college enrollment and completion, and about half of all students enrolled in graduate schools of law and medicine are women. They also hold slightly more than half of the creative class jobs, figures scholar Richard Florida. This state of affairs owes a huge debt to the women's movement, affirmative action, Title IX's prohibition against gender discrimination in education programs and activities, and other initiatives that battled against sex discrimination. Sexism is seen as bad for business, limiting the potential employee talent pool and a surefire way to alienate customers. "A narrowing has occurred between men and women in labor force participation, paid hours of work, hours of work at home, life-time labor force experience, occupations, college majors and education, where there has been an overtaking by females," says Claudia Goldin, Harvard University economic historian in her American Economic Association presidential address, "A Grand Gender Convergence: Its Last Chapter."

Even with making great strides, a troubling gender gap in compensation remains. Women still lag behind men in terms of earning power despite their educational advantages and increased presence in the workplace. For instance, in 2012 women on average made 81 percent of the median earnings of male full-time workers, according to the Bureau of Labor Statistics. Younger female workers face a narrower gender gap. The women-to-men's earnings ratio was 90 percent in 2012 for twenty-five- to thirty-four-year-olds. The comparable ratio for forty-five- to fifty-four-year-olds was 75 percent. Creative-class men out-earn creative-class women by a whopping 70 percent, calculates the Martin Prosperity Institute. In almost every occupation—from management to health care—the median weekly earnings of women are less than those of their male peers.

Compensation equity in the work place is still a goal. Indeed, Goldin's "last chapter" is what will it take to eliminate the last vestiges of such gender inequality. "Like us, today's young women are challenging assumptions and fighting their own, more complicated battles in the workplace," writes Povich. "We are standing in their corner and rooting for their success."

It's a guess, but it seems that the battle against age discrimination in the workplace is at a comparable place to the women's movement in the early 1980s. The era of overt age discrimination is essentially fading, although the EEOC cases are sobering. Many remaining age-related barriers are insidious stereotypes that prevent older workers from flourishing on the job or getting one in the first place. These hurdles will come down as the supply and demand for older workers increases in coming years. Many talented older workers will decide to avoid dealing with management stereotypes by setting up their own business, a brain drain that will erode the bottom line. Old-age advocates are changing the conversation by battling pernicious mindsets. Discrimination will decline with the unfolding of the baby boomer unretirement improv act. "It's a civil rights battle of our era with one quarter of the country held back by discrimination," says Steve Poizner, head of EmpoweredU, a venture capital–backed education firm.

In the vanguard of unretirement are college-educated women. The ranks of college-educated women boomers doubled since the 1970s, and three quarters of boomer women worked outside the home in midlife. They also earned less than men throughout their work lives, and one way the wage penalty shows up is in a lower average retirement income. Educated women also live longer on average than their male peers. A generation of career women is nearing retirement for the first time, the group that marked the revolutionary shift from those earning money they and their families needed to "those who are employed, at least in part, because occupation and employment define one's fundamental identity and societal worth," writes economic historian Goldin in "The Quiet Revolution that Transformed Women's Employment, Education, and Family." "It involved a change from 'jobs' to 'careers,' where the distinction between these two concepts concerns both horizon and human capital investment."

These pioneers are well suited to meet and help define the unretirement challenge. The insights gained from a lifetime of flexible work—moving in and out of the work force, shifting from full-time to part-time and back again—will hold them in good stead when searching for their next chapter. "They're looking for what will be satisfying in the next stage of life," says Betsy Werley, head of the Transition Network, a nonprofit that acts as an encore career resource for professional women fifty and older. "They're saying I want to work, but in a different way."

The women's movement is the most powerful social movement of the past half century. Women helped transform the education system, reshape family relations, and overhaul the workplace. The late Betty Friedan concludes in her last book, *The Fountain of Age*, that an elder movement would lead to even greater changes than feminism. She writes:

> I realized that all the experiences I have had—as daughter, student, youthful radical, reporter, battler for women's rights, wife, mother, grandmother, teacher, leader, friend, and lover, confronting real and imagined enemies and dangers, the terrors of divorce and my own denial of age—all of it, mistakes, triumphs, battles lost and won, and moments of despair and exaltation, is part of me now: *I am myself at this age.* It took me all these years to put the missing pieces together, to confront my own age in terms of integrity and generativity, moving into the unknown future with comfort now, instead of being stuck in the past. I have never felt so free.

Standards of behavior will change. Stereotypes will be punctured. Older people will work longer. The boomer unretirement movement will transform the career expectations and opportunities of younger generations over a lifetime. "Revolutions do not go backwards," said Richard Ely, the progressive era economist. The unretirement revolution will move forward, although not in a straight line.

CHAPTER 7

Retirement, a Brief History of a Radical Idea

It's better to burn out
Than to fade away
　　　　　—Neil Young

"OLD AGE IS AN AGE-OLD PHENOMENON," quips historian Andrew Achenbaum.[1] Most older people could sit down with books portraying life in the elder years written many years ago, in the 1950s, the 1880s, Elizabethan England, the times of the early Greek playwrights and the Bible and identify with many of the observations. Increasing frailty. Aches and pains. The inevitability of death. Powerful memories of distant times. The desire to leave a legacy. Pangs of regrets and moments of gratitude. The insight that comes from a lifetime of experiences, good and bad.

Emotions and memories like these are familiar as we age. What has changed, fundamentally, are the living standards of the elderly, reflecting the nation's underlying economic wealth and social institutions, everyday perceptions of the good life, and widely held expectations for the elder years.

Take the popular image of elders in the early years of the American republic. It was mostly positive for those with financial resources and

family networks. The elderly in an agrarian society were valued members
of the community, treated with respect. Longevity only added to their
moral stature and burnished a reputation for hard-earned wisdom. "In
fact, Americans considered it foolish for the elderly to quit their jobs
merely on account of age: medical and popular writers noted that dete-
rioration in later years less often resulted from natural decay than from
disuse," writes Achenbaum in *Old Age in the New Land.* "The prevailing
notion that the old were seasoned veterans of productivity, whose advice
and participation enhanced prospects for successfully accomplishing
many tasks, justified ascribing to aged persons a variety of important
societal tasks to perform."

This hardly means that the new nation was Eden for the elderly.
Respect and admiration went to elderly farmers and aging town merchants
with property, investments, and an income. Still, it wasn't unusual for
aging farmers to hold on to the ownership of their land while their heirs
worked the fields. No point in putting yourself at risk of being thrown out
of the house. Families were the main safety net for the aged. The community expected adult children to provide a home for aging parents when
their faculties started deteriorating. Caring for elders was a responsibility
children were raised to honor. "The powers and privileges of old age were
firmly anchored in the society," writes historian David Hackett Fischer in
Growing Old in America. "Wherever we turn we find it—in the arrangement of the meeting house, in patterns of office holding and landholding,
in family organization—in fact, the exaltation of age was the central part
of a *system* of age relationships, a set of interlocking parts."

The picture seems morally just, almost romantic. That is, until you
realize Fischer's description of the belief system about the elderly in
agrarian America harshly excluded the aged without savings, without
land, without family. These elderly were typically widows, women who
never married, itinerant workers, single men, the sick, and the disabled.
Towns had some charitable sums set aside for "worthy women unfortu-
nates." As for impoverished men, the community felt it was their fault
they hadn't saved, owned land, or didn't have a family or kin to take care
of them. "The status of the elderly, then, was generally based on the

assets they possessed. Their control of property, occupation, and kin determined how they would be treated. The aging patriarch, of course, was certain to receive respect—but only as long as he retained his authority within his own family," writes historian Carole Haber in *Beyond Sixty-Five: The Dilemma of Old Age in America's Past*. "Those without valued possessions were rarely treated with great honor. For them, in fact, great age could become an overwhelming handicap. Having failed to accumulate enough to guarantee the comfort of their final years, they appeared of little use to the community."

The story of modern retirement, which is where our narrative really begins, comes in three phases. The first period runs from the latter part of the nineteenth century through the early decades of the twentieth century. The idea of offering the elderly financial security became a major part of the political discussion in Europe and the United States during this phase. The signal event was the dawn of old age insurance in the industrial economies, which started in Germany in 1889, thanks to Germany's "Iron Chancellor," Otto von Bismarck. In 1881, he convinced German Emperor William the First to back a social insurance program so that "those who are disabled from work by age and invalidity have a well-grounded claim to care from the state." The mandatory insurance contributions into the system created several years later were made by the state, employers, and employees. A number of other European countries had embraced some form of national old age insurance by the dawn of World War I, including Denmark, Great Britain, France, Luxemburg, and Sweden.[2]

Not the United States. In America this period was defined by agitation and experimentation, exhortation and lobbying for pensions and a social insurance system to provide economic security for older workers. Reformers pushed hard for policies that would allow aging workers to retire without fear of poverty. There was some progress on private and public pensions, but adapting a universal income safety net for the elderly proved elusive.

The economic and social force behind the drive for a retirement system was the potent combination of industrialization and urbanization. America emerged as the world's leading industrial nation in the latter part of the nineteenth century. The era of industrial America was dominated by outsized entrepreneurs like Andrew Carnegie (steel), James Duke (tobacco), John D. Rockefeller (oil), Gustavus Swift (meat-packing), Montgomery Ward (mail-order catalog), and J. P. Morgan (investment banking). People left rural America for jobs in these growing industries concentrated in urban areas. Immigrants came to the United States in record numbers from Ireland, Germany, Scandinavia, and other countries to work the factories, packing into urban tenements to build a new life for themselves and their families. The pace of technological innovation and urbanization was fast and frenetic.

The impact of the Bessemer furnace is a good proxy for capturing the turbulent era. For much of the nineteenth century, railroads relied on cast iron, a brittle material that easily cracked. Steel was too expensive for mass production until Henry Bessemer devised an economical system for mass-producing steel. The Bessemer system replaced wrought iron in the last part of the nineteenth century. Progress came with a steep price tag. "While the Bessemer furnace increased the demand for workers at steel mills, it led to the loss of jobs in iron mills and foundries that could not compete with new steel products. The same kind of turmoil was created in petroleum, meatpacking, textiles, transportation vehicles, and wholesale and retail distribution," writes the late Robert Fogel, Nobel laureate at the University of Chicago, in *The Fourth Great Awakening and the Future of Egalitarianism*. Although far more new jobs were created than old jobs lost, those who obtained new jobs were often new immigrants, and those who lost the old jobs were often either native-born workers or longtime residents.

The rapid pace of change was hard on workers and their families. They had left the farm or another country behind for the city, so fewer families could live off the land during tough economic times. Households increasingly relied on a steady paycheck from their job to pay the bills. A firing, a spell of unemployment, a cut in paid hours was devastating to the typical family's finances. There was no unemployment insurance, workmen's compensation, food stamp program, Social Security and

Medicare and Medicaid to cushion the financial blow. Job insecurity was a harsh fact of life for a majority of American households.

The risk of a job loss loomed particularly large for older workers in the new economy of the time. It was tough to get another job since older workers weren't valued by management and owners. Unemployment for the elderly often translated into a humiliating dependence on family and charity for shelter and food. The emerging social sciences, such as economics and sociology, treated old age and poverty as almost synonymous, each defining and reinforcing the other. The belief in the relationship was something of a self-fulfilling prophecy.

Employers in the emerging industrial society considered the elderly a spent force. Their accumulated knowledge and experience—much appreciated in agrarian times—were worthless in Smokestack America. Older workers were viewed as a burden, unproductive people in an era when industrialists worshipped efficiency. "It is notorious that the insatiable factory wears out its workers with great rapidity. As it scraps machinery so it scraps human beings. The young, the vigorous, the adaptable, the supple of limb, the alert of mind, are in demand," wrote economist Edward Devine in 1909. "Middle age is old age, and the worn-out worker, if he has no children and if he has no savings, becomes an item in the aggregate of the unemployed."

The most famous proselytizer for industrial efficiency was Frederick Winslow Taylor. The gospel of scientific management—a cluster of ideas pushed by Taylor and his peers—obsessed about wasteful motions and underutilized resources. Taylor obsessively broke down tasks into small parts and rearranged jobs so they could be done with the least amount of movement. He and his followers measured everything on the job, eager to eliminate unneeded motions on the factory floor and idle habits among clerical employees. "The principles at the heart of scientific management were clear: break jobs down into their simplest parts; select the most suitable workers to fit the available jobs; turn those workers into specialists, each an expert in his own appointed task; arrange these specialized jobs along an assembly line; and design the right package of incentives (including bonuses and prizes) to ensure that the workers did indeed work," write John Micklethwait and Adrian Wooldridge of the *Economist* in *The Witch Doctors: Making Sense of Management Gurus*. (The late sociologist Daniel Bell captures Taylor's stopwatch mentality in *Work and Its Discontents*: "He couldn't stand to see an idle lathe or an idle man. He never loafed, and he'd be damned if anybody else would. This compulsive character Taylor stamped onto a civilization.")

The efficiency gurus and their clients associated speed and efficiency with youth. A young worker would be better able to keep up with the demanding pace of the assembly line. Medical research reinforced the belief that by middle age creativity was essentially exhausted and, by old age, people were basically worthless, at least from an economic and business point of view. "Because of the developed efficiency standards, so essential to successful business, the wage-earner finds the problem of old age principally one of either increasing inability to find employment or at best employment at low compensation," observed Abraham Epstein, a Russian immigrant and a leading advocate for social insurance in the United States. "After a certain age has been attained, although the worker may still be able to do fair work, if he is no longer able to maintain his former speed, he is likely to be eliminated from industry. The old man finds it difficult to secure work even at low wages," he wrote in 1922 in *Facing Old Age.*[3]

At what age did people become old from an employment perspective? The best scientific research and popular stereotypes converged at the idea that age forty marked the beginning of old age. In the late 1800s, William Osler was physician in chief of Johns Hopkins Hospital in Baltimore, a professor of medicine at the school, and the author of the leading text for clinical medicine. In 1905 he gave a talk built on two key points about aging. "The first is the comparative uselessness of men above forty years of age. This may seem shocking, and yet read aright the world's history bears out the statement," he said. Osler continued. "My second fixed idea is the uselessness of men above sixty years of age."[4]

Osler was essentially in tune with the age. For example, the railroads were among the nation's biggest private employers and a vital industry knitting together the domestic economy. Yet "to get a job on almost any one of our great railroads after one is thirty-five requires a special vote of the board of directors," reported Burton Hendrick in *McClure's* magazine in 1908. "A man who has not established himself definitely in some line at forty is destined almost inevitably to be a wanderer for life. If you apply for work at forty-five you will usually be sent away with the remark that you are 'too old.'"

Forty-five and too old! In his famous Supreme Court decision that upheld the constitutionality of the 1935 Social Security Act, Justice Cardozo included some data on older workers: "In 1930, out of 224 American factories investigated, 71, or almost a third, had fixed maximum hiring age limits; in 4 plants the limit was under 40; in 41 it was under 46. In the other 153 plants there were no fixed limits, but in practice few were hired if they were over 50 years of age." Little wonder with layoffs commonplace in so many businesses that the fear of impoverishment in old age ran deep.

Family remained the principal safety net for the discarded elderly. There is certain nostalgia today about multigenerational households in earlier eras, the nineteenth and early twentieth centuries. Grandpa and grandma, children and grandchildren, all living under one roof. The sentimental glow wasn't widely shared at the time. Multigenerational homes were crowded when dependent parents moved in. Money was tight and old parents were an added expense in an economy already demanding more investment in children if they were to get ahead. Wrote the social insurance advocate Epstein in *Facing Old Age*:

> It seems cruel to any father or mother in this twentieth century to decide between supporting old parents and contenting themselves with a little less food, less room, less clothing, and the curtailment of their children's education; or sending parents to the poor house or charitable agencies, accepting the stigma of pauperism, and thus assuring themselves of more food, more room, and more clothing, and a better education for their children which would help them to become somewhat

more proficient workers. This is a difficult alternative, yet it is certain that thousands of parents in the United States are annually compelled to make such decisions.

The family wasn't as strong a backstop for the elderly for other reasons. America was a highly mobile nation. People constantly picked up stakes seeking work opportunities in a different town or state, with many people joining a steady migration west. The option of moving in with far-flung families often wasn't realistic for the nation's elders. "With increasing rapidity home-ties and family solidarity are being weakened and broken by the mobility so essential to modern industrial development," wrote Epstein. "The migratory and immigrant laborers move from lumber-camps to harvesting fields, railway construction, and public works as the change of employment offers. Thousands of aged workers find themselves in a strange country without friends or relatives."

Pensions, which provide an income at retirement, were relatively rare. One of the first pension plans in the United States was started in 1759 for the benefit of widows and children of Presbyterian ministers. Military veterans got pensions at the end of the Revolutionary War. Payments were limited to soldiers wounded during active military service and veterans and their widows in dire poverty. The railroad freight forwarder American Express Company offered its employees the first formal corporate pension in the United States in 1875, according to Steven Sass in *The Promise of Private Pensions*. Still, he notes, by 1899 only a tiny minority of companies offered their employees a formal private pension plan.

In other words, most aging Americans had to rely on household savings. Like now, the financial demands of everyday life made it very hard for working men and women to save for their old age. Isaac M. Rubinow, an influential writer in the agitation for social insurance in America, laid out the reasons why it was wrong to expect the average person to be able save for a comfortable old age. (The language is from a different era, but his insights about savings still ring true today.) Rubinow was directly taking on the popular sentiment in America that if workers didn't save it was their own fault, a moral failing, a character flaw that deserved condemnation rather than relief. A helping hand would only encourage more "bad" savings behavior.

1. The amount necessary is evidentially greater, for old age is not a brief transitory condition, such as sickness and unemployment may be. It would require a continuous savings for a great many years.

2. The amount necessary is uncertain. There is, after all, the even or almost even chance of early death before old age may be reached. And in addition, the wage-worker has no means at all to know how much he would have to save, nor whether his savings will prove sufficient.

3. It is the final emergency, which in the natural course of events must be preceded by all other emergencies of a workingman's existence. Inevitably the fund of savings would have to be used to meet all these emergencies.

4. The remoteness of the emergency would prevent necessary savings at a time when such savings would be easiest, that is in earliest years.

5. To assume that under these conditions all workingmen could save sufficient to provide them against old age, would be to disregard all real conditions of the wage-worker's existence. Even in the most saving of our States, the average amounts held per depositor in the savings banks are ridiculously small as compared to the amounts needed for a sufficient income at old age.

6. Finally special savings for old age would only be possible through a persistent, systematic, and obstinate disregard of the needs of the workingman's family, which would make the preaching of such special savings a decidedly immoral force.[5]

The dreaded symbol of poverty in old age at the time was the almshouse, or the poorhouse. Not everyone who ended up in an almshouse was elderly, although over time the elderly became a large share of the alms-house population. These institutions also housed the mentally ill and the poor. According to contemporary accounts, conditions in an almshouse ranged from the merely depressing to the Dickensian horrific.

An 1881 article for *Atlantic Monthly* by Octave Thanet, secretary of the Board of Charities, vividly describes visiting a rural almshouse in Illinois. The small almshouse with both women and men was "not the best, and is a long way from being the worst," he wrote in "The Indoor Pauper: A Study." Thanet was greeted at the gate by men in chains. The doctor who ran the place was out, so he was shown around by the doctor's eighteen-year-old daughter. "The sitting-room had a stove, and some pine benches for furniture. On one of these was stretched a hideous old woman, very stout and red, wearing a single blue garment; she seemed to be asleep," he wrote. "'That woman got the dropsy, and she's crazy, too,' said our guide. We asked if any one took care of her. The girl said, 'No, she takes care of herself.'" They continued on their tour of the alms-house. In one bare chamber "a man lay on a comfortless bed, turning so white and haggard a face to the wall that at first glance I thought him dead," writes Thanet. The rest of his narrative is equally dismaying.

The almshouse was harsh on the elderly even in the better institu-tions, as the *Report from the Pennsylvania Commission on Old Age Pensions* in 1919 made clear.

> Most of the inmates looked sullen and wore depressed and downcast mien. Practically all were eager to get out of the place. Even in the best equipped institutions there were no recreational facilities provided for these inmates. Except for a pack of cards, a game of checkers, there was nothing these aged could do to keep their minds occupied and to prevent their nursing of grievances and discontent. This feeling of depres-sion is augmented by the fact that in most Homes no attempt is made to segregate the old people—who have been compelled to go to the almshouse through no fault of their own,—from the feeble-minded, and in many cases the partly insane.

Harper's Weekly famously put a poem about the poorhouse on its cover
in 1871.

> For I'm old and I'm helpless and feeble
> The days of my youth have gone by
> Then over the hill to the poor house
> I wander on there to die

Chilling lines, aren't they? Little wonder no one wanted to end up in
such a place.

The filmmaker D. W. Griffith in 1911 shot a short silent film that
captured a haunting vision of old age in industrial America for the average worker and family. (You can watch it on YouTube.)

The opening scene in *What Should We Do with Our Old?* has a doctor
visiting the ailing wife of an elderly carpenter. The carpenter heads off to
work, but soon the title card reads: "New foreman weeds out the old
hands." He's fired and a much younger man replaces him at the factory.

Upset, discouraged, the carpenter finds out that it is: "Impossible to
obtain employment at his age."

Their savings are quickly exhausted and soon they're facing starva-
tion. His wife is increasingly ill. The worried husband opportunistically
steals some food, but he's caught and arrested. When he comes before
the court, he's convicted and sent to jail.

The judge is a kindly man. He wonders if the old man's story is true.
He sends a policeman to check on the wife. The policeman comes back
from the apartment and confirms the story. The old man is released from
jail. He rushes back home accompanied by the judge. The police with
them are carrying food.

She's dead by the time they get to the apartment. The old man is
distraught, angry. The final storyboard reads: "Nothing for the useful
citizen wounded in the battle of life."

The progressive movement fought for a stronger financial safety net
roughly between the 1890s and 1920s. The political coalition comprised
a loose group of farmers, organized labor, urban lower classes, some

from the middle-class business community, philanthropic leaders, and a number of heads from big business. The progressive movement played a role in the creation of the income tax, the founding of the Federal Reserve, the passage of the Sherman Antitrust Act, the eight-hour work-day, and prohibitions on child labor.

Among the list of progressive reforms was creating a retirement income security system for the elderly. Military veterans had access to pensions ever since the founding of the republic, although the system was capricious and unstable. (For instance, the navy's pension fund from 1775 to 1842 had a "colorful history," going bankrupt three times and each time having to be bailed out by Congress, according to Lee Craig, economist at North Carolina State University.) The federal government offered its civilian employees pension coverage in 1920. States and local governments were slower on the pension front, although twenty-one states by the late 1920s had established formal retirement plans for their public school teachers. Business leaders began embracing pensions after 1900. Private pension coverage expanded rapidly in the first three decades of the twentieth century, with three hundred companies offer-ing them by 1919, covering some 15 percent of the work force, according to Sass in *The Promise of Private Pensions*. The companies that offered pensions to their workers ranked among the largest in the nation, like the railroads.

Why did hard-nosed profit-seeking owners and their managers decide to provide an income for employees no longer on their payroll? For one thing, pensions were a critical part of "welfare capitalism," an approach favored by leading American industrialists and philanthropists. Welfare capitalists wanted to offer economically insecure workers an alternative to socialism. A pension allowed management to shed elderly workers and replace them with younger employees with a modicum of reputa-tional compassion. The elderly needed to be removed from the workplace, and the higher productivity from a younger work force would more than pay for the pension benefits. At least that was the theory.

For another, pensions offered industrial capitalists a number of bottom-line returns. A pension was an instrument of control over their labor force. For their younger workers the promise of a pension helped keep them in line, a force weighing against strikes. Factory jobs were physically demanding and mind-numbing. ("One of the very first requirements for a man who is fit to handle pig iron as a regular occupation," wrote Frederick Taylor, "is that he shall be so stupid and so phlegmatic that he more nearly resembles an ox than any other type.") The risk of losing a pension was yet one more reason for workers to labor hard. The prospect of a pension was an incentive to stay on the job rather than seek better opportunities elsewhere. "Among the largest and most efficient corporations, pension systems are now regarded as good business," writes Hendrick in *McClure's* in 1908. "They largely solve one of their most difficult problems—how to get out of a large labor force the most efficient service."

The pension wasn't guaranteed. Typically granted at age seventy, the pension was controlled by the company, and management wasn't under any obligation to keep paying out to retirees if business took a turn for the worse. Management threatened to cut off the pension income of retired workers unless they returned to the job during strikes, an effective tactic for breaking up protests. A pension could be denied for all kinds of behavior, such as having an affair, smoking, or drinking too much. Historian Carole Haber quotes from a partial list of reasons for being denied a pension at the First National Bank of Chicago, which set up its pension plan in 1899. "In the case of bankruptcy of the pensioner, or of his taking the benefit of any insolvency law, or on his conviction for felony or misdemeanor, or on any judgment entered against, and in the case of any widow, in her misconduct being proved to the satisfaction of the bank, all benefit rights are forfeited," she quotes.[6]

Governments also embraced pensions to manage their work force better. The fear among leading public figures was that workers would stay on the job too long without a pension. By definition, older workers were ineffective workers, wasting taxpayer dollars. The experts warned that children wouldn't get the best teachers, fires and crime wouldn't get the attention they needed, and clerks and laborers on the government payroll would be backward and inefficient, says Haber. She looks at the

Massachusetts *Report of the Commission on Old Age Pensions, Annuities and Insurance* from 1910. The authors were dismayed at how many employees were over sixty-five. "For example, in the cleaning and watering divisions of the street department 35 are employed, of whom all are inefficient: in the cemetery department 16 persons over sixty-five are employed, of whom all are reported as inefficient: in the park department, 27 are employed, of whom 24 are inefficient."

Taken altogether, pensions had a number of attractive features for employers. Pensions allowed management to be decent and ruthless at the same time. Nevertheless, the average older American worker lived with haunting income uncertainty. Despite the rapid expansion in pensions most workers weren't part of the patchwork retirement system. The push to provide a stable safety net for the elderly continued to gather momentum, but it took an epic economic disaster to break the public policy logjam: the Great Depression.

CHAPTER 8

The Rise of Mass Retirement

Sometimes I'd head for the highway
I'm old and the mirrors don't lie
                                    —Leonard Cohen

THE SECOND PHASE OF MODERN RETIREMENT in the United States runs from the Great Depression of the 1930s until the early 1980s. The signal moment—the transition point—was the Social Security Act of 1935. America embraced the idea of a universal income-based safety net for the elderly. Large employers were also more willing to offer their employees a pension plan after the Second World War. The 1965 passage of Medicare created universal health coverage for those sixty-five and over. Medicaid helped out low-income Americans, including the poor elderly.

The rise of mass retirement in the twentieth century transformed the experience of old age for millions of Americans. For many workers it became possible to say good-bye to their colleagues for the last time and enjoy the kind of leisure that for most of history only the wealthy could afford. Thanks to Social Security and Medicare the odds of eking out a penurious existence in old age were dramatically reduced and the financial independence of the elderly truly enhanced. The emergence of modern retirement shaped everyday expectations about the rhythms of life. You went to school. You worked. You retired, meaning you didn't earn a paycheck anymore. Instead, you played. The last stage was something new and different for the mass of American seniors.

The transition to mass retirement might not have happened or at least would have been delayed even more if it weren't for the Great Depression. Despite all the blue-chip commission reports, the election of progressive legislators, the spread of welfare capitalism among big business, not much really happened on a national scale when it comes to retirement until the Great Depression. The downturn was an economic disaster for families. Once again, the less well off elderly, the vulnerable elderly found themselves in dire circumstances. Farmers, skilled workers, and newly emergent middle-class people joined the unemployment lines, too. They watched their savings vanish. The banks foreclosed on their homes. The battle for old age security is rightly told as a fight to help out those treated harshly by an industrial economy. But that's only part of the story. It's also a narrative of increasing financial independence among working and middle-class families suddenly at risk of vaporizing. The specter of the almshouse beckoned once again.

The U.S. economy expanded rapidly if unevenly during the era of agitation for retirement. A growing number of workers joined the new middle class and the quality of everyday life dramatically improved. Robert Gordon, economist at Northwestern University, captures what everyday urban life was like in the late nineteenth century. Gordon writes in *Does the "New Economy" Measure Up to the Great Inventions of the Past?*: "In Kansas City, the stench of patrolling hogs was so penetrating that Oscar Wilde observed, 'They made granite eyes weep.' City streets were piled with animal waste," notes Gordon. "In 1882, only 2 percent of New York City's houses had water connections. Urban apartments were crowded, damp, airless, and often firetraps. Even middle-class apartment buildings were little more than glorified tenements."

The quality of everyday life improved dramatically over the next several decades. An astonishing list of technological and public health innovations transformed urban and rural America, including electric light and electric motors, the internal combustion engine, petroleum, pharmaceuticals, plastics, the telephone, radio, indoor plumbing, and municipal waterworks. By 1900, Gordon notes, urban America was electrified. Electricity not only brought light to city streets and homes, it made washing machines and refrigerators possible. The car and truck changed city streets for the better and tied closer together a restless nation. "By 1929 in urban America the horses were gone, the manure was gone, the pigs no longer roamed the streets, and farm families were no longer isolated," Gordon writes.

The enterprises behind the technological and organizational innovations offered plenty of jobs. Take-home pay rose, too. Brian Gratton, professor of history at Arizona State University, estimates that between 1860 and 1890 the average wage in manufacturing rose by almost 50 percent and another 37 percent from 1890 to 1914, after taking inflation into account. Older workers shared in the prosperity. By 1918, Gratton calculates, men sixty and over earned 75 percent more in inflation-adjusted income than a comparable group did in 1890.[1] The 1920s were truly the go-go years from an economic perspective. "Every worker was producing much more, yet the economy expanded enough to absorb workers displaced by new technologies," writes historian Maury Klein in *Rainbow's End: The Crash of 1929.* "Unemployment scarcely existed, real earnings of wage earners rose about 22 percent, and the workweek shrank, giving workers more leisure time to enjoy their improved income."

The Great Depression threatened to impoverish a nation. Families were scared as the economic security of many crumbled through no fault of their own. The scale of economic disaster during the Great Depression is still terrifying. In 1933, at the height of the Great Depression, more than a quarter of the work force was unemployed and many more were underemployed. The number of banks shrank from more than twenty-five thousand in 1929 to fewer than fifteen thousand in 1933. The Dow Jones Industrial Average plunged by 17 percent in 1929, followed by a 34 percent decline in 1930, a 53 percent drop in 1931, and a 23 percent fall in 1932. Approximately half of the owners of urban homes defaulted on their mortgages. (To put that last figure in context, the combined percentage of loans in foreclosure or at least one mortgage payment past due reached a high of 14 percent in May 2010 according to Richard Revesz, dean of New York University law school.) "Critically, the Great Depression, unlike several earlier downturns which had also sent many thousands of people trampling about the country, dislodged many from the new middle class who held stable, well-paying jobs," writes Claude Fischer in *Made in America: A Social History of American Culture and Character.* "The usual sources of aid for the 'deserving' poor—relatives, fraternal associations, charities, town governments—buckled under the burden. It was hard for many in the middle class to help when they themselves were needy."

These figures only hint at the social distress and personal tragedies of the era. Breadlines snaked around city blocks. Shantytowns called Hoovervilles sprang up on city outskirts. Lives were upended. When my mother was six in the late 1920s she lived on the Caribbean island of Aruba with her mother and her partner, Frank. He worked at the oil refinery Standard Oil had built on the island in the 1920s. He was building a home for them in Mount Kisco, a New York City suburb. The three of them returned to the United States by ship in 1929, docking at the Brooklyn piers. Frank's brother was waiting for them as they arrived. He yelled up to Frank that they were wiped out. The bank with all their savings had failed. Frank disappeared. My grandmother and mother moved to a small property in rural upstate New York where they could eke out a living for much of the Depression. There are millions of similar stories from that era, many of them far worse.

For the elderly, the nation's small pension system didn't cushion the economic downturn much. Pensions weren't common enough, for one thing. For another, nearly 10 percent of employers discontinued or suspended parts of their pension plans and another 10 percent cut benefits. "The private pension in the best of times had been totally inadequate to meet society's old age income requirement," writes pension expert Sass in *The Promise of Private Pensions.* "As the incidence of destitution among the elderly rose dramatically, the corporate instrument became even more peripheral to the national need."

The politics of the Great Depression years were driven by the search to get the economy growing again and to come up with ways of organizing society to create greater economic security. The elderly were at the heart of the political upheaval.

A number of pension-based movements sprang up during the Depression, pushing for a stronger safety net. Groups like Ham and Eggs. Yes, that really was its name. The California-based lobbying organization was founded by a Los Angeles radio commentator (later imprisoned for pro-Nazi sentiments during World War II). He was joined by two brothers who had been convicted of a hair tonic scam. Their economic "guru" was an anti-Semite who believed the Federal Reserve had been created by a secret cabal with links to the Illuminati and the Rothschild banking dynasty. Seriously. I'm not making this up.[2]

Like many of the proposed pension schemes of the time, the underlying idea behind Ham and Eggs was to boost the economy and, at the same time, improve the incomes of aging Americans. The Ham and Eggs impresarios focused their attention on California. The basic idea was for every unemployed California voter age fifty and older to receive a weekly $30 worth of "warrants." The recipient would pay a weekly two-cent sales tax on each warrant, which was worth one dollar. The tax was an incentive to spend the warrants rather than save them. The Ham and Eggs California Pension Plan got on the state ballot in 1938 and received 45 percent of the vote. Close, but not enough to pass.

A far more serious proposal came from a savvy politician—Louisiana senator Huey Long. Better known as the "Kingfish," Long passionately promoted his Share Our Wealth plan. An effective populist at the head of a powerful political machine, Long became governor of Louisiana in 1928 and was elected to the U.S. Senate two years later. In a 1935 radio address, he laid out the key elements of his Share Our Wealth vision and political platform. Every family would own a homestead equal in value to but not less than one third the national average family wealth; no family shall own more than three hundred times the average family wealth; and every family shall have an income equal to at least one third of the average family income. He also wanted a cash bonus for veterans and education for all. As for the elderly, Long said:

> We also propose to give the old-age pensions to the old people, not by taxing them or their children, but by levying the taxes upon the excess fortunes to whittle them down, and on the excess incomes and excess inheritances, so that the people who reach the age of sixty can be retired from the active labor of life and given an opportunity to have surcease and ease for the balance of the life that they have on earth.

The momentum behind Share Our Wealth faded after Long was fatally shot outside the Louisiana governor's office in Baton Rouge in 1935. Carl Weiss, a young doctor, shot Long for reasons that remain shrouded in controversy. Weiss was killed by Long's bodyguards.

The most impressive mass pension movement with a national audience was the Townsend Plan, the "old people crusade." In 1934, Dr. Francis Townsend, a retired physician from Long Beach, California, proposed that everyone sixty and over get a pension of $200 a month. The plan would be funded by a 2 percent sales tax. The monthly pension would have to be spent within thirty days, a boon to the economy. Townsend believed that the old stood in the way of the young. His slogan: "Age for leisure, youth for work."

Townsend created a formidable organization. The mass movement claimed some 3 million club members, 10 million supporters, and the voting power of 25 million. It had its own newspaper, the *Townsend National Weekly*. The near-religious fervor of its members was noticeable; many of its adherents were veterans of the campaign for Prohibition in 1920, repealed in 1933. "That these people have transferred their energies from demon rum to the menace of old-age insecurity is indicated by the frequent references at Townsend meetings to the evils of cigarettes, lipstick, petting-parties and similar evidences of depravity," wrote Richard L. Neuberger and Kelley Loe in 1936 in *Harper's*. "One of the stock arguments for adoption of the Townsend Plan is that it will put

young men and women to work and thus prevent them spending their
time in wild indulgences in liquor, sex and tobacco."

At a 1935 Townsend conference in Chicago, members frequently
burst into song:

> Onward, Townsend soldiers,
> Marching as to war,
> With the Townsend banner
> Going on before
> Our devoted leaders
> Bid depression go;
> Join them in the battle
> Help them fight the foe.

Economists weren't among the swayed. They widely panned the
Townsend plan. Look at it this way: $200 a month or $2,400 a year was
an incredible sum considering average family income in 1934 was
$1,524. Folly or not, the cumulative effect of the various pension
schemes that attracted varying degrees of voter support grabbed attention in Washington, D.C. President Roosevelt promised in 1934 that
his administration would pursue "the great task of furthering the security of the citizen and his family through social insurance." A few
weeks later Roosevelt formed the Committee on Economic Security,
and in 1935 he signed the Social Security Act into law. As Justice
Cardozo put it for the majority when the Supreme Court backed the
constitutionality of the Social Security Act, "The hope behind this stat-
ute is to save men and women from the rigors of the poorhouse as well
as from the haunting fear that such a lot awaits them when journey's
end is near."

A public policy Rubicon was crossed with Social Security. Yes, the law
initially excluded many low-wage workers, such as farmhands, share-
croppers, and home help. The law was overhauled in 1939, creating the
essence of the current Social Security system and covering an expanded
list of workers. (It has been broadened a number of times since then.)

Despite its initial limitations, Social Security is the cornerstone achievement of the New Deal. With Social Security, the elderly were promised an income floor for their old age, a stream of monthly retirement income they couldn't outlive.

The scale of change in the lives of the elderly in the post–World War II economy is astounding, unimaginable to elderly citizens in 1900. Mass retirement was something new. Even today our image of old age and the good retirement is profoundly shaped by those early postwar decades. In addition to Social Security, older Americans gained universal health care coverage with Medicare in 1965. More large corporations offered their workers so-called defined benefit pension plans with payouts during retirement based on a salary level and years-of-service formula. The number of workers on private pension plans rose from 2.7 million, or about 5 percent of the work force in 1930, to 19 million or 28 percent of the work force in 1958. The poverty rate among the elderly plunged from some 35 percent in the late 1950s to less than 15 percent by 1974.

Older men took advantage of the new retirement to leave the job earlier. For men sixty-five and older in the late 1800s the labor force participation rate was near 80 percent. In essence, you worked until you died or were close to death. By 1950, the percentage of older workers still in the labor force fell to some 46 percent, and by the early 1990s the figure reached around 16 percent. Many people started planning on an early retirement. A new leisure class was born: the retired person.

The rise of mass retirement was also spurred by America's golden era of economic growth, 1948 to 1973. The economy grew smartly, wages and incomes rose, and the civilian unemployment rate only breached 6 percent twice. The middle class came of age. Millions of Americans bought homes for the first time, many in new suburbs. Former luxury goods like televisions and range top stoves went mass market. The GI Bill opened the doors of public and private colleges to returning soldiers. Smokestack America thrived, selling mass-produced products across the country and around the world. "If few can cite the figures, everyone knows that we have, per capita, more automobiles, more telephones, more radios, more vacuum cleaners, more electric lights, more bathtubs, more supermarkets and movie palaces and hospitals, than any other nation," wrote historian David Potter in *People of Plenty: Economic Abundance and the American Character.*

The newly affluent seniors developed a distinct lifestyle built around leisure. The popular images of retirement were captured by stories about the mass migration to Sunbelt communities, long mornings on the golf course, and barbecues on the patio in the evening. Age-restricted retirement communities emerged, and Ben Schleifer's development of Youngtown outside Phoenix in 1954 seems to be the first to insist that residents be fifty years or more. Children weren't allowed to be permanent residents and, just in case, there wasn't a school in town. "Schleifer wanted to construct [a retirement community] where retirees could survive on Social Security payments and company pensions," writes Judith Ann Trolander in *From Sun City to the Villages: A History of Active Adult, Age-Restricted Communities.* "In other words, it was Schleifer's goal to create an affordable community where retirees would have autonomy as individuals."

The most famous retirement community is Sun City, also on the outskirts of Phoenix. Built by the developer Del Webb, Sun City opened for business in 1960 and it was immediately swamped with buyers. Four years later after its successful opening, the *New Yorker* writer Calvin Trillin spent ten days in the community. Trillin laid out the rules in "Wake Up and Live." Men had to be at least fifty years old (no age limit on wives) and children were welcome to visit but not live. (There were no schools in Sun City.) Most residents came from the Midwest, Trillin observed. When he was there homes in Sun City went for $10,450 ($77,028 in current dollars) at the low end of the market and rose to $15,950 ($117,569) for the more expensive houses. The population in Sun City was 7,500 in 1964 and Trillin says there were some ninety clubs, including shuffleboard, amateur radio, and lawn bowling. "The formula for happiness in Sun City is activity & friendliness. Residents play shuffleboard, golf, canasta, bridge, go to club meetings & dances with other retired persons," writes Trillin.

Ah, leisure. Retirement was like living at a swank resort. At least, that was the new marketing message ginned up by developers, financial institutions, and advertising agencies. Compare the D. W. Griffith film about the horrors visited on aging workers with a half-hour infomercial created by the Del Webb Corporation in the early 1960s. (You can also watch it on YouTube.) The ad was aimed at encouraging people to retire to Sun City. Like Griffith's *What Should We Do with Our Old*, the Del Webb infomercial is in black and white, but it has sound. The ad begins with the character "Ben Huggins" leaving the office with his coworkers following him singing, "For he's a jolly good fellow."

"I finally made it. No more hurry. No more pressure," says Huggins. He stops his car on the way home, looks at the gold watch he got as a retirement gift from the office, and reads the inscription: TO BEN HUGGINS FOR THIRTY YEARS' SERVICE.

"From now on I'm going to enjoy myself," he says.

Huggins relaxes at home, finishing long-delayed odd jobs around the house. He has fun with craft projects. But before long he and his wife are bored. The neighborhood is changing, with young families and their children moving in. "So this is retirement. Time on your hands and no place to go. Nothing to do," Huggins sighs. "There must be something else. I'm not ready for pasture. I have a lot of living in me."

They get in their car and visit a friend in Sun City. The sign at the entrance to Sun City reads: SUN CITY. AN ACTIVE NEW WAY OF LIFE. GOLF COURSE. ACTIVITY CENTER. COMMUNITY CENTER. RECREATION PARK. SWIMMING POOL. HI-WAY HOUSE. SHOPPING CENTER. They barbecue on the patio of their friend's house and attend an evening dance. The men play a round of golf. The women get their hair done. Their friends encourage them to move to Sun City where there are no kids, no schools, no local taxes, and homes are affordable. Ben and his wife decide to stay. "All the pleasure of country club living," says Ben.

The ad ends with the phrase, "The Beginning."

When I visited Sun City West, a 1978 expansion next to the original Sun City, it was evident little had changed from the original vision. The homes are ranch style and there remains a middle-class "architectural egalitarianism" highlighted by Trillin. The homes differ in size, but not by much. The streets are wide and the sidewalks slope down to the street. Litter? Didn't see any. Walkers? I saw no one on the sidewalks. The town was quiet, maybe because there were no children. Leisure is still the core activity with seven golf courses, four recreation centers, a thirty-lane bowling center, a library, a retail arts and crafts store, and more than one hundred clubs at Sun City West. The main means of transportation is golf carts (a very civilized way to get around).

The private sector created a vision of retirement as leisure on the foundation of Social Security and Medicare, supplemented with pensions, home equity, and other savings. (Ironically, Del Webb wasn't enamored with the lifestyle he brilliantly manufactured. "Del Webb, the hulking, slope-shouldered, long-striding 63-year-old who hates to be called Delbert, could not stand the life in one of his own Sun Cities for more than a few days—or a few hours," reads a *Time* magazine cover story in 1962.) Businesses spent a fortune on advertising to cement the association of retirement and leisure.

The almshouse and retirement communities offered two distinctive mental pictures of old age, images that helped define popular expectations. The journey from the almshouse to Sun City emphasizes the triumph of social insurance in providing economic security to our elders. The 1950s truly marked a new era for the better.

Still, the gap between the retirement vision marketed by industry and the retirement reality of everyday life was wide. Statistically, for example, not that many people retired to an age-restricted community. Only about one in ten Americans age seventy or older lives in a Sun City–like place, according to the Harvard Center for Joint Housing Studies. Elder Americans prefer aging in place, staying in their homes or in the same community with family and friends nearby. The most disturbing crack in the retirement edifice were barriers that excluded black Americans from much of the new economic security system. In the era of Jim Crow, Southern congressional barons backed Social Security, unemployment insurance, the GI Bill, and minimum wage by crafting the bills in ways that guaranteed disparate treatment of blacks and whites. The devil is always in the legislative details.

A classic example is the post–World War II GI Bill of Rights. The GI Bill promoted home ownership, college education, job training, and business start-ups. The law also accommodated Jim Crow. In 1947, of the 3,229 GI Bill–guaranteed loans for homes, businesses, and farms made in Mississippi, only two were offered to black veterans, according to Ira Katznelson, professor of political science and history at Columbia University. "The GI Bill adapted to 'the southern way of life' by accommodating itself to segregation in higher education, to the job ceilings that local officials imposed on returning black soldiers and to a general unwillingness to offer loans to blacks even when such loans were insured by the federal government," writes Katznelson in the *Washington Post*. "At the very moment a wide array of public policies were providing most white Americans with valuable tools to gain protection in their old age, good jobs, economic security, assets and middle-class status, black Americans were mainly left to fend for themselves."

Blacks weren't welcome in retirement communities, for instance. In his 1964 visit to Sun City, Calvin Trillin noted that there are "no Negroes in Sun City." He was told that at all four Del Webb retirement communities the salesmen were instructed to show absolutely no discrimination and "to assure Negro customers that they can buy any house—although 'when it comes to a sale, the sales manager handles it, and he explains to the people what they're getting into, because, let's face it, a Negro would be miserable in Sun City,'" says Tom Breen, one of his guides during his visit.

More broadly, the mantra retirement as leisure wasn't persuasive to everyone—far from it. Many older Americans ended up feeling isolated in retirement, far from former colleagues, family, and friends. *Lifetime Living* magazine, a publication aimed at people forty years and older, couldn't find a corporate head, labor leader, or pension expert in 1952 willing to defend mandatory retirement in a public forum, according to William Graebner in a *History of Retirement*. The television show *The Real McCoys* nicely captured the relationship between work, self-worth, and aging in an episode. The 1950s show starred Walter Brennan, the grandfather of the farming family. His son and daughter-in-law feel he should be able to take it easy in his old age. Their plan to have him retire from farm work badly backfires. "Now, you listen to me and you listen to me close. There are a lot of good years left in me yet. A man is as old as he feels and the way I feel right now I can out-play and out-work the whole gol'darn bunch of you," said grandfather McCoy. When he injures himself, the family once again tries to get him to retire. Feeling useless and rejected, he gets so depressed that they conspire to convince him he's still needed on the farm. Happy, Brennan returns to milking the cows.

The pushback on Madison Avenue's vision of old age didn't come only from a desire to remain useful. The belief that everyone enjoyed financial security in their retirement years is largely misplaced nostalgia or even a myth. Many people labored at companies that didn't offer their workers a pension, especially small businesses. In 1979, only 28 percent of private sector workers were covered by a traditional pension and another 10 percent had a combination of a traditional pension, and a defined contribution plan (much like a 401(k). Workers covered by a pension who suffered through spells of unemployment or changed jobs over the years didn't qualify for a pension or received at most a minimal monthly payment. The traditional pension plan was designed to reward employees for years of service and final pay. Only a minority of workers—10 to 11 percent of private sector employees—ever labored long enough at one company to earn a decent pension in retirement. Traditional pensions did nothing for a majority of private sector workers even at the peak of coverage. "In other words, even in the 'good old days' when 'everybody' supposedly had a pension, the reality is that most workers in the private sector did not," says Nevin Adams, director at the Employee Benefit Research Institute (EBRI). Adds Dallas Salisbury, president of EBRI: "The good old days were true for the elites. They did spend their full careers at one company and they retired with a gold watch and a pension."

The finances underpinning mass retirement were always suspect, especially with gains in average life expectancy. Management consultant Peter Drucker sounded an early alarm in the 1950s. In an article for

Harper's, he argued that Social Security and pensions should be "the roof on the house of old age rather than the foundation." He goes on:

> In a society which, like ours, will contain a high population of able-minded and able-bodied older people, the foundation must be an effective policy to make the older people productive and keep them employed. Without the roof of pensions the building would be open to the elements. Yet if we do not underpin the roof with a solid foundation, it will most certainly fall in.

Drucker's insight was prescient. It brings us to the third major phase in the evolution of retirement in America: The emergence of unretirement.

CHAPTER 9

Rewriting the Social Compact

Life gets mighty precious
When there's less of it to waste
                                   —Bonnie Raitt

ONE OF THE BEST LINES in economics comes from the opening sentences of *The Armchair Economist* by Steven Landsburg, professor at the University of Rochester. "Most of economics can be summarized in four words: 'People respond to incentives.' The rest is commentary."

The public policy message about old age shouldn't be the current mantra of "we can't afford retirement" and, therefore, government and businesses need to cut, cut, cut. The unretirement mindset starts from a far more positive place. Older workers are educated and healthy, on average. Boomers have expressed a strong desire to remain engaged in the market economy. They still want to make a difference. They're a creative force for change. "What additional incentives would make it practical and desirable for more people to work longer? Think about incentives to keep the human capital in the workforce," says University of Minnesota economist Art Rolnick. Laura Carstensen, head of the Stanford Center on Longevity, agrees. "We need to change the incentive structure," she says.

The public policy and commercial enterprise focus should be on designing incentives to realistically bolster prospects for unretirement.

Older workers may choose to stick with full-time work. They might embrace part-time jobs, bridge jobs, contract labor, and, in a surprising number of cases, starting their own business. There are so many potential options and policymakers should get on the bandwagon instead of sticking to the current approach of ignoring older employees and aging entrepreneurs. My goal in this chapter is to put forward a handful of initiatives that I think might accelerate unretirement. Of course, legislative changes are difficult to consider even before taking into account the bitter dysfunction and ideological divides in Washington, D.C., and many state capitals. You may like all, a handful, or none of my suggestions. Hopefully, taken altogether, the ideas will spark a conversation about what's possible and desirable for encouraging unretirement and encore careers. "The story about people working longer is going to happen. Maybe not as much as it should or as fast, but it's already happening," says Eugene Steuerle in an interview in his Urban Institute office. "The question is, do we do it well or poorly?"

I vote for both speeding up the unretirement process and doing the transition well.

That said, in suggesting unretirement initiatives I don't want to jump from one stereotype of the aged (they're unproductive, uncreative, and incapable of making it in today's fast-paced work world) to another prejudice (everyone's healthy, educated, and wise, willing to work until they drop). Aging workers are a diverse group by definition. Aging is much more than chronology, birth, and death and the time in between, a clock ticking in the background of our lives and generations. Yes, our birthdays remind us we're getting older every year. The AARP tells us when we reach fifty, sending us a letter urging us to join the advocate for the elderly and get senior discounts to boot! (I like the comment about passing the fifty-year milestone by Paul DiMaggio, sociologist at Princeton University. When asked how he felt about turning fifty, DiMaggio quipped he could no longer be an enfant terrible. He would have to be content being, simply, terrible.)

The aging experience reflects our narratives, the stories we tell ourselves and others. Our aging selves reflect our joys, our disappointments, and our memories. Something that happened forty years ago may live vividly in our minds, while what we did yesterday is vague—and vice versa. Generations share defining memories. Boomers came of age during the early decades of the post–World War II era, a time of rapid economic growth. Boomers lived through the Cold War, the civil rights era, the Vietnam War, the women's movement, the fall of the Berlin Wall, the rise of the personal computer and the Internet, the decline of traditional pensions and the spread of 401(k)s, and the emergence of an integrated global economy. Boomers enjoy a common cultural vocabulary, conversational shorthand, remembrances of events past, even if we weren't actually there. I was still in high school when Woodstock, the defining rock festival of the sixties, drew some half a million people to a farm in New York State. I didn't go. I was too young to even try. Instead, my friends and I saw the movie *Woodstock* many times when it came out a year later in 1970. (Obviously, this was in the pre-VCR era, let alone Netflix. You had to go to the theater to watch a film again.)

The range of experiences lived by people who make up a generation also differ greatly. Look at leading-edge boomers, those now at an age to file for Social Security and Medicare benefits. Some are veterans; others protested the war in Vietnam. Some grew up in the Jim Crow South; others were raised on farms in rural Minnesota. Some got divorced; others stayed married for half a century. Some had children; others were childless. Some enjoyed an occasional drink; others ended up in rehab. Some moved here from another country; others were born in the United States. The gap in experiences is often a matter of a few years. My brother is four years older than I am. For his group of graduating high school seniors the Vietnam War and the draft dominated everything. I took a class my senior year in high school laying out options for dealing with the draft, but by the time I was handed my high school diploma the draft was essentially over.

Critically, the gap in economic circumstances and opportunities has widened in recent decades, especially between those with a college education and those without. The ratio of median hourly wages for those with a bachelor's degree and median hourly wages for those with only a high school diploma has widened since the early 1980s. The earnings premium for graduating from college rose from 40 percent in the eighties to around 84 percent currently. Some form of postsecondary education has become a necessary although not sufficient condition for getting the kind of job and career that comes with retirement and health care benefits. In sharp contrast, aging low-skill workers in retail, warehouses, home health care, and similar jobs have typically earned little and haven't had access to employer-sponsored benefits. The thought of working longer in low-wage jobs or after putting in hard years on the assembly line is painful for some. "It's one thing to say to a thirty-year-old that you're going to work longer, but it's different with someone fifty-five years," says Mary Rosenthal, age sixty-one and director of Healthcare Workforce Development in Minnesota. "Now they're fifty-five years old, realize they have to work another ten to fifteen years with a body that may be burned out and they weren't told that might be the case when they were thirty. It's an ugly thing."

Social commentator H. L. Mencken powerfully captured her sentiments back in 1922. "If he got no reward whatever, the artist would go on working just the same; his actual reward, in fact, is often so little that he almost starves," he wrote. "But suppose a garment-worker got nothing for his labor: would he go on working just the same? Can one imagine his submitting voluntarily to hardship and sore want that he might express his soul in 200 more pairs of ladies' pants?"

Point well taken. Yet even here the story is more complex than the averages captured by the income, wage, and education statistics. (Averages can mask great variations. The classic example is the statistician who drowns while crossing a river that was—on average—only three feet deep. Oops.) Look at the experience of Tom Fossum, age sixty. He was a concrete laborer for some three decades, helping to construct commercial buildings through the Twin Cities, including the Mall of America, a monumental citadel to consumerism. Concrete is a tough business, hard on the body. In an interview with Adam Belz of the *Minneapolis Star Tribune*, Fossum said his back went first. His knees went next. He had to retire at fifty-four years old. Since then, Fossum has had two knee replacements. Fossum's pension is about two thirds less than what it would have been if he had been able to work until age sixty-two. Still, he misses work, and not just for the money. "You get out every day, and meet friends and you work all day," Fossum told Belz. "Time goes by fast."

Richard Wagner is a former navy officer on his second career. He's head of the Dunwoody College of Technology, a hundred-year-old trade school housed in a large dark redbrick building in downtown Minneapolis. I met with Wagner since I had heard that Dunwoody is seeing more fiftysomething students. It's true. He gave me a tour of the facilities and while we watched students practice on machine tools in the building's basement (manufacturing jobs are hot) Wagner noted that factory work "requires less and less physical labor." Employers are looking for a better-educated work force with computers and automated equipment doing much of the hard labor. More than a third of workers in manufacturing have at least some college, triple the number three decades ago. Older students come to Dunwoody to get a certificate that enables them to stay employed, he added. A good example is an electrician. It's a wearing job, climbing up and down ladders, lugging heavy equipment around and installing wiring. Older electricians eventually grow weary of the physical demands of the job. What they then do is get qualified to become an estimator on the electrical work for projects, said Wagner. "Former electricians are really good estimators," he said. "Older workers are looking for a career that will give them a steady income."

That said, putting work at the core of framing policy initiatives for an aging work force is optimistic on the job front, a perspective in short supply these days. Far too many workers of all ages remain unemployed and underemployed, earning some income here and a job there, discouraged by their fading prospects of finding a steady paycheck, seemingly stuck on the fringes of the labor market. The challenges are real, but we should remember the lesson of 1979, says Narayana Kocherlakota, president of the Federal Reserve Bank of Minneapolis. He notes that in October of that year, Paul Volcker, the new chairman of the Federal Reserve Board, gave a speech about inflation, "A Time of Testing." Inflation rates had been increasing over the past fifteen years, and at the time of his talk it was running at more than a 9 percent annual rate. Many economists believed the best that could be accomplished was to stabilize inflation at around 10 percent, recalls Michael Boskin, head of the White House Council of Economic Advisers during the first Bush presidency. Several days before Volcker's talk, his predecessor Arthur Burns gave a speech with the depressing message that he doubted central bankers had the "practical capacity for curbing an inflation" that is persistent. Inflation was the democratic disease.

Volcker's response? In essence, nonsense. He took a series of tough actions that not only brought inflation rates down but also broke widespread expectations that high inflation was inevitable. More than three decades later the Federal Reserve follows a realistic target range for inflation of 2 percent. Kocherlakota argues that the United States is at a comparable moment in our history. He also called his 2013 talk "A Time of Testing" to underscore that we "are again confronted with a severe test—but this time a test created by low *employment* and low *employment expectations.*"

Unretirement is a critical part of the much bigger story of repairing the job market. The current time of testing involves reviving the goal of a full employment economy, a catchphrase from another era largely relegated to economic history. (An exception is two eminent Washington, D.C.–based economists, Jared Bernstein and Dean Baker. They published *Getting Back to Full Employment: A Better Bargain for Working People* in 2013 and *Getting to Full Employment* in 2003.) Full employment is usually defined as somewhere between 1 percent and 2 percent unemployment, a figure that reflects the normal ebb and flow of the work force as people are laid off and leave jobs for better opportunities. However, in the United States a full-employment economy more realistically may be closer to the 3 percent to 4 percent level, a marker reached only a handful of times during the past half century: in the fifties, the latter part of the sixties, and during the heady years of the dot-com boom in the nineties. A 2 percent to 4 percent unemployment rate is a reasonable goal to embrace. (After all, North Dakota in 2014 had an unemployment rate below 3 percent.)

The post–World War II embrace of full employment was in reaction to the trauma and high unemployment rates of the Great Depression.

The ambition eventually foundered on the double-digit inflation rates of the 1970s. Economists at the time became convinced the only way to keep inflation down was to tolerate higher rates of unemployment. Economists didn't ever quite put it this way, but too much economic growth and too much employment was bad for the overall price level. A reserve army of unemployed and underemployed workers is good for holding down inflation rates. But the conventional wisdom that says low unemployment is inflationary is wrong.

Throughout U.S. history, periods of rapid economic growth and technological innovation have often been times of declining inflation rates. Technological advances, productivity improvements, and open borders can hike growth prospects and still keep overall prices stable (the experience of the late nineteenth century and late 1990s). "It is simply not logical (or correct) to argue that an increase in production will foster a general rise of prices. Concerns that faster total growth of output in the economy will cause a fall in the purchasing power of money—inflation—are simply wrong," writes Jerry Jordan, former president of the Federal Reserve Bank of Cleveland. "Similarly, it is false to say that 'too many people working' or 'too low unemployment' can 'cause inflation.'"[1]

What counts with inflation is that the Fed maintains the credibility of its commitment to price stability, currently defined as a target rate of 2 percent. Seared by the experience of the 1970s, the Fed and its network of monetary mandarins throughout academia and global finance centers have developed a deep understanding of how to keep inflationary pressures in check. The Fed might err for a short period of time, but it has the knowledge and the will to lean against a sustained rise in the price level. Hence, the underlying trend toward subdued inflation over the past three decades.

The human toll from long spells of unemployment and underemployment is too high for all workers, young, middle-aged, and old, men and women, highly educated and less skilled. The damage runs much deeper than difficulties paying the bills, and that's bad enough. People lose purpose. Their health deteriorates. Families break apart. Laid-off workers can't save for retirement. They borrow too much to stay afloat, a debt burden that eventually makes their financial circumstances even worse. The unemployed lose a sense of attachment and belonging to a much larger community and society. A robust job market is the preferred solution to reducing poverty, increasing economic opportunities, and transforming retirement into unretirement.

The most important reforms for encouraging longer careers involve the two big safety nets, the retirement savings system and health care. Let's start with retirement savings. It's high time to acknowledge that the system is not only broken but is unsuited for the new world of unretirement. The typical value of 401(k)s and IRAs for workers nearing retirement was about $120,000 in 2010, according to the Federal Reserve. That sum would provide a mere $575 in monthly income, assuming a couple bought a joint-and-survivor annuity, calculates Alicia Munnell, director of the Center for Retirement Research at Boston College. (When you buy an annuity you get an income for life, depending on how much you put into it. An annuity with a joint-and-survivor clause lowers the monthly payout because the payments continue until both are dead.) The figure will improve with working longer, of course. But the finances of the future unretired—younger boomers, gen Xers, and millennials— would benefit enormously from an improved low-cost and universal retirement savings system. Most important, a better designed retirement savings system would greatly enhance the ability of workers to embrace variety and flexibility throughout their career.

The lack of savings isn't because Americans have a "shop till they drop" mentality, although we are world-class consumers. Far more important in defining the struggle to save is the slow growth in incomes for the average American household. The typical income for working-age households fell by 12.4 percent between 2000 and 2011, from $63,535 to $55,640, calculates the Economic Policy Institute. Worker wages have stagnated even as people struggle to meet the mortgage tab, build up emergency savings, set money aside for their children's college education, and pay more of the health care bill. The current retirement system doesn't take enough into account that many people lose their jobs and suffer spells of unemployment.

Just ask the Sauberts of Muncie, Indiana. Muncie is better known as Middletown, the title of a famous book by sociologists Helen and Robert Lynd. The Lynds lived in Muncie in 1924 to study the "typical" American town. Their 1929 book *Middletown* became a national bestseller. Muncie was a thriving smokestack town when the Lynds were there, a manufacturing hub with the Ball Brothers glass jar company, a General Motors transmission plant, a number of other auto parts manufacturers, and more glassmakers.

Like many midwestern towns, Muncie fell on hard times in the 1970s, the beginning of manufacturing's long decline. The auto parts maker BorgWarner opened its Muncie plant in 1928, a sprawling, redbrick factory on the outskirts of town. The plant once employed more than a thousand people on four shifts, but by the early 2000s the work force had shrunk to a few hundred. Charles Saubert worked there. His father had worked at GM for nearly thirty-nine years and, after high school, Charles went to work at BorgWarner in 1983 (when it was called Warner Gear). But Saubert lost his job in 2008 at age fifty-three. He had clocked twenty-five years at the auto transmission parts maker. BorgWarner closed the factory a year later, so there was no going back. The dream of a good pension and comfortable retirement vanished because he was five years shy of putting in thirty years on the job.

The Sauberts are solidly middle class. His wife, Pam, held a variety of jobs over the years, such as a hospital technical worker, tax preparer, substitute teacher, Girl Scout employee, and volunteer. They have a house and cars, raised a daughter, paid their bills, took vacations, participated in a 401(k), and, with the demands on their money, found it hard to save. Sound familiar? Two years after being laid off, Charles Saubert was still out of work. The kind of factory work he knew was scarce and there were plenty of laid-off assembly-line workers ready to jump at any opening. "What's gonna hurt is the ones that are older, Charlie's age," said his wife, Pam. "All they know is factory work."

The Sauberts eventually dipped into his 401(k) to pay off their house. This way they no longer had to take painful phone calls from the mortgage company when they fell behind on their payments. Pam went back to school to get her teaching degree and is now a substitute teacher, hoping for a full-time job. Charlie is stocking the shelves and performing maintenance at Meijer, the grocery store. He's making about half what he did at BorgWarner. He also gets a monthly pension income of $344 after taxes. He does some odds and ends work in people's homes. "It is tight but we manage," says Pam.

When it comes to understanding the difficulties in saving for our elder years, stories like the Sauberts' are a critical part of the narrative. Retirement savings also suffered when a number of corporations during the great recession reduced or even eliminated the company match into the 401(k). Employees found defined contribution plans like 401(k)s, where the employee makes the decision to participate and where to invest (within the limits of the employer's plan), difficult to manage well. However, the most disturbing number is that only 42 percent of private sector workers ages twenty-five to sixty-four have any pension coverage in their current job. The result, according to the Center for Retirement Research at Boston College, is that more than one third of households end up with no coverage during their working years while others moving in and out of coverage accumulate small 401(k) balances. In short, the current system doesn't even come close to universal coverage for the private economy.

Alarm bells are also going off in the one sector of the work force with essentially universal coverage: government. State, local, and federal government pensions cover their full-time employees. The backbone of the public retirement system remains the traditional defined benefit pension plan, the same one that most private companies have abandoned. Problem is the financial meltdown and great recession made apparent what many experts have long known: Too many state and local governments routinely underfunded their pension plans while the future cost of their retirement payout promises swelled. The generosity of many public pensions is now an incendiary topic, with taxpayers potentially on the hook for billions in unfunded promises. "The next decade will be one of fundamental reform in public sector pensions," says Robert Clark, economics professor at North Carolina State University.

Most states have passed some kind of pension overhaul in recent years, although the changes have largely concentrated on reducing costs and have been mostly marginal initiatives—a bit of tinkering, really. For instance, governments are pushing employees (especially new hires) to contribute more into their savings plan. The biggest flaw with these plans has little to do with employees, however. It's that politicians across the country have failed to adequately fund these plans to pay the bill of future obligations. Corporations moved away from defined benefit pension plans after the 1974 Employee Retirement Income Security Act (ERISA) required companies to more fully fund their plans, raising the cost of offering long-term employees a pension. Rather than pay up, management turned to much cheaper 401(k) and similar defined contribution pension plans. (Talk about the law of unintended consequences!) My guess is that financial pressures will similarly push government leaders to also shift over time to defined contribution plans. (Existing defined benefit plans will remain as legacy obligations that will fade away as aging retirees die off.) The change seems inevitable because politicians will remain reluctant to adequately fund them.

What's more, public sector defined contribution plans will spread because they reflect the needs of a modern work force. Over the past twenty-five years the median tenure of all wage and salary workers age thirty or over at an employer has been around five years. The 401(k) and comparable plans are "portable," meaning employees can roll the savings into an IRA or into their new employer's plan when they change jobs. The 401(k) offers faster "vesting" than traditional pension plans, a fancy way of saying the money is yours quickly. Employees can contribute money into their employer-sponsored plan so long as they're working at the company, well into their eighties if they want. There is no set retirement age or early retirement incentive with the 401(k). The average tenure in state jobs is only 6.4 years. Many public sector workers don't enjoy in full the long-term promised benefit. "Public sector retirement plans cannot provide full retirement security for people who don't spend a full career in government employment," says Roger Ferguson, chief executive of TIAA-CREF. "But we still need to provide opportunities for them to save and experience a reasonable outcome after a lifetime of working across society."

Defined-contribution savings plans can be made better. Much has been learned over the past three decades. We know that the 401(k) asked too much of people. They had to voluntarily join, a difficult decision for lower-income workers living off tight budgets. Many employees found themselves overwhelmed by having to choose from page after page of mutual fund options. High fees eroded the returns workers earned off their savings. The good news is that plan design is improving. New employees are now automatically enrolled (they have the opportunity to opt out of the plan, a choice very few take), and the menu of offerings has been narrowed. Many employer-sponsored plans offer well-diversified investment choices such as target date funds and lifecycle funds that automatically shift toward a more conservative portfolio as the date of retirement nears. Some plans automatically increase contributions to the maximum allowed over a period of years. Although most participants in private sector 401(k) plans still don't have the option of receiving payments from their plans as a stream of annuitized income in retirement they can't outlive, it's widely recognized that plans need to offer their near retirees the choice. (It's a more common option among nonprofit defined contribution savings plans.) "We know what plan design works," said Larry D. Zimpleman, chairman of the Principal Financial Group at the Employee Benefit Research Institute's seventy-third annual policy forum. "We know what plan design doesn't."

An intriguing simulation created by Jack VanDerhei, research director of EBRI, illustrates the power of good design. Assume the goal is for 401(k) participants to replace 70 percent of their preretirement income after they say good-bye to their colleagues for the last time at age sixty-five. With voluntary participation in a 401(k)—combined with current Social Security benefits—76 percent of lower-income workers ages twenty-five to twenty-nine in a 401(k) will achieve that measure of success at retirement. At an 80 percent income-replacement rate, the threshold success rate falls to 67 percent. Not good. For the same workers with automatic enrollment and automatic escalation of contributions the success figure rises to 90 percent with a 70 percent replacement-rate gauge and 85 percent with an 80 percent goal. Much better.[2] "We are on the cusp of being able to make defined contribution plans work for everyone, but we really have to act differently and think differently and we really need to get at it in the next five years," Zimpleman said.

He's right. Lawmakers should transform defined contribution savings plans into a best practices retirement savings product: automatic enrollment; automatic escalation; limited investment choice, low fees, and an annuity option for retirees. Sure, employees can keep the choice of opting out of the plan, but experience suggests that most won't exercise the right. The government could open up to private companies that don't offer a retirement plan to their workers—usually smaller firms— the federal government's Thrift Savings Plan (TSP). The contributions could be made through payroll deduction so the cost to firms of participating would be minimal. The TSP is one of the world's best designed defined contribution savings plans with nearly $400 billion in assets under management and more than 4.6 million participants (as of December 31, 2013). The TSP offers five broad-based investment funds—government bond fund, fixed income fund, large-cap stock fund, small-cap stock fund, and an international stock fund—along with the option of a lifecycle fund created out of the other five funds. The annual expense ratio was an extremely low 0.027 percent in 2012, meaning for each fund the cost was about 27 cents per $1,000 of investment. "What's the downside?" asks Dean Baker, codirector at the Center for Economic and Policy Research, during an interview at his office. "It's common sense."

Better yet, lawmakers could create a universal retirement plan attached to the individual. There have been a number of proposals over the years along these lines. For instance, the government could automatically enroll every worker in an IRA through automatic payroll deduction. Retirement experts in academia and finance are also looking to learn from the various mandatory retirement savings schemes in Australia, Britain, and Israel, even though the term "mandatory" is toxic in Washington, D.C., at the moment. Nevertheless, retirement savings promotes individual responsibility and bolsters household choice in the elder years. Retirement savings lowers the demand for government resources and charitable services among an aging population. It also provides an additional financial cushion for those experimenting with jobs during their unretirement years.

Okay, what about health care, the most divisive public policy issue in America in several generations? The United States spends some 18 percent of GDP on health care, more than any other nation. (To put that number in context, Ezekiel Emanuel, chair of medical ethics and health policy, University of Pennsylvania, writes that "the United States spends on health care alone what the 65 million people in France spend on everything: education, defense, the environment, scientific research, vacations, food, housing, cars, clothes and health care. In other words, our health care spending is the fifth largest economy in the world.") The U.S. health care system is going through a period of massive, controversial change called the Affordable Care Act, or Obamacare.

Let's briefly review the history of health insurance in America. Coverage for health services started in the United States some two hundred years ago with hospital care for sailors paid through compulsory wage deductions. The retailing giant Montgomery Ward purchased from London Guarantee and Accident Company what's considered the nation's first group health insurance policy in 1910, according to Laura Scofea in *The Development and Growth of Employer-Provided Health Insurance*. Still, less than 10 percent of the population had some form of health insurance by 1940. The turning point was World War II. Wages were frozen during the war but not employee benefits. Companies found it prudent to bid for scarce labor by improving medical benefits for their employees and, almost by default, employer-sponsored health insurance became the linchpin of the nation's health care system. The number of individuals covered by the employer benefit jumped from 20.6 million in 1950 to 142.3 million in 1960. A major factor behind the rapid expansion of employer-based health care group plans was that contributions by the employer into the plan were exempt from employee taxable income. The same tax treatment didn't hold for individual health plans. The individual health insurance market never really offered a competitive product with premiums high and coverage sparse.

The United States never really embraced universal coverage, despite multiple attempts over the years. A key plank in Theodore Roosevelt's losing presidential campaign of 1912 was national health insurance. President Harry Truman tried for universal health insurance after World War II with his Fair Deal. President Clinton's universal health care initiative collapsed early in his first term. Nevertheless, a patchwork quilt of coverage made up of employer-sponsored plans, nonprofits like Blue Cross and Blue Shield, Medicare for the elderly, and Medicaid for the poor did a reasonably good job with coverage. But the threads holding together this health insurance quilt became increasingly frayed. While most large companies still offer their employees a health benefit, nearly two thirds of firms with up to twenty-four employees don't. Between 2000 and 2010, the share of Americans under the age of sixty-five with employer-sponsored health insurance declined for the tenth year in a row, from 69.2 percent to 58.6 percent, according to the Economic Policy Institute in Washington, D.C. Little wonder the ranks of the uninsured grew rapidly. Medical costs spiraled higher even as the United States performed poorly on most health quality measures compared to other major industrial nations. Americans paid more for less, the definition of a bad deal.

From the perspective of workers and economic vitality, a major drawback to an employer-based system is that the company owns the policy rather than the worker. Even though workers don't own the plan, they paid the full cost of the benefit through reduced wages. A layoff translated into lost health insurance coverage for the worker and family. The reality of being without health insurance was particularly painful for, say, fifty-five-year-old workers handed a pink slip. It was hard to get another job with health insurance, the individual health market was a bad option (expensive premiums and poor coverage), and yet it would be many years before qualifying for Medicare. Another bad side effect of the employer-based system is what economists call "job lock." The term captures when workers stay at a job they don't like because they're afraid if they leave their next job won't come with health insurance.

"Entrepreneurial lock" also exists. A Kauffman-RAND Institute for Entrepreneurship Public Policy study looked into whether people with employer-based insurance were more likely to become self-employed if they could get their health insurance through a spouse. Their estimate suggests that the health insurance "entrepreneurial lock" for men is just over one percentage point relative to an annual base business creation of 3 percent. The fear among women of losing health insurance reduced their business creation somewhat. The scholars also tested the thesis by looking at eligibility for universal coverage under Medicare. The business ownership rate for men at age sixty-four was 26.5 percent. The figure jumped to 28.7 percent at age sixty-five. This part of their study did not focus on women, but researchers did find a large increase in female business ownerships rates at age sixty-five. "The availability of affordable health insurance for the self-employed has an important impact on whether individuals are likely to become entrepreneurs," concludes economist Robert Fairlie and his coauthors in their 2010 study, "Is Employer-Based Health Insurance a Barrier to Entrepreneurship?"

It would be far better if workers of all ages were free to shift careers, explore new job opportunities, find a bridge job, and start their own company throughout their work lives without worrying about losing their health insurance. It's a smart way to encourage entrepreneurship. "I tell anybody who will listen: The single biggest barrier, bar none, the single biggest barrier to creativity, entrepreneurship, innovation, productive capacity in this country is employer-based health insurance," says Jeremy Neuner of NextSpace. "Because you have all these people who would much rather be doing something differently, but won't make the leap because 'my kids need health insurance; I need health insurance.'"

Neuner tells the story of a NextSpace member, an engineer. He wanted to create high-end architectural LED lighting for homes and offices. But the engineer took forever to make the leap from his W-2-based job for his 1099 venture. "Not because he didn't have a good product, not because the product didn't have a really huge market, not because he didn't have funding," says Neuner. "He had everything he needed except stupid health insurance. So think about that."

Enter the Obama administration's signature legislation, the Affordable Care Act. The nation's most significant social legislation since the 1935 Social Security Act, it tries to address the flaws in the existing system. The law marks a fundamental divide in America's hundred-plus-year debate over national health care. The United States embraced universal coverage by essentially abandoning an approach that excluded people from the mainstream health insurance market based on preexisting conditions.

Despite the incendiary charges against the Affordable Care Act, it's a deeply centrist bill that took ideas from the moderate wing of the Republican Party, merged them with mainstream technocratic health care insights, and included the liberal dream of universal coverage. The Affordable Care Act keeps the employer-based system, Medicare, and Medicaid. The blueprint for reform was designed by the Heritage Foundation in 1999, brought into reality in Massachusetts in late 2004 by Mitt Romney, the state's Republican governor, and later embraced with additional changes by President Obama. The Heritage-Romney-Obama health insurance plan stitched back together the patchwork quilt of different health insurance markets into a near-universal system. The two key changes in the legislation are expanding Medicaid to broaden coverage among lower-income families and establishing the state-based health insurance exchanges. The latter are designed to improve the choice and policy coverage in the individual health insurance market.

Of course, the Affordable Care Act is anathema—how's that for an understatement?—to its conservative opponents. A number of states delayed setting up the insurance exchange, a tactic that forced the federal government to take up the responsibility. The rollout of the exchanges was initially disastrous. Some states refused to accept the terms of expanded Medicaid coverage. Conservatives fought to repeal Obamacare. But the Supreme Court let the law stand and other court cases failed to stop the rollout. Most important, Obama won reelection in 2012. The exchanges are being fixed and the initial goal for signing up people was met despite problems. Once the remaining glitches are worked out people should find it easier than ever to shop for insurance. Buyers of individual policies will receive more benefits to offset premium costs, including guaranteed coverage, limits on out-of-pocket expenses, and comprehensive medical coverage. "Something like 25 million citizens, more than half of those who are currently uninsured, will enter into a relationship with a medical practice within the next few years," writes David Warsh, veteran economic journalist and founder of the online weekly EconomicPrincipals.com. "They'll join more than 250 million Americans who are currently insured in the biggest undertaking to improve public health since the days of city sanitation and the war on communicable disease more than a century ago."

Despite its flaws, Obamacare is a step in the right direction for the new economy of unretirement. There's no going back to a health care system based on preexisting conditions and millions of uninsured Americans. Even vehement opponents of Obamacare reluctantly have come to realize this. Of course, the Affordable Care Act will evolve and adapt over the years. There are still too many holes and the market isn't competitive enough. Over the long haul, say, the next two decades, the legislation has probably set in motion the eventual demise of our employer-based health care system (which had been slowing unfolding even before Obamacare). No one should weep for the extinction of an inefficient and inequitable system. Almost all health care economists—conservative and liberal alike—agree that attaching the plan to the individual or household is a smarter approach. The health care experts differ significantly on the design details of that plan—catastrophic insurance? single payer? global budget? tax credits? value-added tax?—but not on the direction of reform.

What about the commonly voiced fear that while a stronger retirement and health social safety net may be just, the price is too high because it will also discourage entrepreneurship and risk-taking, the wellsprings of economic growth? The opposite should be the case in the twenty-first century economy, especially if the overhaul is designed with additional work incentives throughout an adult's career, including the unretirement years. Modern finance theory—hardly a bastion of socialist thinking—suggests that strong safety nets that minimize the downside from bets gone bad can actually encourage greater risk taking.

Without a safety net they can rely on, "people are afraid to venture out into the rapids where real achievement is possible," writes Yale University economist Robert Shiller in *The New Financial Order: Risk in the 21st Century*. "Brilliant careers go untried because of the fear of economic setback." So do second and third encore careers.

Modern finance theory shines when it comes to insights about managing risks. It represents a rich set of ideas for hedging away risks you don't want, minimizing the impact of inherent risks, and embracing the bets you desire. Investment analysts Scott L. Lummer and Mark W. Rieppe nicely captured the critical role of risk management this way. In *Pudd'nhead Wilson*, Mark Twain wrote, "The wise man saith, 'Put all your eggs in the one basket and—WATCH that basket.'" Miguel de Cervantes in *Don Quixote* believed, "'Tis the part of a wise man to keep himself today for tomorrow, and not venture all his eggs in one basket." The finance authors rightly emphasize that Cervantes and Twain were both great writers, but Cervantes would have made for a better investor.

Fledgling elderly entrepreneurs and laid-off older workers without family wealth to tap would have every incentive to try their hand at starting their own business or trying a different career if they were confident of having health insurance and some form of retirement savings in their old age. Who knows how many Horatio Algers are stuck in a cubicle, developing their business plan in their garage at night yet unable to pull the trigger, worried about retirement savings and medical bills? In an economy where lifetime employment with one company exists mostly in the history books, where freelancers and contingent workers comprise about a third of the work force, with older workers eager to find part-time jobs and create bridge careers before they qualify for Medicare, health insurance and retirement benefits shouldn't be tied to the employer. Instead, we should focus on constructing a universal safety net that encourages working and risk-taking over a lifetime. Taken altogether, "it's a concept of social insurance with work at its core," says University of Arizona sociologist Lane Kenworthy.

That's a suitable public policy mantra for the age of unretirement. What other types of incentives might bolster prospects for the rapid spread of unretirement? Here's an intriguing idea for encouraging later filing for Social Security. What if the extra income boost from delaying filing for Social Security benefits came in a lump sum rather than in an annuity paid out over time? That's the question posed by Jingjing Chai, Raimond Maurer, and Ralph Rogalla of Goethe University and Olivia Mitchell of the Wharton School at the University of Pennsylvania in "Exchanging Delayed Social Security Benefits for Lump Sums: Could This Incentivize Longer Work Careers?"

The scholars give this example: Workers who delay claiming their Social Security benefit until after their so-called normal retirement age could be entitled to a benefit increase of about 8 percent every year retirement is deferred, up to age seventy. In their example, older workers decide to stay on the job until age sixty-six, rather than retire at age sixty-five, their normal retirement age. At age sixty-six, they would get a lump sum worth 1.2 times the age sixty-five benefit and would also receive the age sixty-five annuity stream of income for life when filing for benefits at age sixty-six. Those who wait until age seventy would get a lump sum worth some six times their starting-age annual benefit payment, plus the age sixty-five benefit stream for life.

So what? Well, their research suggests that people like lump sum payouts for a variety of reasons. Among the attractions of a lump sum are financial flexibility, the option of leaving money to heirs, and—for "financially sophisticated individuals"—the opportunity to invest the money. The lure of the lump sum would encourage workers to voluntarily stay on the job, on average by about one and a half to two years longer, the researchers calculate. Nevertheless, the workers' Social Security benefits wouldn't be cut, they would still have a lifetime annuity to live on, and Social Security's finances would remain essentially the same.

Try this one out: payroll tax relief. A leading proponent is John Shoven, economist at Stanford University. The current benefit formula is based on a calculation that takes into account a worker's highest thirty-five years of earnings. Once thirty-five years have been put in, the incentive to stay on the job weakens, especially since older workers usually take home less pay than they did in middle age, the peak earning years. Why not declare that older workers are "paid up" for Social Security after forty years, asks Shoven? Why not indeed? There are a number of proposed variations on the idea, but they all converge on the notion that eliminating the employee share of the payroll tax is an immediate boost to an aging worker's take-home pay while getting rid of the employer's contribution lowers the cost of employing older workers. The change seems like a win-win situation from the unretirement perspective. "It's an incentive for people to work longer," says Richard Burkhauser, professor of policy analysis at Cornell University.

I'd also change the rules concerning required minimum distributions (RMD) in 401(k)s, IRAs, and the like at age seventy and a half. The requirements are Byzantine anyway. For instance, with a traditional IRA, the RMD is April 1 following the year you reach seventy and six months, even if you are still working. The withdrawal requirement includes IRAs offered through an employer, such as the SIMPLE IRA and a SEP IRA. The same withdrawal date applies with a 401(k), unless you continue working for the same employer. There is no RMD with a Roth IRA. Got all this? A pet peeve of mine is how unnecessarily complicated the rules are with retirement savings plans. Washington could raise the required minimum distribution rules on all plans to, say, eighty years or eighty-five years. Then again, Washington could simply eliminate the RMD altogether. Again, it's a small shift in policy that would add to a cluster of incentives making unretirement increasingly attractive.

Disability is another part of the safety net ripe for work-centered reform. The number of people filing for disability has soared even though the percentage of middle-aged adults reporting a disability has been roughly stable for two decades, averaging about 10 percent. Between 1998 and 2008 the fraction of middle-aged men and women ages forty to fifty-nine receiving Social Security Disability Insurance (SSDI) increased by 45 percent among men (from 3.9 percent to 5.6 percent) and 159 percent among women (1.9 percent to 5 percent), according to economists David Autor of MIT and Mark Duggan of the University of Maryland in "Supporting Work: A Proposal for Modernizing the U.S. Disability Insurance System." The scholars rightly highlight a major problem with the existing disability program: It discourages work. For example, Social Security Disability Insurance only pays benefits to fully disabled workers who have not been gainfully employed for at least five months. There are no partial disability benefits. Outside of a handful of minor exceptions, early vocational rehabilitation services aren't available. "Thus, it's paramount that the United States disability insurance system be reoriented toward supporting employment—opposite its current configuration," write scholars Autor and Duggan.

The experience of the Netherlands is instructive. The numbers of disabled workers in the Netherlands were high and rising until the country began a series of changes, overhauling its disability program around encouraging work. Among the reforms, all Dutch companies must now fund the first two years of disability benefits to their workers. What's more, the employer, worker, and a consulting physician put together a return-to-work plan with a case manager overseeing the process. Since the reforms, fewer workers with disabilities are joining the public disability program. Autor and Duggan's proposed changes mirror the Dutch experience. Richard Burkhauser of Cornell has laid out a similar overhaul package. "These reforms provided incentives for employers, who are in the best position to offer accommodation and rehabilitation, to do so in lieu of moving workers with disabilities onto cash transfers," says Burkhauser.

A work-incentive approach would reinforce the powerful insight of the 1990 Americans with Disabilities Act. "Physical or mental disabilities in no way diminish a person's right to fully participate in all aspects of society." Older workers are more susceptible to the ravages of time, from aching backs to sore knees, and a disability insurance system that focuses on supporting people with disabilities to stay employed offers benefits to individuals and society. "Specifically, we believe that the goal of SSDI reform should be to increase the odds that individuals with work-limiting disabilities remain in the labor force," say Autor and Duggan. "This will raise their well-being and reduce the odds that they apply for long-term SSDI benefits. The cost savings that we envision under this proposal accrue from better supporting individuals with disabilities in the workplace rather than denying them benefits months or years after they have exited the labor force."

Unemployment insurance also could be overhauled to keep more workers attached to the labor market. In the United States, unemployment insurance offers a small income for a period of time after being laid off. Germany has a very different model: job sharing. Economist Baker lays out the basic idea with this example: The economy is tanking, business is bad, and a German firm faces the need to lay off 20 percent of its work force. The German government has created incentives for the firm to cut hours by 20 percent instead. The government replaces 60 percent of lost wages, the company replaces another 20 percent, and the worker takes home 4 percent less while working 20 percent fewer hours. "From the standpoint of employers, they have workers available whose hours can be quickly increased if demand picks up. This saves them the need to find and train new workers," writes Baker. "From the standpoint of workers, this keeps them employed and tied to the workforce." The cost? About the same as America's unemployment insurance program, Baker adds.[3]

Economists have done plenty of work on using tax credits, wage subsidies, and similar incentives to encourage employers to add people to their payroll. These policies aren't directly targeted at older workers. Rather, the gains apply to all employees, young and old alike, and have their biggest impact on the economically disadvantaged of any age. In his Nobel Prize lecture, economist Edmund Phelps passionately argued that "suitably designed employment subsidies would restore the bourgeois culture, revive the ethic of self-support, and increase prosperity in low-wage communities. That would boost a country's dynamism, not weaken it, and also strengthen popular support for capitalist institutions." I'd add that so would encouraging an aging population to stay employed longer and to start their own businesses.

CHAPTER 10

The Us Generation

Every silver lining's got a
Touch of grey
　　　　　　　—Grateful Dead

SHiFT IS AN ENCORE-CAREER NONPROFIT organization in the Twin Cities. It holds many meetings during the year, usually in the first-floor cafeteria at the Twin Cities branch of Minnesota State University, Mankato. The large fluorescent-lit room is full of durable, circular linoleum tables with ten or so plastic chairs at each. The typical gatherings I've attended have sixty to a hundred participants, mostly in their late forties to early sixties. A number are there because they've been laid off. Others are burned out on their careers or eager to find jobs with greater psychological and emotional rewards. "For most it's a combination of economic pressure and the desire for meaningful work," says Jan Hively, an eightysomething serial social entrepreneur and driving force behind the creation of SHiFT.

Harry "Rick" Moody, director of academic affairs for the AARP, spoke at a SHiFT event about an unexpected (at least to me) subject: the seventeenth-century painter Rembrandt. Moody illustrated his talk with slides showing the long trajectory of Rembrandt's art over his forty-five-year career. Moody's thesis was that Rembrandt was not only a great artist. He was an entrepreneur who adapted his creativity to changes in the economy and shifts in market demand as he aged. Phyllis Moen, a scholar of retirement and aging at the University of Minnesota, also spoke. She picked up on the Rembrandt theme in her remarks. "You all need to be innovators," she said. "We become what we believe and what we do."

Those sentences resonate with Tene Wells. She didn't expect to lose her job in 2009. Wells was the decade-long president of WomenVenture, a St. Paul, Minnesota, nonprofit that offers business expertise and consulting services to women-owned enterprises. Times were tough and her departure was sudden. Age fifty-eight, Wells had to get away to grieve, to repair, and to clear her head.

A close friend and local restaurant owner has a home in Seattle. The two of them drove to her house overlooking Puget Sound. Shortly after they arrived, her friend handed Wells the car keys, the house keys, and told her there was plenty of wine in the cellar and she'd be back in several weeks. Wells read. She relaxed. She thought about what she should do next. Wells eventually hit on becoming a social entrepreneur, bringing her business skills to bear on a major social issue, perhaps globally. When she got back to the Twin Cities she started investigating various possibilities with friends and acquaintances. "I used the wealth of contacts I had built up over the years," said Wells. "I met lots of people for coffee."

When I met Wells she was sixty years old and a Bush Foundation fellow, a two-year funded program for developing leadership skills. She was still exploring her social venture options and thinking it might pay for her to attend a midcareer program, something like Harvard University's Kennedy School of Government. Wells was on a panel I moderated on encore careers in 2013. The other participants were Marci Alboher, author of *The Encore Career Handbook: How to Make a Living and a Difference in the Second Half of Life*; social entrepreneur Todd Bol, cofounder of the Little Free Library; and Jodi Harpstead, a twenty-three-year management veteran of the medical device multinational Medtronic and currently chief executive officer at Lutheran Social Services.

The panelists offered much practical information to the audience about thinking through the realities of making a transition to a new job, a new career, or starting your own business. Savings help. Getting health insurance is critical. Don't drain retirement savings to fund a start-up. Nothing surprising, but it's always helpful to review the basics.

What stood out during the panel discussion is how each of them found conversation invaluable to their transition. Specifically, each panelist relayed how they found their network of family, friends, colleagues, mentors, and acquaintances invaluable for thinking through various scenarios and trade-offs, especially during the inevitable dark weeks of doubt.

These network conversations are an underappreciated asset for aging boomers with unretirement. Tom Wolfe memorably and sarcastically called boomers the "me" generation: spoiled, narcissistic, and self-absorbed. Yet the "us" generation seems a more apt description as boomers age, with older workers mining existing connections and establishing new ones in their unretirement years. Older workers typically have a reasonably rich network to tap, thanks to the passage of time. It's a smart move, too, since scholarly research has established that at least half of all jobs come through connections. Additionally, studies convincingly demonstrate that workers who get a job through the informal channels of friends and colleagues express higher overall job satisfaction.

The experience of Cris Siebenlist in Kansas City, Kansas, highlights the critical role of networks. She spent much of her thirty-five-year career teaching special education. Siebenlist loved her work, but toward the end of her career she found it harder to keep going back to the time pressures of the job. "The deadlines used to be stimulating," she says. "Then, not so much."

Not long after Siebenlist retired, a friend from the nearby Penn Valley Metropolitan Community College got in touch with her. The friend needed to fill a part-time job teaching special education kids. Siebenlist ended up taking the job for two years, twelve hours a week. Another part-time job came up about the same time from another friend, this one at a local YWCA. Her friend wondered if Siebenlist would work with women interested in nontraditional jobs, in particular careers in the field of sustainability. Siebenlist jumped at the opportunity. The post lasted about a year, and she wrote the online curriculum, Exploring Green Jobs. Among other activities she is on the board of Friends of Kaw Point Park and regularly rides her bike up to twenty miles, two times a week in good weather.

Notice a theme? Every job she got—paid and volunteer—was through her connections. "I think whether you want to volunteer or work, the network is essential," says Siebenlist. "That's how we find jobs. It's through networking. It isn't through ads and online."

Of course, some of us have better networks than others. It's also useful to step outside your network to get additional insights and ideas. The good news is a new industry is emerging to help older workers figure out what comes next. The organizations offer networking opportunities and guides to resources for planning your unretirement, an encore career. Aging boomers don't have to rely solely on their own contacts for sketching out the next stage of life. "What are the ingredients that go into this rethinking of your life so that even though individual practitioners don't provide the whole service, they recognize the needs and can connect through referrals to the expertise that may be of greater assistance," says Doug Dickson, president at Discovering What's Next, based in the greater Boston area. "Nobody's quite figured it out yet. There's a lot of experimentation going on. The challenge is to create a sustainable business model for providing services to people."

Unretirement activity is bubbling up everywhere. Business should be brisk with workers fifty-five and older projected to account for 25 percent of the labor force in 2020, up from 12 percent in 1990, according to the Stanford Center on Longevity. For the age group sixty-five to seventy-four the 2020 projection is 35 percent for men and 28 percent of women. The unretirement and encore career perspective is that those figures are too conservative. Some of the names involved in the unretirement business are well-established brands, such as the AARP with its Life Reimagined for Work initiative. As we've seen, Marc Freedman's Encore.org based in San Francisco is a leading force in encouraging encore careers. The organization is also a key resource for nonprofits around the country plunging into the encore business. The pioneer Ken

Dychtwald and his wife, Maddy Dychtwald, formed Age Wave in 1986 to consult with large companies and governments about the impact of aging boomers. The Transition Network is in a number of major metropolitan areas, creating communities for professional women fifty and over. ReServe is a New York City–based nonprofit with branches in several cities. It matches fifty-five-plus professionals with local nonprofit organizations, public institutions, and government agencies that need their expertise. Many unretirement programs have forged partnerships with federal, state, and local governments, the private sector, community colleges, and libraries.

The industry is developing its own research network, although not all the scholarly studies and conferences focus on aging workers. Among the big centers are the Sloan Center on Aging and Work at Boston College, the Center for Retirement Research at Boston College, the John J. Heldrich Center for Workforce Development at Rutgers University, and the Stanford Center on Longevity at Stanford University. Career coaches, financial advisers, and lifestyle consultants are increasingly targeting the older worker market. So are temp agencies that concentrate on seniors, like Retirementjobs.com and RetiredBrains.com. The list of players is long. "There's no way to Google to get to all of them. What we're all trying to do is organize these ideas and options and opportunities into some sort of coherent suite of services that people can connect to," says Dickson.

The experience of Life by Design NW (LBD) in Portland is typical. The nonprofit was created in 2005 with the involvement of seven organizations, including Portland Community College and Hands On Greater Portland. LBD NW received a grant from Atlantic Philanthropies to concentrate on helping aging boomers in the area think through what to do when retirement looms. The nonprofit initially put its resources toward surveying Portland boomers. The great recession pushed LBD NW to shift its efforts toward boosting the job skills of unemployed and underemployed boomers. Money was tight in 2012, so the nonprofit moved into Portland Community College. The boomer nonprofit is now part of CLIMB Center for Advancement at Portland Community College.

CLIMB stands for Continuous Learning for Individuals, Management and Business. Once again LBD NW has adjusted its mandate, broadening its portfolio of offerings to work with aging boomers seeking answers in their next act.

Much of this emerging industry activity is concentrated among aging boomers with at least some financial resources. The environment is tougher for low-income older workers, with relatively spare and under-funded government and community college programs available for those seeking new employment opportunities. The Senior Community Service Employment Program (SCSEP) is for workers fifty-five and older with an income less than 125 percent of the federal poverty guideline (translated into earnings, that equals less than $15,000 annually for an individual). The program is run by government agencies around the country. The participants do community service work and are paid the federal mini-mum wage (or the state minimum wage if it's higher) while in the program. They can stay with the SCSEP for up to forty-eight months with a goal of finding an unsubsidized job. Sadly, according to the Center for Labor Market Studies at Northeastern University, an estimated nine million people between the ages of fifty-five and seventy-four were eligi-ble for the program—some one hundred times the number of people served by SCSEP recently.

Among the ranks of aging low-income workers who could benefit from training are many immigrants. The modern wave of immigration to America is one of the great human dramas in our history. New York, Miami, Los Angeles, and other major metropolitan areas are immigrant capitals. Venture almost anywhere into the heartland and you'll run into foreign accents. America's foreign-born population sixty-five and older is around five million, 12 percent of the nation's forty million immigrants. Many of these aging immigrants toiled in low-wage jobs, often two or three at a time. Their employers typically didn't offer a retirement savings plan and they may have worked off the books. "This population is very vulnerable," says Yunju Nam, an associate professor at the University of Buffalo, State University of New York. "I am really concerned about their financial future."

Programs are responding to the challenge, though. For instance, the nonprofit organization Self-Help for the Elderly in San Francisco offers a number of services to the aging Chinese community, including afford-able housing for independent seniors, residential care facilities for the aging, health insurance counseling, and senior centers for meals, exer-cise, and other activities. It also runs an on-the-books employment agency that focuses on Chinese workers in their fifties. Many low-income aging Chinese immigrants don't speak English well, but Self-Help concentrates on vocational training and job placement where fluency isn't a requirement, such as home health care, home cleaning, janitorial services, and hospitality work. On-staff counselors act as interpreters with employers when needed. The idea is for aging Chinese workers to earn at least forty quarters of employment, the minimum necessary to file for Social Security benefits. "My goal is to create more job opportuni-ties for older immigrants," says Anni Chung, the organization's sixty-two-year-old head. "San Francisco is so expensive it will be hard to stay here without work."

The evolution of the financial planning industry offers an intriguing parallel, at least up to a point. The current state of unretirement planning seems to be in a similar place that financial planners were four decades ago. There had long been wealth advisers, accountants, brokers, trust managers, and other professionals serving the financial needs of the well-heeled. However, a group of advisers felt the business needed higher standards and certification of professional competence. The new certi-fied financial planning profession held its first meeting in December 1969 at an airport hotel room. The College for Financial Planning and the International Association for Financial Planners were created by the thirteen attendees—far from an auspicious beginning. "Most discourag-ing of all, the fledgling movement had only the vaguest of action plans," write E. Denby Brandon Jr. and H. Oliver Welch in *The History of Financial Planning.* "And yet, despite huge odds, financial planning—the first new profession in the last four centuries—did exceed beyond the most fervent hopes of the revolution's founders, not just in the United States but around the world."

I think there is a big difference between the emerging unretirement industry and the certified financial planning profession. The latter almost exclusively caters to the well-off. The former is far more democratic and inclusive.

The rise of unretirement should usher in a new market of products and services geared toward the working elderly. The business of catering to an aging population is mostly associated with coping with disabilities among the elderly, selling products such as Depend undergarments and Fixodent denture cream. The financial services industry still focuses mostly on accumulating assets for retirement savings and less on smart ways to draw on the money, less useful especially for an aging population that won't retire in the traditional way. Technology companies don't pay much heed to aging workers except, perhaps, to poke fun at their supposed, highly stereotyped high-tech ineptness. Yet the market for the fifty-plus population in the United States is an estimated three trillion dollars. The economic prospects associated with unretirement are dazzling. "When you look at an aging workplace it's an opportunity," says MIT's Coughlin. "The demand will be there for innovation."

His message resonates with Dr. Katy Fike. A former business analyst at Lehman Brothers, Fike changed careers to gerontology in 2004 (a stroke of good timing) and she received her Ph.D. in the field from the University of Southern California's Davis School of Gerontology. She is a serial entrepreneur and one of her ventures is the San Francisco–based Aging2.o. The company's mission is to bridge the gap between entrepreneurs and the fifty-and-over market. Entrepreneurs are realizing there is money to be made coming up with innovative products and services that are nothing like the ones marketed on late-night cable television. Many of the best products are specifically aimed at the aging (think universal design and the Aeron chair) but appeal across generations. A classic example is the easy-to-use universal-design Oxo kitchen line, from salad spinner to can opener. The Apple iPad and competitive tablets is another example of a high-tech product with a large contingent of aging buyers. Among the efforts spearheaded by Aging2.o are organizing events in major metropolitan areas to bring together the entrepreneurial community and the aged community. With the same goal in mind, Fike and a New York City–based partner have started a business accelerator called GENerator. "What is happening now, as America gets older, is that standards are going up," she says. "We are seeing a better industry for the older consumer."

Much as business fortunes were made off the association of leisure and old age in the decades following the Second World War, so will entrepreneurs and managements of established companies race to profit from the rise of unretirement and the spread of encore careers. Office furniture makers with ergonomically sound products are potential beneficiaries. Older workers will probably continue to treat themselves after a long day at the office, taking advantage of high-quality, healthier offerings, such as grocery store takeout. Appearances and mobility are important to older workers, a boon to dental suppliers, joint replacement companies, health clubs, and cosmetic companies. The prospects for education programs geared toward the work needs of encore careers are intriguing. Savvy financial planners will find it pays to help their clients figure out their work goals and the next stage of life rather than the current emphasis on asset allocation and asset accumulation. Technology and health care companies will oversee a revolution in remote sensors and movement devices that will creatively support new visions of aging and not just offer increased safety and monitoring to geriatrics. The list of profitable possibilities with unretirement is long. My bet is that a common theme among older workers and younger workers will be that they share similar tastes in products and services, from technology to music. Call it a universal-design mentality expressed throughout everyday life. Many older workers and aging entrepreneurs won't buy "old people's" products. "Making things easier to use but make them pleasurable—people want that," says Gianfranco Zaccai of the design firm Continuum. "Things that keep you active."

Of course, there's always a dark side to any expanding business. The lure of making money off an older working population is stoking various schemes. Take the antiaging industry. Some of it is okay, essentially cosmetic changes that help people feel young, such as hair coloring, antiwrinkle cream, and denture work. Unfortunately, the hustlers of the antiaging business also sell youth by promoting products that are expensive and, at best, don't live up to their billing. Yes, the science of aging is fascinating, and researchers are coming up with results that suggest therapies that could eventually slow down the aging process and, more important, improve the quality of life during the extra years of longevity. The operative word is "future." At the 2013 annual meeting of the Gerontological Society of America in New Orleans, I attended a session with a panel of experts on prospects for longevity. They differed in their relative optimism and pessimism, but the scholars and scientists were unanimous in condemning much of the current fad behind antiaging marketing. "If they are selling it now, it doesn't exist," said S. Jay Olshansky, professor in the School of Public Health at the University of Illinois at Chicago. Daniel Perry, president of the Alliance for Aging Research, was harsher in his concern. "I think the antiaging industry is a greater threat than we think. The charlatans have tarnished the kind of research that is coming out now."

The unretirement trend will exert an impact on the biggest asset of the average American household: their home. Unretirement will shape how older people approach housing and how developers think about market opportunities. The dominant image of housing and old age is people picking up stakes and moving to a warm climate. The reality is that most elders actually "age in place." Many seniors want to stay near family and friends. Younger people move more frequently, seeking out job and career opportunities. Those of retirement age are about half as likely to move long distances as the rest of the population. In Georgia, for example, the senior population is predicted to increase by more than 40 percent from 2010 to 2020 from the aging of the existing population, compared to less than 3 percent from elder migrants to the Peach State, according to William H. Frey of the Brookings Institution.

Older Americans essentially stopped moving during the great housing bust of 2006 through 2012. The home ownership rate of those ages sixty-five to eighty-four exceeds 80 percent, and many who wanted to go elsewhere couldn't sell their homes. Older people are more likely to stay in their community going forward, even when the housing market is vibrant. Older workers will find it easier to land a job and find engaging volunteer opportunities by staying put and tapping into their local network of friends, family members, colleagues, and acquaintances. Their network increases the odds that a soon-to-be retiree will get a part-time consulting contract, an opportunity to use hard-earned know-how at a local business, a chance to draw on a private sector experience to help out a nonprofit venture, and a base of customers to build a start-up business.

The drawback to leaving the Twin Cities for Orlando, New York for Phoenix, Washington, D.C., for Winston-Salem, and so on is that valuable community networks are suddenly useless. It's possible to create new networks, but that takes time, a scarce commodity among elders. The wealthy can build a new network fast since they have the money to be invited on local boards and may make contacts from attending industry conferences over the years. But for most people the smart move is to stay put and take advantage of their local connections.

Aging in place is a rich concept. It doesn't necessarily mean staying in your current home. There are a number of alternatives that will keep you in your community. A savvy choice is moving to a smaller home, condo, or townhouse. Large homes cost significantly more to maintain and property taxes are higher. Plus, as we age, most of us are less inclined to do maintenance. It's increasingly risky to climb up a ladder and clean the gutters. Smaller yards and one-floor homes take much less care. So do condominiums and townhomes where the maintenance is contracted out. The savings from running a small home compound over time. Cooperative housing has been a fringe movement, but it's becoming mainstream with ventures springing up around the country, some formal and others informal. The common space, such as kitchen and dining room, is typically shared, but homes or apartments remain private.

A senior community that locates everything from independent living to nursing home care in one place is another option. A continuous care community offers independent living when you're healthy enough to be active, say, at work and volunteering. There's assisted living facilities for when you're less well and nursing home care when deeply ill. There are nearly two thousand currently in operation around the country with a great deal of variety among the types of living arrangements, from apartments to townhomes to duplexes. Mother-in-law apartments, granny flats, garage apartments, and other "accessory dwelling units" (the arid social science designation) are popular, especially with middle-aged adults raising children and minding aging parents. Zoning restrictions in many single-family neighborhoods may prohibit or make this kind of living arrangement difficult. But with an aging population, the trend is toward relaxing the rules in a growing number of neighborhoods.

Still, surveys show that most homeowners want to stay in their current homes. Everyone knows the real estate catchphrase: location, location, location. The comparable mantra for aging homeowners will be remodel, remodel, remodel. There's plenty of good remodeling design that's also age-friendly, such as universal design. For example, lights with increased illumination and lighting controls can be incorporated into a kitchen home-improvement project. European showers look sophisticated but they have the added advantage of no lip, allowing for easier wheelchair access sometime in the future (but useful, too, for washing plants and the dog in the meantime).

The combination of aging-in-place and working longer will hike the demand for improved public transportation (a boon for bus and train manufacturers). Young people are leading the trend toward less driving. Instead of driving a car, in many parts of the country younger people are biking, car pooling, and taking public transportation to work. Internet shopping and telecommuting are having an impact on transportation choices, too. Why get in a car when you can shop at the keyboard or commute from the bedroom to the home office in slippers? Baby boomers may well make similar choices after spending much of their so-called leisure time behind the wheel of a car transporting kids to school events and driving to the job. (Economists count the time spent at the wheel as leisure time!)

A major reason for believing an aging work force will attract additional commercial and public investment is that the business of unretirement is global. The United States is far from alone in dealing with an aging population. Much of the world is aging and living longer. For instance, the global population age sixty-five and older is expected to triple from 2010 to 2050—from half a billion to 1.5 billion. The population sixty-five and older in the European Union is forecast to account for some 30 percent of the region, up from 17.5 percent in 2011. Japan is aging faster than any nation in history. In the Land of the Rising Sun those sixty-five and older comprise a quarter of the population currently, and it's projected that seniors will account for 38 percent in 2050. (The United States has one of the youngest overall populations.)

Concerns over the growing numbers of seniors at the moment are highest in the major industrial nations, but not exclusively. China is going through its own gray revolution. China's sixty-five and older group is expected to comprise 24 percent of its population in 2050, up from 8 percent in 2005. South Korea will be home to the world's second-oldest population with 35 percent over the age of sixty-five in 2050. "Yet even in much of the developing world, where the old typically live with the young, falling birthrates and growing life spans are combining with industrialization and urbanization to create new stresses," writes Richard Jackson, adjunct fellow, Global Aging Initiative for the Center for Strategic and International Studies in "The Global Retirement Crisis: The Threat to World Stability and What to Do About It." "Almost everywhere, countries will have to race against time to ensure their economic and social fabric against the 'shock' of global aging."

A controversial political focus in many nations is reforming their social welfare and pension systems designed to encourage retirement. Less appreciated is how much progress is being made with unretirement in a number of countries in the major industrial nations. Take Europe. European nations are gradually raising retirement ages. Germany's retirement age is sixty-five, but for those born after 1964 it has been raised to sixty-seven. In Denmark, the current age of retirement is sixty-five, slated to rise to sixty-seven beginning in 2024 and, after that, retirement age will be indexed to life expectancy. In France, age sixty-two is the minimum age for a full pension for most workers so long as they contributed into the system for 41.5 years. The French government has increased the contribution period to 43 years by 2035 (and most boomers will have retired by then). The European Union is trying to reduce other barriers to longer work lives. The EU required its member nations to come up with anti–age discrimination legislation by 2006, although the directive has been adhered to with varying degrees of enthusiasm. "The baby boomers in Europe are about ten years behind the baby boomers in the United States," says Jan Hively, the septuagenarian American social entrepreneur. "The rapid change in attitude about working longer in the U.S. hasn't happened there. The change has been rapid in the United States."

Attitudes are changing, however. The European Union declared 2012 the year of active, healthy aging, a good year for the European School of Management and Training and the International Leadership Association to jointly sponsor a conference in Berlin on older workers. Among the experts was Jan Hively. She says the European business leaders at the conference had a traditional perspective on what constitutes an "old" worker. The professor who spoke before her said older workers don't want to work past sixty. When it was Hively's turn to talk, she asked those in the audience who were over fifty to raise their hands. About a dozen hands were raised out of an audience of some four hundred, she estimates. She asked, "How many don't want to stop working before age sixty-five?" Most raised their hands. "I said to the professor," chuckles Hively, "the times are a changin' in Europe."

The progress is showing up in the numbers. The elderly labor-force participation rate in Europe is much higher than just a decade ago (although from a very low base). The only European countries where the elderly labor-force participation rate has not risen are Italy and Poland. Indeed, from a global perspective, very few countries aren't seeing later retirements. According to the Center for Strategic and International Studies. Russia, Brazil, China, India, Japan, Mexico, and South Korea are the only countries that haven't witnessed an increase in older workers and, critically, with the exception of Russia all of these nations have relatively high numbers of seniors already in the work force.[1]

Japan is intriguing. The island nation is often portrayed by demographic fearmongers as the poster child for the coming modern demographic apocalypse. A projection that shows up frequently in demographic discussions about Japan is how adult diapers should outsell baby diapers by 2020. No question that Japan's economy has struggled with slow growth and deflationary pressures ever since its asset bubble burst in the late 1980s. (The Japanese bubble economy was fueled by debt. Japanese financiers borrowed on their stock holdings to buy everything from Van Gogh paintings to U.S. golf courses. Companies borrowed to expand their manufacturing capacity with abandon. Leverage financed Japan's real estate speculation. The land beneath the Imperial Palace in Tokyo was estimated to be worth more than all of California before the bubble burst.) However, the demographically informed doom and gloom about Japan's future is exaggerated. Japanese society and economy are adjusting to an aging population. Importantly, for the unretirement story, "the average age for Japanese to quit work is in their late sixties, three to four years above the OECD average," writes David Pilling, Asia editor for the *Financial Times*. "Women, as well as men, work until they are surprisingly old. Many of Japan's elderly, in other words, are producers as well as consumers," he adds in "How Japan Stood Up to Old Age."

It's worth quoting from an interview Pilling had with seventy-two-year-old Makoto Hashimoto. He works part time at a bike-rental lot in Sakura Shinmachi, or Cherry Blossom New Town, southwest of Tokyo.

> He looked trim and sturdy, certainly more than capable of working the 25 hours a week he spends at the lot. "I was in the printing industry," he said. "When I turned 60 I retired but spent two years moping around the house. I put on weight and realised that it was not a healthy lifestyle. Normally it's difficult for people over 60 to get a job. So I thought, let's go Silver," he said, referring to Silver Human Resources, a nationwide government-subsidised work programme. "The legal retirement age is 65 but at that age we are still fit and able to work."
>
> There were hundreds of such lots in Tokyo, each with space for several thousand bikes. Many were staffed by people

between 60 and 80 years old. "We do whatever is required. Even if we need to build something, we do it. Some of us put up shrubbery or trim it," he said, pointing to a hedge that wouldn't look out of place at Hampton Court. "They are little jobs. But they need to be done." For Hashimoto, who had a pension from his printing firm, money didn't seem to be the main motivation. He described the $600 or so a month he earns as "play money"—for eating out or for taking a trip to a nearby hot spring resort.

Remember the opening lyrics to the Buffalo Springfield song "For What It's Worth": "There's something happening here / What it is ain't exactly clear." There is much exciting experimentation going on over redefining retirement and old age, not just in the United States but in much of the global economy.

CHAPTER 11

Third-Age Entrepreneurs

Gee, ain't it funny
How time slips away
            —Willie Nelson

THE MOST FAMOUS NAMES IN BUSINESS are entrepreneurs who've transformed the way we live and work, from Andrew Carnegie to Sean Combs. America's entrepreneurial dynamism extends well beyond game-changing legends. Millions of small business owners, sole proprietors, freelancers, and other independent operators add to the economy's vitality; the immigrant starting a corner deli, the chef opening her restaurant, and the middle manager trying his hand as a consultant out of a home office. Facebook founder and chief executive Mark Zuckerberg captured a major reason why the notion of owning your own business exerts such a powerful pull on many Americans when he said that the popular catch-phrase at Facebook is "the riskiest thing is to take no risks."

When it comes to older workers taking a risk with their career or job, that's a phrase worth thinking through. It captures an aspect of how many of us feel during times of transition, seeking out a new career or greater meaning in our work. In a wonderful passage in *Walden*, Henry David Thoreau eloquently expresses the risk-based idea of "what are you waiting for?" Thoreau disdains the man who dreams of becoming a poet, but first must make his fortune. Poetry, the conventional wisdom says, can wait for retirement. "This spending of the best part of one's life earning money in order to enjoy a questionable liberty during the least valuable part of it, reminds me of the Englishman who went to India to make a fortune first, in order that he might return to England to live the life of a poet," he writes. "He should have gone up garret at once."

We know marrying the returns from career and job risk-taking with the reality of our finances is hard. Money is tight. The mortgage has to be paid and retirement savings increased. Perhaps most sobering, we know from everyday experience that taking a risk doesn't mean it will pay off. It's in the nature of the beast. The word "risk" comes from an old Italian word, *risicare*—to dare. "To dare reminds us that the essence of risk is about making decisions or choices with unknown outcomes," writes the late Peter Bernstein in his *Against the Gods: The Remarkable Story of Risk*. The outcome could be disastrous.

The financial risks associated with entrepreneurship are why youth and starting your own business are often thought of as synonymous. The young have less to lose, fewer responsibilities and more time to recover if the business bet goes bad. When we think of entrepreneurship, we remember Bill Gates of Microsoft and the late Steve Jobs of Apple creating the personal computer revolution in the 1980s and Mark Zuckerberg of Facebook and Jack Dorsey of Twitter building social media enterprises in the 2000s.

Think again. The Kauffman Foundation promotes entrepreneurship, and its research shows that older people start businesses more than any other age group. The share of new business formation by the fifty-five- to sixty-four-year-old age group rose from about 14 percent in 1996 to nearly one-quarter in 2013. Over this same time period the fifty-five to sixty-four age group has started new businesses at a higher rate than those in their twenties and thirties. Other data sets tell a similar story. Looking at 2003 Census data, those sixty-five and over had a total self-employment rate of 26.9 percent, calculates Edward Rogoff, economist at Baruch College. For the age group fifty-five to sixty-four, the total self-employment rate is 17.8 percent, he adds. A survey by the nonprofit

Encore suggests that approximately 25 million people—one in four Americans ages forty-four to seventy—are interested in starting a business or launching a nonprofit venture in the next five to ten years. These aspiring entrepreneurs had an average of thirty-one years of work experience and twelve years of community involvement. Even though many of these potential entrepreneurs won't follow through on their goal, the response is indicative of the powerful lure of being your own boss.

Numbers like these convince Dane Stangler, vice president, research and policy at the Kauffman Foundation, that the United States could be on the cusp of an entrepreneurship boom—not in spite of an aging population but because of it. I had a wide-ranging conversation with Stangler in a small conference room at the Foundation's stunningly beautiful, prairie modern building in Kansas City, Missouri. The bottom line from our conversation was that "many different strands and trends are feeding into entrepreneurship with older people." Ting Zhang is an economist at the Jacob France Institute in the Merrick School of Business at the University of Baltimore. The author of *Elderly Entrepreneurship in an Aging US Economy: It's Never Too Late,* Zhang has focused much of her economic research on aging entrepreneurs. When we met at a Chinese restaurant in Rockville, Maryland, she readily endorsed the older entrepreneur thesis. "Some older workers have been cherishing a dream, wanting to start their own business, and the time is now," she says. "Aging is a new opportunity to be an entrepreneur." (I recommend conducting an interview over Chinese food.)

The lure of entrepreneurship among seniors could get even stronger. Self-employment offers greater flexibility than a traditional wage-and-salary job. Surveys show that the older entrepreneurs clearly enjoy what they're doing. The self-employed tend to retire later than their wage-and-salary peers. The average planned retirement age of small business owners with sales from $100,000 to $10 million surveyed by Barlow Research Associates in 2012 was sixty-seven years. "Entrepreneurship is flexible, allowing individuals to design their ventures to suit their needs, whether limiting work hours, working alone or with partners, concentrating on current income or building future value, or focusing on long- or short-term goals," writes Rogoff in *The Issues and Opportunities of Entrepreneurship After Age 50.* "For older workers who prefer traditional employment, entrepreneurship becomes a choice when they encounter age discrimination, face an unwanted prospect of relocation, or find the available options unattractive because of low pay."

I like how Elizabeth Isele, one of the cofounders along with Rogoff of the nonprofit Senior Entrepreneurship Works, captured what is happening: "Elderly entrepreneurship is now a movement."

Visit TechTown, a business incubator on the edge of Wayne State University in downtown Detroit, for a sense of the eager older entrepreneur. Incubators offer a number of services for fledgling entrepreneurs, including the basics of finance, marketing, and business plan development. Many of the incubator's students are boomers, so it's fitting that the story of TechTown is one of renewal.

TechTown is housed in a five-story cream-colored building designed by Albert Kahn, America's foremost industrial architect during Detroit's heyday. Among his factories were two giants of the era, Ford Motor Company's Highland Park factory erected in 1903 and the Ford River Rouge complex in Dearborn built in 1917. A decade later, Kahn designed the headquarters for Oakland Motors, later the Pontiac division of General Motors. The building became the Chevrolet Creative Services building. It's where General Motors designed the Corvette. Auto show displays were also built there. The building was abandoned in the 1950s, an empty hulk for decades.

In 1997, Dr. Irvin Reid became president of Wayne State University. Jack Smith was the head of General Motors. It was tradition for the head of Wayne State to lunch with the CEOs of the major automakers. During lunch at GM, Smith offered Reid the abandoned Chevrolet Creative Services building for Wayne State. Reid took it.

Once he figured out what to do with the building—create a business incubator—the drawbacks of the place forced Reid to move in floor by floor. He raised money by tapping a variety of public and private resources, including selling historic renovation tax credits to commercial enterprises. "The building is so large and so steady that it actually had a two-lane road that went from the first floor all the way up to the top floor," recalls Reid. "Well, today, that road is where a lot of the mechanicals are housed."

TechTown opened for business in 2004, when Dr. Reid was over seventy years old. The redesigned interior has the classic feel of a Silicon Valley office building, with large windows, bright colors, small conference rooms, and cubicles. The symbolism is apt: TechTown and its risk-taking entrepreneurs work out of a building once owned by the auto industry, housing workers with traditional defined benefit pension plans. Randal Charlton, the executive director from 2007 to 2011—from age sixty-seven to seventy-one—put his stamp on the incubator. Charlton has had a varied career (to put it mildly): science journalist, tending dairy cows for a Saudi sheik, jazz club owner in Florida, consultant to the World Bank, and founder of multiple companies, not all successful. Although not by plan—TechTown is open to anyone—there are more fledgling entrepreneurs over age fifty than under.

Among them is Pat Harris. She opened the Bottom Line Coffee House in Detroit's Midtown neighborhood in 2012, along with her husband, Al, and son, Kyle. The coffee shop isn't far from TechTown. Harris worked for some twenty years in human resources at Eastern Michigan University, in Ypsilanti, Michigan. But the fiftysomething Harris wanted to try something new and, at the same time, help to revitalize Detroit, the deeply troubled city she grew up in. "We were empty nesters and it was a time of our lives where we could go for something we've been wanting," says Harris. "I have been really excited about transitioning out of what I used to do and do something different."

The coffee shop is a family affair. Harris's husband is an experienced entrepreneur who owns a signage and graphics company. He also works as a project manager on historic renovations. The Bottom Line is located on the ground floor of an old apartment building he helped rehabilitate. Most of the apartment dwellers are students at Wayne State. Al Harris oversees the whole operation of the coffee shop, the equivalent of the company's chairman. Pat runs the business. She's the chief executive, and she also works part time at Bed Bath & Beyond for a steady income and to learn more about the retail business. Their son Kyle, a 2011 graduate of Syracuse University, is the manager of Bottom Line and lives in the apartment building.

The coffee shop is meeting its bills. It's experimenting with different techniques for attracting more customers, such as trying out a curbside coffee delivery business and a catering service. Local is an important theme. Their coffee beans are roasted locally. They serve locally produced sandwiches, salads, and baked goods. They've contracted with a woman for soups after discovering her at a nearby farmers' market. Harris has learned that running a business and working within a large organization are very different. "What I've learned and what I am seeing is how we need to work to keep our business going and we have to make decisions quickly. You can't have a thousand committees and say, 'Well what do you think?' It's almost like, 'Let's try this. Let's go for it and let's see.'"

When Harris became involved with TechTown, she and her husband had already developed their business plan. She received at TechTown coaching and advice from experienced entrepreneurs. She and her husband invested in the business, along with a variety of local funders. "What I've found is that people are really willing to help when they see that you're trying something new," says Harris. "People are willing to help, or at least offer suggestions or ideas or encouragement."

Harris had looked into two businesses—health care and retail—before deciding on a coffee shop. The former idea reflected the experience she and her husband had gained over twelve years' caring for her father-in-law, who had dementia and, later on, terminal cancer. While caring for him she became actively involved with the Alzheimer's Association as a speaker and support group leader. Meanwhile, the owner of the Beethoven building had approached them to see if they wanted to open a business. They assessed the neighborhood and decided a coffee shop was the best option. Harris went with a retail business over health care mainly because she was burned out as a caregiver.

Opening the coffee shop took a leap of faith. She had worked for one employer for twenty years. "My mom worked for her organization for forty years. God bless her, I'm glad she was able to do that," says Harris.

"But when I talk to her now about what we're going through in starting this business, she just can't relate. 'You're starting a business? And you're in the middle of your life? You should be thinking about settling and retiring.' It's kind of crazy for her." I wondered aloud if her mother might have a point. "You've got to go for it," replied Harris. "You can't be afraid of failure. Some days you say, 'What did I get myself into?' But it just draws you in. I can't describe it any other way. It's invigorating. There's something about it that's cool."

Harris highlighted an aspect of business ownership she likes: She's responsible. At a larger company she notes that you're part of the process. It's important to be involved and do good work, of course. But that's a very different experience from running your own company. "In your own business, when you make a decision it affects literally your own personal bottom line," she says. A business owner has to take responsibility for all aspects of the business, even if you don't necessarily wear that hat. The hardest part of the business, she's found, is keeping family roles and business responsibilities separate. Her husband is her life partner, but now he's also the company leader. Sometimes Harris has to tell her son to do something as a business owner, not as a mother. "It's definitely a work in progress," she laughs.

Milton Roye, age fifty-six, has also started his own company and it's also a work in progress. A graduate of Harvard and MIT, he had a long career as an auto industry executive, including sixteen years with General Motors. His last job was with a division of Tata Motors, the Indian car company, when it aimed at expanding into the U.S. market. When he saw Tata put the brakes on its U.S. ambitions, he started exploring what to do next. "I was way too young to even think of stopping working," he says. "I thought maybe it was time to start my own company."

Roye formed ENRG Power Systems, a Grand Rapids, Michigan, start-up in 2009. ENRG markets a plasma ignition system designed by a New York–based inventor that improves nondiesel engine truck and van fuel economy by up to 21 percent. A plasma ignition system is more expensive to install, but saves fuel costs over time. The initial market he's targeted is businesses with a fleet of pickup trucks and other comparable trucks. Roye twice won in his sector in the Accelerate Michigan Innovation Competition—a business competition that brings together later-stage entrepreneurial companies with investors—securing $50,000 in funding. He's still looking for his first customer, though, quipping that everyone wants to be his second customer. Still, he's far from discouraged. "All my background has gone into this," he says.

Like Harris, Roye has been struck by the difference between being an employee and an owner. He remembers how instructors at TechTown pushed him to boil down his business plan from more than one hundred pages to less than a dozen pages. "When you come from a big company the path is laid out. The question is how well do you execute it? That's all that counts. Execution," he says. "When you're an entrepreneur, it's 'write a business plan to get a direction' and, as soon as you hit save, your direction is going to change. Hopefully by degrees, but it will change at least 45 degrees. There is no straight line in entrepreneurship."

Older entrepreneurs create all kinds of businesses, "from supplementing income to wanting to start the next Facebook," says Stangler of the Kauffman Foundation. Technology has made it much easier for entrepreneurs to get a business up and running. They can work out of the house, the coffee shop, the shared office space. Business software lowers the cost of running the business. Information technologies dramatically increase the potential reach of a start-up. "You can start a business without a great deal of money these days," says William Zinke, the serial entrepreneur and president of the Center for Productive Longevity.

People with plenty of entrepreneurial experience tend to favor building more durable enterprises with human resource departments and capital budgets. They might even attract angel investors and venture capital, money from well-heeled investors willing to take a chance on a new enterprise. Older entrepreneurs do well competing in markets where experience, credibility, and contacts are invaluable. "Older people with experience have an entrepreneurial edge in a knowledge-based economy," says economist Zhang.

Mac Lewis is chief executive officer and cofounder of FieldSolutions. Working with a network of more than twenty-seven thousand independent contractors, the Minnetonka, Minnesota, company provides field service technicians to large technology companies throughout North America. Lewis started the company in 2006 at age sixty. He had worked at IBM in various capacities for fourteen years. When he left IBM he created, ran, and invested in a number of high-tech companies, spending the previous ten years before he started FieldSolutions as founder and partner in a venture capital fund. He could easily have retired and managed his money, but "rather than invest in something, I wanted to get my hand in it," he says. "People with experience know how to support their customers and how to price their product."

Many start-ups founded by older entrepreneurs aren't the kind of job-generating gazelles that populate new business creation hotspots such as Silicon Valley, Boston's Route 128, and the Austin tech hub. No, many new companies founded by senior entrepreneurs are better known as Schedule Cs, businesses established by an aging accountant, a laid-off middle manager turned consultant, or an outsourced accounting special-ist. They're sole proprietors with a handful of employees at most. "We see that an aging work force has to supplement their incomes," says Dennis Ceru, a serial entrepreneur, angel investor, and professor of entre-preneurship at Babson College. "It might be part-time work, full-time work, or turning a hobby into a business."

Marene Austin lives in Memphis, Tennessee. She retired from FedEx in 2002. She had worked at the package delivery company's headquar-ters in Memphis for twenty years, most recently as an operations manager. Before going to FedEx, Austin had a long, varied work history, including factory work, floor clerk at Sears, Roebuck and Company, real estate agent, and dissector of cats in a science lab (seriously). Some three years after retiring, Austin wrote a motivational book, life lessons to pass along to her grandchildren. She also created her own jewelry business, called Celebrate. "I am at the stage of life, my kids are all grown-up, my husband passed away. I can do fun stuff," she says. "I'm a young sixty-five. I run with the young ladies. I run with the forty-five-year-olds."

Austin receives a pension from FedEx and Social Security. The busi-ness nicely supplements her income, she says. Austin found a community to help her launch her jewelry business: the Center for Entrepreneurship and Innovation at the University of Memphis, run by Kelly Penwell. Like TechTown, the business incubator works with fledgling entrepreneurs. (Penwell herself has had several careers, from running a family ice business in eastern Long Island to high school teacher to university professor to director of an incubator.) Austin learned about marketing her jewelry at the Center. She sells out of her home. Austin always has some jewelry in the trunk of her car. She sets up booths around town at events. You can buy Celebrate jewelry online. She's considering a catalog option next. The Center helps keep her up on technology and she enjoys working with students. "Live all your life," she says. "Don't just retire and sit down."

That could well be Jan Hively's motto. She too has had a number of careers. Hively is a serial entrepreneur in the nonprofit sector. The desire among a segment of older workers to create nonprofit businesses that address social ills is strong. An Encore survey of potential social entrepreneurs reports that the top areas for social activism are social services, poverty alleviation, health care, economic development, at-risk youth, and the environment.

Hively had a two-decade career in government and education before attending the University of Minnesota to get a Ph.D., awarded in 2001 when she was sixty-nine years old. She has since helped create three nonprofits: the Vital Aging Network, the Minnesota Creative Arts and Aging Network, and SHiFT, the Twin Cities–based clearinghouse of information and resources for encore careers. "My focus shifted to the meaning of work," she says. "Living well and working well is a lifelong effort. My mantra is to take meaningful work—paid and unpaid—to the last breath."

Boss boomer has a nice ring to it, no? Yet entrepreneurship isn't for everyone. Ceru notes that every year he doesn't really know if he will make enough money to meet his business expenses. He doesn't get a regular paycheck. The financial uncertainty is hard to deal with at any age, but especially difficult when there is less time remaining to make up any shortfall. You also have to be realistic about how much money you'll make. "I turned sixty this last year," Ceru says. "I think there is this collective fantasy everybody is supposed to have two BMWs, a home somewhere in a warm climate, and only work twenty hours a week for it."

The investment money for a small business is often a bootstrap operation and most third-age entrepreneurs have modest financing needs, according to Encore. Older workers should be extremely wary of dipping into their retirement savings plans to fund a business. Two out of three of those surveyed by Encore say they need $50,000 or less to get started. Almost half of those surveyed said they expected to tap personal savings to launch their ventures. The main sources of funding for most small businesses are household savings, family, and friends. Home-grown entrepreneurs are also raising some money from everyday financiers through online fund-raising portals like Kickstarter. (I'd love to see families adopt a model used by Berry Gordy when he launched the record label that would become Motown in 1959. He grew up in a family of ten, and they were all entrepreneurs. The family had a loan fund to which each family member contributed $10 a month. The money could be used to start a business. "Gordy took out an $800 loan (estimated at $6,000 in today's dollars) after being approved by a family vote, to be paid back in one year at six percent interest," writes Yana Chernyak for Students for Liberty, a libertarian organization. A smart investment!) There are also ways to test out some business ideas along the way without spending much money upfront. In recent years, microentrepreneurs have tapped into the Internet and the share economy to sell craftwork and artwork, rent out a room or mother in law apartment, and sell accumulated stuff over the next decades.

Peter Bernstein, the late dean of finance economists, wisely emphasized in his writings on money and finance that no one can pierce the fog of the future. You can't get rid of the uncertainty. The key question to ask, therefore, is, "What if you're wrong?" For older workers with an entrepreneurial bent, the question is, "What's your downside if your small business idea goes bad?"

Fiftysomething Elizabeth Campbell confronted the chance that her dream would go bad. The former nurse opened Yoga Gem in Montgomery, Alabama, in 2013. Campbell graduated from nursing school in 1979. She worked for seven or eight years as a nurse, for much of the time the sole support for her family of four. (She later divorced.) Campbell stayed a nurse, but she joined the air force for greater financial stability. She officially retired on January 1, 2009, as a lieutenant colonel. Campbell wanted to keep active, but the idea of returning as a nurse in the private sector didn't appeal to her. Instead, she used the GI Bill to pay for her yoga training, a passion of hers. She worked at a yoga studio in Montgomery and eventually decided to open her own studio business. The yoga she teaches emphasizes healing. Campbell had some money in the stock market and pulled out about $60,000. She lives frugally and she has a pension. "I opened the doors, and I would wait all day," she recalls. "One or two students showed up. 'What have I done? I signed a three-year lease. What a fool I was,'" she thought.

Not really. Business at her studio picked up by the second month. Word of mouth worked in her favor. So did her competitive pricing, she says. Campbell can pay the rent and her bills. She isn't drawing a salary yet and she's teaching three to four classes a day. Still, she has hired three teachers and the studio has about 250 student visits a month. "You see people change with yoga," she says. "This is how you change the world."

The unretirement industry offers resources to tap into before taking the leap into entrepreneurship, such as business incubators like TechTown. There are a number of federal, state, and local government programs, typically managed in partnership with other organizations, such as industry groups, nonprofit organizations, and colleges. Trade shows and conferences in the business that intrigues you are an efficient way to gather information. The most valuable information vein to mine, however, is the knowledge of experienced entrepreneurs. Veteran entrepreneurs are generous with their know-how. Entrepreneurs may have a reputation as loners, people who prefer to report to no one but themselves. Yet in my experience they're incredibly eager to share their insights and accumulated experience to anyone interested in listening. They're realistically supportive. TechTown, for example, has about 120 entrepreneurs actively helping out their potential small business owners. "There are more people willing to participate for free than you would imagine," says Leslie Smith, president and CEO of TechTown. "They just want to help create value."

When I asked Harris of the Bottom Line Coffee House if she would recommend other people give entrepreneurship a try, she replied:

> Don't be afraid. If you really believe that you have this idea in you and you want to pursue it—go with your gut. The second thing I would say is don't let money stop you. We did invest in ourselves, but we didn't have a lot of money. A lot of it is really being passionate about what you believe in and what you want to do. The other thing I would say is reach out and find a really good support system. If starting a business is what you what they want to do, charge forward, develop a great business plan, find the resources that will help you, and do it.

The thought of starting a business is intimidating to many older workers. It isn't the right option for many aging boomers. Nevertheless, it seems to me investigating the possibility of starting your own business might push older workers closer to figuring out what it is they really want to do in the next stage of life. That's the really valuable insight. Once you've got that, the rest is effort.

CHAPTER 12

Aging Boomers on the Job

Everybody knows
Time flies when you're having fun
　　　　—Smokey Robinson

STEVE POIZNER IS A SILICON VALLEY serial entrepreneur. Poizner's latest venture is the venture capital–backed EmpoweredU, a bet that there's money to be made educating older workers. Headquartered in Campbell, California, the company is a joint venture with the Sherry Lansing Foundation, Creative Artists Agency, and UCLA Extension, the higher education arm of the University of California, Los Angeles. "We think there are hundreds of thousands of boomers that need to enhance or switch their careers out of necessity and there are hundreds of thousands of boomers who need to switch their careers out of desire," he says. "So this is a very large opportunity, and we're hoping to be a key instigator."

I met Poizner at company headquarters, a ninth-floor office suite in a glass-sheathed commercial building off California's Highway 17, near San Jose. When I got off the elevator in the fall of 2012, the nearby office suites were empty with FOR LEASE signs in the doorway. EmpoweredU's office was nothing special, a typical Silicon Valley start-up. A long room lined with similar desks and high-end office chairs, whiteboards on the wall, a soccer game in a corner, a small refrigerator. Most of the employees seemed young. No suits. No ties.

Toward the back of the room with the same desk and chair as everyone else sat Poizner. We got some water from the kitchen and headed into a conference room. He spoke about the new venture with quiet, modest passion. No fireworks. No revolutionary slogans. Yet like many Silicon Valley entrepreneurs the ambition driving the business is breathtaking: "We need to change the culture of the country," he says.

Considering its location, it's hardly surprising that information technology is a key part to the EmpoweredU education experience.

The company focuses largely on building the technology that runs mobile online classrooms. But in its work with UCLA Extension, EmpoweredU has identified a number of growing fields for older workers. Among the certificate programs are: Global Sustainability, Health Care Management, Nonprofit Management, IT Management, Patient Advocacy, College Counseling, Project Management, Financial Planning, Human Resources, and Marketing and New Media.

College counseling is an example of an encore career. Some form of postsecondary education—from a community college certificate to a business school MBA—is a passport to material success in America today. A college diploma is increasingly what philosophers call a necessary but not sufficient condition for entry into middle-class jobs, the kind that come with benefits. The demand for counselors who can navigate the postsecondary universe comes from a number of sources, including public schools, charter schools, and private schools. A growing number of parents are turning to college counseling experts for guidance on managing the college application process for their student, an opportunity for entrepreneurs to hang out a shingle or, more likely, a website. Salaries in the college counseling occupation are in the $40,000 to $50,000 range at nonprofit organizations, according to the Bureau of Labor Statistics. The return from working with private clients is potentially much higher, $50,000 to $80,000. "There are jobs in the area and there is a huge need," says Poizner. "It's a great encore career for a boomer."

Health care management is another intriguing opportunity. For customers of our Byzantine health care system, demand is growing for professionals to help families navigate the complicated process of making it through a medical crisis. The professional deals with every-thing from filing health insurance claims to understanding hospital procedures. "It's a career where your age and your wisdom and your life experiences are strengths—competitive advantages," says Poizner.

Another proponent of investing in additional education to turn the lure of a new career into reality is Ralph "Jake" Warner. He's the founder of Nolo.com, the self-help legal organization, and author of *Get a Life: You Don't Need a Million to Retire Well.* "What is it that you want to do?" he asks. "Go back to school and attend some classes. It can change your life."

That's what Fred Henry told me he did when I interviewed him for a *Businessweek* story years ago. A Harvard MBA, he had worked for three decades at Bechtel Corp., the giant engineering and construction company, by the early 1990s. He was a project manager in the company's power plant business and sales were down at the time. In his late fifties, Harvey was itching for a change, he recalled. He mulled over different options for building on his Bechtel experience. But on an airplane flight he read an article about a financial planner, and said to himself, "That's what I want to do." Harvey enrolled in financial planning courses at UCLA, left Bechtel, and became a certified financial planner with a book of clients. "I wanted to get out of corporate life, and do something I'm interested in, and be independent," he says. The transition worked out well for him.

Of course, some occupations are older-worker friendlier than others. Silicon Valley information technology companies are notorious for their bias toward youth. At the other end of the spectrum, workers sixty-five and older make up nearly a third of all funeral services employees. It's the occupation with the highest share of older workers (no joke), accord-ing to Richard Johnson, Gordon Mermin, and Eric Toder for the Urban Institute. Pat Patton, along with his wife, Sue, owns Patton-Schad Funeral and Cremation Services in Sauk Centre, Minnesota, birthplace of Sinclair Lewis and inspiration for Gopher Prairie, the fictional setting of his 1920 novel, *Main Street.* Patton is also on the Executive Board of the National

Funeral Directors Association. "A lot of support staff in the industry is retired full-time workers that now want something different," he says. "Older workers are possibly more understanding about what the people in the funeral home are going through."

Jerry Beddow has worked for Patton-Schad since 1996, a year after retiring as a high school principal. He works about three to four hours a day, helping position the casket at the funeral home, carrying flowers, talking to grieving families, and driving the hearse. He's seventy-four years old, thoughtful and considerate during our conversation. "As long as I am feeling okay I will keep doing it," he says. "It keeps me off the streets," he laughs.

The AARP publishes a biannual beauty pageant, highlighting the fifty best employers for people over fifty. The AARP first ten employers for 2013:

> National Institutes of Health (NIH)
> Scripps Health
> Atlantic Health System
> The University of Texas MD Anderson Cancer Center
> Mercy Health System
> The YMCA of Greater Rochester
> West Virginia University
> Bon Secours Virginia
> National Rural Electric Cooperative Association
> WellStar Health System

Clearly, employers in the government, health care, and education fields do well by older workers, at least compared with some other fields. A 2011 survey by Encore.org of experienced adults currently working in a second career had 30 percent in education, 25 percent in health care, another 25 percent in government, and 11 percent in nonprofit organizations. The Urban Institute looked into finding occupations that were both growing and with an above-average share of workers fifty-five and over. Their list of occupations included home health aides, nurses, postsecondary teachers, social workers, management analysts, and coun-selors.[1] Take nursing. The average age of registered nurses is forty-five and the nation's 2.7 million nurses work throughout the health care industry, including in hospitals, clinics, eldercare, and home care. "Most nurses will continue working as long as they can," says Lori Blatzheim.

She should know. Blatzheim was a nurse for forty-six years, mostly in California. She specialized in caring for children, including pediatric rehabilitation. When she was in her early sixties she had a conversation with her nurse manager. "We talked about working and getting older. My husband wanted me to retire. But it was hard. I have a lot of education. I've done a lot of things. I've been in leadership positions. So why should I retire?" she recalled saying. "I loved my work." Still, she began to feel it was time for a change, to try something new after more than four decades as a nurse. She and her husband focused on getting their finances in good shape, and at age sixty-eight she retired.

In many cases, older workers find that it pays to take their skills into a different sector of the economy. There's the creative boost from trying something different coupled with the reassurance that comes from tapping into existing strengths. "For example, a registered nurse might move from a major hospital to a community clinic; a computer systems analyst at a private software company might take a job in local govern-ment; a civil engineer at a private construction firm might work on a state government highway project," speculate Barry Bluestone of Northeastern University and Mark Melnik of the Boston Redevelopment Authority in their research report, *After the Recovery: Help Needed: The Coming Labor Shortage and How People in Encore Careers Can Help Solve It*.

Their insight resonates with Scott Kariya. He was an information technology recruiter for twenty-three years, earning a good living. The combination of a healthy income and a hefty stock portfolio allowed him to "retire" at age fifty-two in 2006—really unretire. Quickly bored, Kariya started working for ReServe, a New York City–based nonprofit with branches in a number of other cities including Miami, Newark, and Baltimore. ReServe matches fifty-five-plus professionals with local nonprofit organizations, public institutions, and government agencies that need their expertise. The professional typically works between ten and twenty hours a week for a $10 an hour stipend, well below what they could charge in the marketplace. The ReServe work force consisted almost exclusively of retirees several years ago, but more recently older workers who want to stay engaged in their profession are signing up. Kariya's talent-recruitment background fits well at the nonprofit. "Everyone wants to stay busy," says Kariya. "But I think a lot of people get tired of the fifty-hour workweek."

Kariya recently has made another job shift, this time a more radical change. A self-described computer "geek," he decided it was time to recharge his batteries by embracing a different career direction. Kariya now heads up ReServe's information technology operations, running everything from the help desk to software maintenance. Kariya is enjoying his new responsibilities while, at the same time, he gets to continue working in an organization with a mission he believes in. His advice for anyone interested in a similar change at work is to convince your colleagues you're up to the task, building on your reputation within an organization. "It's difficult to make a switch into a new field and a new environment," he says. "But the people in the organization knew me. They knew I am a geek. So they were receptive to the switch."

Sometimes, older workers have little choice but to learn a new skill set. That's what John Willis, age fifty-four, did.

Willis has always worked. When he graduated from high school he went to community college, but after a year he left to take a job at Vanity Fair, the apparel company (now VF Corporation) in Greensboro, North Carolina. Willis was at Vanity Fair for twenty-three years, 1979 to 2001. He worked his way up to front-line supervisor. But in 2001, Vanity Fair closed his plant—one of thirty factories that management shut down—when it moved its U.S. production to Asia. Willis got a similar supervisor job at a Hanes Corporation (now called Hanesbrands) facility making $22 an hour. The Hanes plant was closed in 2008. The American textile industry has largely shifted its factory work to cheaper parts of the world, like China, Bangladesh, and Vietnam.

Two years of tight budgets followed for his family. His wife is a part-time housekeeper. Willis was considered a dislocated worker by the federal government because he lost his job to foreign competition. The designation qualified him for a variety of government-funded services, including paid tuition at nearby Danville Community College. He got his degree in warehouse specialization and Willis now works for British-based tea giant Twinings as a warehouse associate, loading, unloading, and stocking shelves. He doesn't see "a lot of room for growth" in this particular job, but he has talked to his supervisor about his desire to move up into positions of more responsibility as the company expands its operations. He makes $17 an hour, but he can increase his hourly pay to almost what he made at Hanes with overtime.

Duane Whittaker also found out that he needed to add a skill to stay employed. A charismatic, trim fifty-seven-year-old, he went to Concordia University in St. Paul, Minnesota, for two years. He enjoyed playing college football, but the academics didn't hold his interest. In 1978 he left college to enlist in the air force. Whittaker worked on supply teams for four years and then he qualified as a military fire fighter. His air force fire fighting duties took him to a number of bases in the United States, as well as France, England, Ireland, Iraq, Korea, and Guam. His three children are all in their thirties with good careers of their own—military, air traffic controller, and owner of a refrigerator sales business. His wife is a full-time cultural liaison for the Osseo school district, a small town not far from Minneapolis.

When he left the air force in the 1980s, Whittaker worked for a company that serviced printers. One of the firm's clients was HealthPartners, a nonprofit health maintenance organization. He got a job in hardware and software support at HealthPartners in 1988. His department expanded as HealthPartners absorbed other health care providers in the region, but Whittaker found himself laid off in April 2006. His severance paid his salary and health insurance through the end of the year. He became an information technology contract worker. His income went down considerably. He had been earning in the low $60,000 level at HealthPartners, but as a contractor he could charge only $18 to

$25 an hour for three-month to six-month full-time contracts. (At an average of $20 an hour full time for a year in contract work he would make over $40,000 but, as anyone who has done contract works knows, there is plenty of downtime during the year.) He also earned two-year certificates in information technology and health and fitness at the Minnesota School of Business. The tuition was subsidized by his veteran's benefit. "I regret that I didn't take school seriously when I had the chance," he says. "But I've been to school a lot since. I've accomplished that goal now."

A contract client of his was Fairview Health Services, a giant Minneapolis-based medical complex. Fairview offered him a part-time job in the spring of 2012. The rhythm of his new work life goes like this: He's at Fairview from 7:30 A.M. to 12:30 P.M. every work day. He's a personal trainer at LA Fitness from 2:30 to 7:30, typically training six to ten members a day. "I like talking to people and helping people," he says. He enjoys it so much he turned down a recent opportunity to work full-time at Fairview. "Being a coach is something I wanted to do since high school," he says. "Now I'm doing what is right for me."

Retirement? Sixty used to be the magic date for him. Now he plans on working to at least sixty-two, perhaps sixty-five, adding that it "depends how things are going."

More companies and nonprofit agencies are specializing in placing seniors in full-time and temp work. Large, well-known employment agencies like Manpower have created divisions that focus on senior workers. Other companies target the fifty-plus employee, companies like Senior4Hire, RetiredBrains, and RetirementJobs. The market is also expanding with firms focusing on narrow occupation segments for seniors. For instance, RetirementJobs, the temp agency for workers fifty and over, recently created a sister company, Mature Caregivers. The Bureau of Labor Statistics predicts that employment of home health aides will grow by 69 percent from 2010 to 2020, far faster than the average for all other occupations. Employment of personal care aides is expected to expand by 70 percent over the same time period. The job isn't easy. Caregivers spend time navigating and coordinating health care for their aging customers. The medical establishment has outsourced many traditional nursing tasks to caregivers, too, such as managing medications, administering intravenous fluids and injections, changing bandages and cleaning surgical wounds, and so on. "Caregiving is a job type that happens to be growing quickly," says Tim Driver, head of ReplacementJobs.com. "It's also the type of work where age discrimination is nonexistent."

Of course the price of flexibility for young or older employees who choose to work fewer hours or who involuntarily work part-time is a smaller paycheck. "The jobs are there," says Arthur Koff, founder of Retired Brains. "Most of the jobs that are available are temporary, part-time work. They do pay less." However, the overall pay picture for the unretired is improving somewhat. Brookings Institution economist Gary Burtless investigated whether workers—men and women—postponing retirement earned below-average wages compared to workers in the thirty-five- to fifty-four-year age group. The simple answer is yes. That said, the trend in pay shows progress with time. The pay gap narrowed between older workers and their younger peers from the 2004 to 2010 period compared to 1985 to 1991. Measured against previous generations, the financial penalty for postponing retirement is declining. "Clearly, the relative hourly earnings of older women and men have improved compared with those of prime-age workers," writes Burtless.[2] "One reason that the average hourly pay of older workers has improved compared with that of prime-age workers is that older workers are now relatively better educated than older workers in the past." A decade from now the pay difference should be even less considering that there are currently more college graduates under age fifty than over age fifty.

The supply of aging workers willing and able to contribute to their employer will swell in coming decades. What about the demand for older workers? Employers will become far more aware of the advantages of senior workers in coming years, especially with the share of the labor force fifty-five and over projected to rise from 19.5 percent in 2010 to 25 percent by 2020. Management will also realize that older workers are productive, creative employees as negative stereotypes fall by the wayside. The employer conversation about older workers will increasingly shift toward redesigning corporate benefits to help keep talent on the payroll longer. Already, older workers are a hot topic among human resource professionals, although progress on the benefits front has been slowed by the bad economy of recent years. Employer benefits were trimmed during the great recession, and management was under little pressure to do more for their employees—old and young alike— since most people were glad to have a job. Motivated older workers found themselves negotiating ad hoc arrangements with the human resources department or their boss for a gradual exit out of the company, perhaps with a part-time contract in hand. "If employers would accelerate the drive for flexible work arrangements everyone would be better off," says Richard Johnson, labor market expert at the Urban Institute. "Flexibility is important."

Managements have made some strides toward offering their employees greater job flexibility. A Bank of America Merrill Lynch Workplace Benefits Report is suggestive. The survey includes responses from 650 C-level executives and human resources and benefit plan leaders. Virtually all the surveyed employers—94 percent—said it was important to keep older workers on the job longer because of their talent and skills. To retain these employees, half of the surveyed employers said they offer flexible or customized work schedules to retain older workers. A third have started education programs around retirement income and health care topics. A third offer continuing education and development opportunities while 22 percent allow employees to work remotely and 21 percent are offering extended benefits to older employees.

The unretirement conversation is starting to show up in employer discussions about improving retirement benefits. Until fairly recently, the retirement discussion at work focused almost exclusively on the employer-sponsored retirement savings plan, such as a 401(k). Companies have put a lot of effort into educational initiatives on managing a retirement portfolio well. The term *retirement* also signaled the day an older employee left the organization. Retirement marked the moment when an employee left the world of work for a lifestyle of leisure. At least that was the image. A number of far-sighted managements now recognize the work-and-retirement divide is less true today, and the realization should affect the design of employee benefits.

Case in point: Intel Corporation. Like all big, dynamic companies, the Silicon Valley behemoth Intel Corporation offers its employees a good benefits package, including retirement savings. Intel also supports employees phasing into retirement. Recently Intel has experimented with several new pilot programs. Through one of the programs, U.S. employees eligible to retire can apply for an Encore Career Fellowship. This program helps employees ease into the next stage of their life. They have the opportunity to leverage their skills, evoke their passions, and have an impact in their community by working with a local nonprofit organization. Intel has also piloted programs supporting employees interested in learning new skills, exploring entrepreneurship, and becoming public school teachers. "Creating a culture that supports our employees as they prepare and plan for retirement is important," says Amber Wiseley, Intel Retirement Benefits Strategist. "Our employees are looking for different options to reimagine retirement and are seeking opportunities to continue to have an impact on society."

A comparable conversation is taking place far from Silicon Valley at Herman Miller in Zeeland, Michigan. About a quarter of the company's work force is fifty-five plus, not uncommon for an American manufacturing company. (Herman Miller does all its manufacturing in the United States.) Does that mean in five years Miller will suffer an enormous outflow of employees heading into retirement? Doubtful. "The old model that people will retire at sixty-two and they'll pack up their belongings and move to Florida is really dated," says Tony Cortese, senior vice president for human resources. "I don't think that's the reality we confront."

Still, Miller worries about losing its older employees' skills and knowledge too quickly. The company has responded to the concern by instituting a number of programs with built-in flexibility. For example, workers get to take six to twelve consecutive weeks off during the year. Employees aren't paid during that time, but they keep their benefits and length of service. You don't have to be an older worker to take advantage of the program, but most participants are getting up in age. "We don't care what it's for. If you just want to go to the beach and lay out for twelve weeks, we do not care. We've had people take time off to go to school. We've had people take time off because their body needs a break from the manufacturing floor. Maybe their wife has arthritis and they want to go south because it gets too cold in the winter," says Cortese. "We've had people who are fifty-five or older say, 'I don't know if I'm ready for retirement but I'm going to try this instead.' They come back, saying, 'I want to do that next year. I'm not ready for retirement, I don't want to go part-time, but this is working out really good for me.'"

Miller recently rolled out a "flex retirement" plan. An employee must be sixty years or over with five years of service at the company to qualify for the program. Flex retirement allows for planning an exit from Miller over a period lasting six months to two years. The retirement decision is irreversible and, in return for the planned reduction in hours, employees put together a knowledge transfer plan to teach the ropes of the job to their replacement. Observes Cortese: "They say, 'I'm ready to retire, but I'm not ready to go today. I'm going to phase out over a two-year time frame and as I do that I'm going to put together a knowledge transfer plan and I'm going to go from forty hours to thirty hours to twenty hours.'"

Other companies have earned reputations as good employers for aging workers. For example, Baptist Health South Florida, the largest not-for-profit health care organization in the region, is well known for its flextime, job sharing, telecommuting, and compressed work schedules. It offers bonuses to experienced nurses who coach newer colleagues. Employees who are at least fifty-nine-and-six-months who have been with the company for ten years or more can begin drawing on their retirement savings and still work part-time. Another example is AGL Resources, a natural gas distribution company based in Atlanta, Georgia. AGL allows its retired workers to return on a part-time or project basis and participate in company benefits. The National Institutes of Health in Bethesda, Maryland, has a rich menu of options, including flexible work schedules, telecommuting policies, and mentoring opportunities. These employers represent just the beginning of a trend that will gather momentum as unretirement and encore careers become part of the expected and desired lifecycle among an aging workforce. Benefits like these are good for employees and employers. Says Coughlin of MIT's AgeLab: "In the near future the 'new kid down the hall' may, in fact, be someone's grandmother in the next stage of her multiact life."

Unretirement is a realistic option for many professionals. Aging professionals often try to stay engaged but put in fewer hours on the job. Over the years I've interviewed a number of older financial planners who have downshifted to a few favored accounts. The planner is still engaged in the business, which they enjoy. They earn a reduced income, of course, yet they also enjoy more free time to travel, volunteer, and spend with grandchildren. Lawyers can take years to wind down their practice and afterward they may teach as adjunct faculty at a law school or make a part-time living as a mediation specialist.

However, the unretirement movement could have a larger impact on the professional experience later in life with a little encouragement. Take attorneys sixty-five and older. A series of changes in the legal market-place has reduced the demand for aging boomer attorneys. The growth in legal services has been driven by corporations and organizations that use large firms less reliant on senior lawyers, and the demands for legal advice by individuals who traditionally hire smaller firms to represent them is down. "Thus, just at a time when the demographics of the legal profession have produced a very large pool of senior lawyers, the proportion of the legal profession that is needed to remain in senior positions to supervise paid work and to be well compensated for this work is declining," observe Kenneth G. Dau-Schmidt, Esther Lardent, Reena Glazer, and Kellen Ressmeyer in *Old and Making Hay*, a research paper for the Maurer School of Law at Indiana University, Bloomington.

The solution, these legal experts say, is for firms to establish "second act" programs for their senior attorneys. Senior lawyers would concentrate much of their energies on the firm's pro bono work. The scholars calculate that even if a mere 5 percent of practicing attorneys over age sixty-five participated in a pro bono second act, the number of attorneys working primarily on public interest work would double. The deal would be that older lawyers accepting the second act path would put in fewer hours and get paid less. "The legal profession has a golden opportunity to do well by its members, itself, and society at large," they write. "The aging of the Baby Boom generation presents society with a large population of idealistic and talented lawyers who have succeeded in their careers and now have the opportunity to better themselves and the less fortunate by under-taking a 'second act' in pro bono work before they retire."

Here's another thought, this time for elderly certified financial planners. Imagine if these financial planning experts took their money knowledge and helped out ordinary families with budgeting, home ownership, debts, and managing retirement accounts. The typical hourly charge for a fee-only certified financial planner is in the $150 to $350 range. The average price tag for developing a plan for a family is between $1,500 and $3,500. Yale University Nobel laureate Robert Shiller roughly calculates that some fifty million Americans who can't afford a certified financial planner would benefit from a consultation with one. Clearly, the need is there. What if successful CFPs in their unretirement years reached out to these millions of Americans that could use their advice and charged them a modest fee—a fraction of what their well-heeled clients paid? They would do good, but still have some money coming in.

What's exciting about all these and other experimentations is that they will evolve. Boomers are trying out different ideas, essentially seeing what unretirement business and lifestyle models pay off, putting pressure on managements to create more flexibility into the workplace and economy. Managements, in turn, are trying to learn what kinds of job transitions and benefit packages will boost the bottom line and improve the caliber of their work force. Better yet, Gen Xers, millennials, and future generations of workers will learn from these baby boomer unretirement trials and errors. The main lesson younger generations will take from the unretirement improv act is that they will have much more time to try different career paths, to alternate the rhythm of their work lives, sometimes pushing themselves deep into the job and at others kicking back a bit, perhaps starting their own companies and, at another time, joining organizations with a mission that touches their hearts. "I think young people will benefit enormously from the transition of working longer," says Stanford's Laura Carstensen. That's the true tantalizing and enticing promise of the unretirement movement, a goal that should motivate aging boomers to launch their next act now.

CHAPTER 13

Planning for Unretirement

I'm a Jack of all trades, we'll be alright
—Bruce Springsteen

THE LATE ED KOCH, THE irrepressible three-term mayor of New York City, used to ask everyone he met, "How'm I doin'?" Once, I emerged from the subway station onto the sidewalk and there was Koch, asking his trademark question. A memorable moment. I think I gave him a thumbs-up. Koch was also a role model for unretirement. He left office at age sixty-five in 1989 and he subsequently led an active life as a television judge, radio talk show host, author, law partner, newspaper columnist, professor, commercial pitchman, among other things, before dying at age eighty-eight in 2013. Whew!

When it comes to retirement savings, the answer to Koch's question seems to be for many Americans, "not that good." Many experts agree. Teresa Ghilarducci, professor of economics at the New School for Social Research, takes a particularly stark view of the average American's retirement future. "The specter of downward mobility in retirement is a looming reality for both middle- and higher-income workers," she writes in the *New York Times*. "Almost half of middle-class workers, 49 percent, will be poor or near-poor in retirement, living on a food budget of about $5 a day."

Hold on. The retirement wealth and income picture is complicated, but much of the hand-wringing about aging boomers is misplaced. Yes, the median 401(k)s and IRAs for workers nearing retirement was some $120,000 in 2010 and the retirement savings system in the United States is deeply flawed. Nevertheless, I'm skeptical that the finances of middle- and upper-income households are so dire that poverty or near-poverty is in the cards for almost half. For one thing, just as applying the term "crisis" to Social Security's future finances is wrong, so is labeling the average American's retirement prospects a crisis misleading. For another, unretirement and encore careers will boost the household finances in the elder years for a majority of aging workers. As we've seen, the income gains from working longer are routinely underestimated. Finally, the pessimists underestimate the household gains in quality of life from embracing frugality not out of cheapness but by deliberate choice. More and more people are learning that they want fewer things while desiring more experiences and social connections. The economic returns from frugality are considerable.

A minority of older workers are at risk, with the most vulnerable concentrated among low-income households. This is the population most dependent on Social Security in their old age. It's also why calls to reduce Social Security benefits are wrong. Instead, benefits should be increased.

A more optimistic perspective informs the scholarly report *How Did the Recession of 2007–2009 Affect the Wealth and Retirement of the Near Retirement Age Population in the Health and Retirement Study?* The inflation-adjusted wealth of people nearing retirement—those ages fifty-three to fifty-eight in 2006—declined by a relatively modest 2.8 percent from the onset of the great recession to 2010, calculate economist Alan Gustman of Dartmouth University, economist Thomas Steinmeier at Texas Tech University, and research associate Nahid Tabatabai at Dartmouth. Of course, in more normal times the wealth of early boomers would have grown rather than contracted. Nevertheless, a 2.8 percent decline is hardly a catastrophic figure. "We thought the early boomers would be an enormously vulnerable group," says Gustman. "So we looked back and the answer was: not much happened."

Say what? I was doubtful. Unlike studies that focus on the state of 401(k), IRA and similar retirement savings plans, the scholars took a much broader look at the finances of early boomers. Their figures include the present value of projected lifetime Social Security benefits; defined benefit pensions and defined contribution plans such as the 401(k); the value of a primary home, net of mortgage debt; the worth of other real estate, mostly vacation homes; business assets; vehicles; financial assets such as stock holdings; and IRAs. (The researchers excluded the top 1 percent and bottom 1 percent of households from their database.) Okay, their conclusion is believable. Surprisingly, an intriguing part of the explanation behind why this particular group of boomers came out of the downturn relatively unscathed is that many owned their homes for a long time. They had built up sufficient equity in the homes over the years so that when the housing bubble burst only 5 percent found themselves "underwater"—owing more than their home was worth, the scholars say.

Of course, this is just one study, however carefully constructed. But the results echo comparable insights from other broad-based examinations. All these studies go beyond a narrow focus on retirement savings plans. An example is *The Assets and Liabilities of Cohorts: The Antecedents of Retirement Security* by J. Michael Collins, John Karl Scholz, and Ananth Seshadri from the University of Wisconsin, Madison. They used the Survey of Consumer Finances—the gold standard for wealth data in the United States—to focus on the cohort born in 1929 to 1943 (sixty-seven to eighty-one years old in 2010) and those born in 1944 to 1958 (ages fifty-two to sixty-six by 2010). Their calculations include net wealth (assets minus liabilities), financial assets (excluding vehicles, real estate, businesses, and other relatively illiquid assets), and total debt. Their results suggest that net wealth for Depression-era babies and baby boomers are relatively similar. The younger generation does have more debt, mostly mortgage debt. Among the current generation of retirees and the generation about to enter the retirement years, their net wealth and financial assets don't show any particularly troubling trends, the scholars believe. "We do not see strong evidence of the Baby Boom cohort struggling to keep up in terms of net wealth, nor is this recent age cohort suffering from undue exposure to default risks related to higher levels of borrowing," they write. Even more striking, they expect the updated results of this particular study will improve as successive age cohorts gain more education.

Here's another generation-based study. In *This Is Not Your Parents' Retirement: Comparing Retirement Income Across Generations*, Barbara Butrica and Karen Smith, research associates at the Urban Institute, and Howard Iams, senior research adviser to the Social Security Administration, try to get at this question: How is retirement income at age sixty-seven likely to change for baby boomers and the following gen Xers compared to current retirees? For answers they look at five cohorts at age sixty-seven. They are Depression-era babies (1926–1935), war babies (1936–1945), leading boomers (1946–1955), trailing boomers (1956–1965), and gen Xers (1966–1975). The results of the model and projections are rich and dense, with plenty of nuance. A key highlight is their conclusion that future retirees will have higher incomes and lower poverty rates than the current generation of retirees. That's the good news. The bad news is that their simulation predicts future retirement inequality will increase with much of the projected income gains going to the better-off segments of society.

They also expect that boomers and gen X-future retirees won't have the amount of income in retirement needed to maintain their preretirement living standards. For example, they predict the typical gen X retiree at age sixty-seven will have an income of $46,000. The comparable Depression baby at age sixty-seven had an income of $28,000—a third less. At the same time, the gen X retiree is projected to replace 84 percent of their preretirement income, less than the 95 percent replacement rate for Depression-era retirees. The projected decline in replacement rates reflects a number of factors coming together, including changes in women's earnings, differences in historic investment returns, and savings habits. (However, I expect their projections will prove too pessimistic if younger generations pursue an unretirement path.)

Let's take one more academic-type study into account, *The Success of the U.S. Retirement System.* It's by Peter Brady, Kimberly Burham, and Sarah Holden of the Investment Company Institute, the Washington, D.C.–based trade group for the investment industry. The source of the study makes me read it critically. The people who profit from the 401(k) and IRA retirement savings system find that the 401(k) and IRA work well. Surprise, right?

Still, even reading through the report with a skeptical eye, I like an aspect of it. The traditional metaphor for the U.S. retirement system is a three-legged stool—Social Security, employer-sponsored pension plans, and private savings. They argue the metaphor is too limited. Instead, they offer up the concept of a pyramid, with Social Security the foundation and additional layers representing home ownership, employer-sponsored retirement plans (private sector and government, defined benefit and defined contribution), IRAs, and other assets, such as bank deposits and mutual funds owned outside tax-sheltered retirement accounts. The composition of the retirement resource pyramid varies across households. "Available data and research show that when the majority of U.S. households retire they are able to maintain their standard of living, and more recent cohorts tend to have more resources than previous cohorts as they enter retirement," concludes the report.

All these studies emphasize that there is a group of vulnerable, aging workers. Collins, Scholz, and Seshadri highlight that the financial situation is worrisome among minority households. The authors of *The Success of the U.S. Retirement System* tempers its overall optimism, too. "Research indicates that people who retire earlier than expected due to poor health, groups that often have limited work histories, unmarried people (never married, divorced, or widowed), and those with low levels of education have lower levels of resources for retirement than others," they note. The Urban Institute scholars agree: "Regardless of the measure of well-being, certain baby boom and Gen X subgroups will remain economically vulnerable, including unmarried retirees, non-Hispanic blacks, high school dropouts, those with weak labor force attachments, and those with the lowest lifetime earnings."

Social Security is the pension plan for low-income Americans. Social

Security accounts for some 55 percent of total wealth among those
approaching retirement, but 79 percent for those in the bottom fourth
of the wealth spectrum, according to Gustman, Steinmeier, and
Tabatabai. Workers with an average salary of $30,000 a year can nearly
double their annual retirement income from Social Security by putting
in an extra eight years, from age sixty-two to seventy. Even delaying
filing for one or two years pays off. What's more, with the exception of
the very wealthy, Social Security is a critical financial foundation for
the elder years. The results from all the studies I've cited deteriorate
significantly if Social Security benefits are reduced.

The personal finances of the typical boomer should improve in
coming years, thanks to some welcome tailwinds. Boomers have the
opportunity to shore up their finances—reduce debt, increase savings,
or, most likely, a combination of the two. Progress is already being made.
Retirement account balances in the aggregate are up since 2009, surpass-
ing $10 trillion for the first time in the first quarter of 2013, according to
the Urban Institute. The Washington, D.C.–based think tank calculated
that retirement account balances were 16 percent above their 2007 peak
and 5 percent above the peak after adjusting for inflation. The nightmare
on Main Street is over. To be sure, it will take years for the housing
market to regain its health. Nevertheless, the housing market is recover-
ing, home equity is being rebuilt, and homebuilders and remodelers are
busy again. My own sense is that the economic conditions of a region
will reassert their power over real estate prices. The ebb and flow of
home values will once again depend largely on local job and income
growth. In the words of a Bloomberg Businessweek story, it's "back to
blissful boredom." Let's hope so.

Household balance sheets in the aggregate are healthier. Workers
and their families adapted to hard economic times by consuming less,
paying down debts, and putting more money into savings. The restraint
hasn't been easy, but a great deal of progress was made. For instance,
the financial obligations ratio is down sharply. This ratio calculated by
the Federal Reserve measures household debt payments to disposable
personal income. The debt ledger includes mortgage and consumer

debt payments, automobile leases, and homeowner's insurance. It's the typical household's monthly outlay for debts, the kind written out at the proverbial kitchen table. The financial obligations ratio hit a record high in the third quarter of 2007 (no surprise). By the early months of 2013 the ratio was down to the levels of the early 1980s. (The series starts in 1980.)

Household finances should continue to show gains in the aggregate. Certainly, odds are that borrowing among older workers will remain restrained. The household debt crisis of the past few years emphasized the risks of borrowing too much. Older workers will focus much more on saving. Retirement is no longer an abstraction, something that happens far down the road. No, the clock is ticking and the elder years are getting closer. Older workers are also at a stage of life when saving for retirement is realistic. A big difference is that the kids are grown, out of the house (mostly), and launching their own lives and careers. According to *The Success of the U.S. Retirement System*, household survey data from 2010 shows only 14 percent of households with a head younger than thirty-five saving primarily for retirement. Instead, a third of these households were mostly saving for education, homes, and similar big-ticket items. What about households ages fifty to sixty-four? Nearly half said retirement was the main savings goal. A mere 15 percent responded that they were saving for education and other major purchases. A majority of older Americans will be on a reasonable path for the last third of life, especially assuming unretirement. "There is no need to live in fear that you are going to be penniless in retirement," says Meir Statman, finance professor at Santa Clara University and author of *What Investors Really Want*. "Most people grow up reasonably responsible financially."

The dire portraits of the average elderly boomer falling into abject penury don't take into account the financial returns to working longer. The pessimists also miss the potential lifestyle gains from moving away from buying things to sharing experiences. Put somewhat differently: significant numbers of aging Americans will gladly adopt a thrifty or frugal mindset. The commonplace assumption is that thrift is something forced on aging Americans, the result of harsh circumstances that pushed them to become cheapskates and penny pinchers. Instead, frugality and thrift reflects mindfulness about relationships and the social good, the result of thinking through the question, "What really matters to me?"

Several years ago I picked up a book published in 1920 by Simon Wilson Straus, president of the American Society for Thrift. His description of the popular image of thrift in *History of the Thrift Movement in America* still rings true nearly a century later. "Penny-counting, cheese-paring, money-hoarding practices were looked upon by the public as the ideals sought by those who tried to encourage thrift," wrote Straus. "The man who practiced this virtue, it was felt, was he who hoarded his earnings to such an extent that he thrust aside every other consideration in order to keep from spending his pennies, his dimes, and his dollars."

Who wants to live a "cheese-paring" life? Sounds bad, doesn't it?

An emphasis on thrift doesn't mean living cheaply—far from it. Thrift or frugality is really shorthand for an approach grounded in matching our money with our values. Straus defines thrift this way: "It is the thrift that recognizes that the finer things of life must be encouraged," he writes. "The skilled workman, the artist, the musician, the landscape gardener, the designer of beautiful furniture, the members of the professions—all those, in fact, who, through the devotion of their abilities, contribute to the real betterment of mankind, must be given support through our judicious expenditures."

David Starr Jordan, founding president of Stanford University, similarly defined thrift at the 1915 International Congress for Thrift in San Francisco. He told the assembled audience that thrift "does not involve stinginess, which is an abuse of thrift, nor does it require that each item of savings should be financial investments; the money that is spent on the education of one's self or of one's family, in travel, in music, in art, or in helpfulness to others, if it brings real returns in personal development or in a better understanding of the world we live in, is in accordance with the spirit of thrift."

Who didn't have a moment during the great recession of looking around their home or apartment, opening closets and drawers, gazing into a garage and storage bins, and wondered, "Why did I buy that? Is this how I want to live? I'm paying off credit card debt for that?" Modern marketers have done a bang-up job equating the good life with owning lots of stuff, much of it paid for on the installment plan. The financial services industry stokes the fear of not having enough by depicting the American Dream during the traditional retirement years as an expensive moment, time spent paying big bucks for homes, the golf course, cruises, and exotic travel. Didn't we always know this image wasn't quite right, at least in the back of our minds? Thrift is really a mindset for trying to match spending and values. "In some ways, that's what financial independence is. You don't have to answer to anyone because you have enough," says certified financial planner Ross Levin. "When I am working with clients as they get older or near the end of life, they talk about the things they wish they had done. They talk about their regrets, and the regrets always focus on experiences. It's always something like 'I wish I had done more with the kids when they were younger.' It's never 'I wish I had bought a Mercedes.'"

By thinking through "What do I value?" the unretired will come up with far more sensible and fiscally prudent answers to the question "How much do I really need?" Harry West, the former CEO of Continuum and current senior partner at Prophet, hit on the thrift mindset. In our conversation he remarked on the flexibility and options that come with minimal expenses and debts. "When you talk to boomers, what you find is that freedom is really, really important. And you think about that because they grew up in the sixties or were born in the sixties, which was a time of freedom," says West. "Freedom is a low overhead." That expression should be a mantra for young and old workers alike. (West's wisdom reminds me of a joke a former colleague loved to tell. A fisherman lives on an island. He makes a living taking people out on his boat to fish. He loves the water, the rhythm of his days, the simplicity and beauty of everyday life. Life is good. One day he takes a multimillionaire out to fish. The multimillionaire chatters on about how beautiful is the sea. This is what life is all about, he pronounces. He proceeds to tell the fisherman that he should borrow lots of money and buy a fleet of fishing boats. "Why should I do that?"

asks the fisherman. "Well, you would work hard but eventually you would make so much money that you could take a vacation and enjoy the water and fishing! Like me!" As a Shaker hymn beautifully says, "It's a gift to be simple and a gift to be free.")

Frugality has implications for thinking about the replacement rate, a workhorse concept in financial planning for retirement. The basic rule of thumb is that replacement rates should be in the 70 to 85 percent range. I know you have to start from some kind of baseline, but this is a classic example where averages are highly misleading. The percentage of income that could work for me might be very different from your target range. More important, with frugality the desired replacement rate may be much less than figures routinely touted by the financial services industry.

The frugal mindset is spreading from society's tributaries into the mainstream, largely thanks to growing awareness of sustainability. The catchphrase "sustainability" has many shades of meaning, but several themes have emerged. Concerns over global warming. Fears of environmental degradation. The desire to cut down on waste. Worries over the health of communities. My favorite definition of sustainability comes from the late actor and nonprofit entrepreneur Paul Newman: "We are such spendthrifts with our lives," said Newman. "The trick of living is to slip on and off the planet with the least fuss you can muster. I'm not running for sainthood. I just happen to think that in life we need to be a little like the farmer, who puts back into the soil what he takes out." For many people, frugal is green and green is frugal.

The urban scholar Richard Florida, in his book *The Great Reset*, looked at potential economic and social changes coming in the United States following the great recession. Despite the undeniable traumas of the downturn and its immediate aftermath, Florida saw some welcome changes unfolding in future years. His bottom-line forecast could have been addressed to the personal finances of aging workers and the future unretired. "The promise of the current Reset is the opportunity for a life made better not by ownership of real estate, appliances, cars, and all manner of material goods, but by greater flexibility and lower levels of debt, more time with family and friends, greater promise of personal development, and access to more and better experiences." Florida has captured the promise that lies in the unretirement movement, particularly for younger generations that will learn from an older generation's example.

Unretirement will reshape how we think about retirement planning. Over the past three decades the baby boom generation has been taught to equate preparing for retirement with investing in the markets. In essence, the retirement planning mantra has been stocks for the long haul, asset allocation, and picking mutual funds. The equation has always been somewhat wrong and, deep down, we've always known we shouldn't rely on Wall Street's lush return promises. Our doubts were largely kept at bay through the persuasive genius of the Wall Street marketing machine. It took two bear markets and two recessions in less than a decade for boomers to realize what many had sensed all along: The core of retirement planning isn't investing, it's jobs.

The new retirement planning mantra: Encore jobs, networking, and delay filing for Social Security benefits. My advice is to put down yearend retirement portfolio results. Set aside market predictions and mutual fund performance charts. Turn off your computer and tablet. Instead, focus on what kind of job and career you'd like to do as you get older. Invest in your human capital, maintain your skills, and add to your education. Investigate your options by picking up a book like Marci Alboher's *The Encore Career Handbook: How to Make a Living and a Difference in the Second Half of Life* or Kerry Hannon's *Great Jobs for Everyone 50+: Finding Work That Keeps You Happy and Healthy . . And Pays the Bills.* "You should be looking for the kind of jobs you could do that are challenging and interesting and offer an acceptable income," says Arthur Koff, the septuagenarian founder of Retired Brains, an online portal for retirees and near-retirees. "The time to do it is while you're working, yet a lot of people don't make the plan."

Next Chapter in Kansas City, Kansas, is housed in a modest brick structure in a section of town where the courts are located. Karen Hostetler is director of Next Chapter. She turned sixty-five in 2013. Next

Chapter is a small grassroots organization with a mission of helping older workers in transition toward unretirement. I met with Next Chapter activists Pat Brune, Cris Siebenlist, and Hostetler in a conference room in the fall of 2013. There was a lively conversation and at one point planning for unretirement came up.

> SIEBENLIST: Frankly, not everyone will figure it out. They'll do a little bit of this and a little bit of that. Other people will float around for a while and say, Is this all there is?
>
> HOSTETLER: You need to plan. It takes commitment to figure it out.
>
> BRUNE: If I could change my transition to what I did, it would have been to be more intentional. I said yes to what came along.
>
> HOSTETLER: Don't jump into the first thing that comes along.
>
> BRUNE: I only see my intentions looking back. It's only later that I see how the dots are connected.

Invest in your networks of family, friends, colleagues, and acquaintances. Scholars have documented that about half or more of all jobs come through such informal channels and connections. You'll want to reach out to others in similar circumstances, people who are also trying to figure out their next stage of life.

Ralph Warner is the founder of Nolo.com, a self-help legal guide business, and author of *Get a Life: You Don't Need a Million to Retire Well*. He gives this example: Let's say it's a dream of yours to work on environmental causes. The pressures of daily life stop you from getting engaged, however. You'll get to it tomorrow. Now you're sixty-five or seventy years old. You head toward an environmental organization you admire and say, "Here I am. How can I help you?' The answer is going to be probably not much," says Warner. "Yes, you'll be able to help out with the phones or mailings as a volunteer. There's nothing wrong with that. But what if you want more?" he asks. "Now, take that same person who in their forties or fifties gets involved with several local environmental groups and at age seventy is a respected senior person. They're valued and they're needed. They earned it." And, I would add, if you need an income at that moment, you're worth it. You've just won the aging boomer trifecta: An income, a community, and a mission.

Don't get me wrong: Saving is important. Max out your 401(k) and IRA. Create a well-diversified, low-fee retirement savings portfolio. Savings is your margin of safety because life has a way of upending well-thought-out plans. An unexpectedly ill parent. A divorced child moving back in with parents. For Robert Lawrence, it was a detached retina.

Lawrence was a teacher at Jefferson Community College, part of the Kentucky Community and Technical College system in Louisville. He taught there for about twenty years, commuting up to ten weeks every year to visit his partner in New York City. Lawrence planned on retiring at age sixty-six. Just after his sixty-fourth birthday, he stopped by a colleague's office for a brief hello and ended up listening to a long, detailed explanation of why his colleague planned to keep working until age seventy. The conversation convinced Lawrence to hold off retirement for another six years.

That is, until two months later. His retina detached and several surgical repairs didn't hold. He retired at age sixty-five in 2005, sold his home, downsized, and moved into his partner's condo in Jackson Heights, Queens. His partner, age seventy-five, is a consulting engineer, often putting in forty-hour workweeks. "If it had not been for health reasons I certainly would have been working," says Lawrence.

A surgeon in New York fixed his retina. Lawrence is busy. He volunteers at a hospice in Manhattan, visits with grieving caregivers after the death of a loved one, and helps out at his local church. With a comfortable pension and some savings he chose flexibility over pay. The main reason: Lawrence and his partner are railroad "rare mileage" collectors. "We're railroad fanatics," he says. They ride the rails throughout the United States, often seeking out obscure lines to collect their miles. "The only reason I did not seek out teaching in New York is my partner didn't want me to because of these trips," adds Lawrence. "He's in command of his own time as a consultant. If you're teaching, you're not."

When it comes to retirement planning the goal should be to put your savings on autopilot as much as possible. Instead, spend your time creating opportunities for an income and meaning throughout a lifetime. The return on the unretirement investment will dwarf anything you'll get from picking a good mutual fund.

CHAPTER 14

The Economic Possibilities for Grandparents

We can never know about the days to come
But we think about them anyway
                                    —Carly Simon

COULD JOHN MAYNARD KEYNES BE RIGHT about 2030? No, not the Depression-era Keynes who wrote the playbook policy makers still consult for ideas on how to combat recessions. Instead, the Keynes of the bold forecast that the "economic problem" of insufficient wealth to meet everyone's everyday needs would be solved in a hundred years. Keynes made the prediction that economic abundance would replace economic scarcity in a 1930 article, "Economic Possibilities for our Grandchildren."

The essay opens with the gloomy impact of the Great Depression:

> We are suffering just now from a bad attack of economic pessi-
> mism. It is common to hear people say that the epoch of
> enormous economic progress which characterized the nine-
> teenth century is over; the rapid improvement in the standard
> of living is now going to slow down ... That a decline in

prosperity is more likely than an improvement in the decade
which lies ahead of us.

Sound familiar? Keynes didn't buy the conventional miserable outlook.

> We are suffering, not from the rheumatics of old age, but from
> the growing-pains of over-rapid changes, from the painfulness
> of readjustment between one economic period and another . . .
> The prevailing world depression, the enormous anomaly of
> unemployment in a world full of wants, the disastrous mistakes
> we have made, blind us to what is going on under the surface—
> to the true interpretation of the trend of things.

"What," he memorably asks, "are the economic possibilities for our
grandchildren?"

Keynes was optimistic about their prospects. The economy over the
next hundred years would benefit from a number of factors. Strong
productivity growth in manufacturing, agriculture, and mining was critical to his outlook. So were striking improvements in transportation
networks and increases in capital invested in new equipment and technologies. Taken altogether, Keynes predicted that the standard of living
in developed nations would be between four and eight times as high as
it was when his essay was published. Not bad for a reasoned guesstimate,
considering in the United States income per person is roughly six times
what the figure was in 1930, noted Ben Bernanke when he was head of
the Federal Reserve.

Once again we're living through a period of pessimism. Forecasts of
permanently high unemployment and long-term economic stagnation
are commonplace. Deepening the job gloom are the writings of economists, technologists, and hedge-fund managers who see middle-class jobs
wiped out by automation, robots, artificial intelligence, and digital
networks. It isn't hard to imagine a dystopian future defined by technological unemployment and underemployment for the mass of workers,
young and old alike. Every day, it seems, we hear another story about

automation taking away jobs, and not just menial labor. Think high-speed trading on Wall Street. The lightning-quick trades account for much of the volume on the major stock exchanges, yet the action is driven by computers and software communicating with other computers and software, supervised and monitored by at most a relative handful of highly compensated workers. Years ago, the trading activity would have been supported by a small army of people, including junior traders, clerks, market makers, and floor brokers.

The anxiety about our economic future is understandable considering the trauma of the recent past. The need for more paid positions, lots of them, is apparent. And not just any job, but engaging work that pays decent wages and offers workers prospects for improvement and creative expression. Of course, it's impossible to say what lies ahead. (The legendary movie mogul Samuel Goldwyn once quipped, "Never make predictions, especially about the future.") Still, Keynes's framework for thinking about the future economy suggests that we're witnessing another painful adjustment from one economic period into another era. Scholars like Erik Brynjolfsson and Andrew McAfee of MIT; W. Brian Arthur, visiting researcher with the Intelligent Systems Lab at the Palo Alto Research Center; creative-class theorist Richard Florida; *Wired* cofounder and senior maverick at the magazine Kevin Kelly; and, more recently, economist Tyler Cowen of George Mason University, have made a strong case that we're not only living through a transition toward an economy dominated by a digital ecosystem but that the future is vibrant. They differ on the timing, but they all foresee the potential for healthy wealth creation from innovation in the new economy. "Technological progress—in particular, improvements in computer hardware, software, and networks—has been so rapid and so surprising that many present-day organizations, institutions, policies, and mindsets are not keeping up," write Brynjolfsson and McAfee, scholars at the MIT Sloan School of Management in *Race Against the Machine*. Adds W. Brian Arthur in "The Second Economy," an article for McKinsey & Company: "Is this the biggest change since the Industrial Revolution? Well, without sticking my neck out too far, I believe so."

The central feature of the digital economy at the moment is the rapid evolution of information technologies. The personal computer entered the workplace about three decades ago. The commercial dawn of the Web took place in 1995 with the initial public offering of Netscape. Since then computing power and digital networks have expanded exponentially. For example, in fifteen of the U.S. economy's seventeen sectors, companies with more than a thousand employees store more than 235 terabytes of data, on average—more data than in the Library of Congress, according to McKinsey. By the time you read that figure the number will be much larger.

The digital economy is a major force behind advances in biotechnology and medical treatments. Powerful computers and robots are critical in developing solar power and other clean-energy technologies. All kinds of organizations are using Big Data techniques to boost efficiencies and customize their products and services. Each transformation feeds off the other, reaching deep into everyday economic life, creating new possibilities and profit opportunities, such as Google's driverless software-controlled car and the Watson supercomputer designed to play *Jeopardy!* "It's helping architects design buildings, it's tracking sales and inventory, getting goods from here to there, executing trades and banking operations, controlling manufacturing equipment, making design calculations, billing clients, navigating aircraft, helping diagnose patients, and guiding laparoscopic surgeries," writes Arthur in "The Second Economy." Add Brnjolfsson and McAfee in "Winning the Race with Ever-Smarter Machines": "Digitization, in other words, is not a single project providing one-time benefits. Instead, it's an ongoing process of creative destruction; innovators use both new and established technologies to make deep changes at the level of the task, the job, the process—and even the organization itself."

Simply put: You ain't see nothin' yet.

Of course, not everyone buys the vision of future economic dynamism and vibrant innovation. A thoughtful digital-boom skeptic is Robert Gordon, economist at Northwestern University. In two scholarly papers, "Is U.S. Economic Growth Over? Faltering Innovation Confronts the Six

Headwinds" and "The Demise of U.S. Economic Gorwth: Restatement, Rebuttal, and Reflections," Gordon argues that the United States is doomed to slow growth for a long time. The core of his perspective is that digital-based innovations pale in their economic and social impact compared with the wave of transformational innovations that started in the nineteenth century, such as electricity, the internal combustion engine, the telephone, and municipal waterworks. Even if you don't buy his innovation skepticism, Gordon also believes an aging population, faltering education gains, rising income inequality, and government debt are such daunting headwinds that economic growth in the United States will remain at sub-par levels.

Gordon raises a number of powerful cautions against simplistic techo-optimism. But after reading his papers I think he underestimates the depth of the latest creative advances in software, robotics, and related technologies. He downplays how the digital transformation is gathering momentum, spreading throughout the economy. Imagine, only three decades ago, the Internet was an obscure network, mostly for researchers; today almost 2 billion people worldwide are connected, with nearly $8 trillion traded through e-commerce. What might the digitally networked global economy look like in another three decades?

Think of it this way: There is no shortage of potential ideas that could become products and services. Economic growth theorist Paul Romer recommends that skeptics imagine one hundred jars. Each jar contains one element from the periodic table. (Remember memorizing the periodic table?) A simple calculation (well, simple for him) shows that sampling from the jars and mixing the elements together allows for ten raised to the thirtieth power of different mixtures. No matter how you look at it, that's a big number. What's more, there are actually many more possibilities than this calculation suggests because you could test out the various combinations at different pressures and temperatures, he adds. "In fact," writes Romer, "if each of the 5 billion or so people on earth had tried one new mixture every second since the Big Bang, we would only have tried about 5 percent of the possibilities." Okay, it's a really big number.[1]

Romer draws a similar lesson from a deck of cards. There are about ten to the sixty-eighth power ways to order a deck of cards. Strange as it may seem, Romer says it's mathematically easy for us to hold a deck of cards arranged in a way that never existed before. "For reasons that seem to spring from some deep feature of human psychology, we find it difficult to believe that so many possibilities could emerge from familiar objects such as decks of cards or collections of jars," he writes. "We therefore tend to agree with the pessimist who argues, for example, that almost all the good mixtures from the elements of the periodic table have already been found. But if we have tried only a vanishingly small fraction of the mixtures, how could we possibly have found all the good ones?" In an increasingly digitally networked, evolving global economy with ever-greater exchanges of information and ideas, we've barely touched on the economic possibilities. Economics is not a dismal science!

One message in the periodic table and a deck of cards is that jobs will be created that we can't even picture at the moment. The march of technological innovation both destroys and creates jobs. Joseph Schumpeter, a twentieth-century economist, captured the dynamic with his evocative metaphor of "creative destruction." The catchphrase captures the process by which new technologies, new markets, and new organizations supplant the old. We tend to celebrate that creativity and process and underplay the destruction side of the equation. The dynamism of technological innovation is devastatingly painful. In 1800, some three quarters of the labor force worked in agriculture. By 1910, agricultural jobs had declined to less than a third of the total work force, according to Susan Carter at the Center for Social and Economic Policy, University of California, Riverside. Meanwhile, manufacturing employed one in five workers. Smokestack America dominated the global economy in the 1950s and 1960s, but many factory workers never recovered from losing well-paying manufacturing jobs as industrial companies moved from the Northeast and Midwest to cheaper sites in the South and West and then to emerging markets like China.

When I visited the Hilton Cincinnati Netherland Plaza in downtown Cincinnati a few years ago I saw pictures of the job upheaval. The hotel opened in 1931, a premier example of French art deco in America. (The building influenced the design of the Empire State Building.) In one corner of the lobby are striking photographs from the early years. One photo shows a long line of women handling a bank of hotel phones. Another picture has a group of men in the basement running a printing press for the hotel's daily newsletter and menus. These jobs are long gone, replaced by e-mail and desktop publishing, yet plenty of jobs have been created since then. Fast forward to the early 2000s. A quarter of American workers were employed in jobs that weren't listed in the Census Bureau's occupation codes in 1967. Among the unimagined jobs is Webmaster. The job title didn't really exist until the midnineties with the commercial expansion of the Internet. The same goes for app developer with the advent of Apple's iPhone in 2007. "What's unpredictable are the physical gizmos that will trigger a multiplier effect with employment," says Amar Bhidé, professor of international business at the Fletcher School of Law and Diplomacy, Tufts University. Says Mark Thoma, economist at the University of Oregon: "There will be jobs we can't imagine right now."

Even if you don't buy the story that information technologies will generate healthy job creation, it isn't hard to see where jobs will emerge, assuming modest levels of economic activity. Job prospects look good in many service-sector occupations, such as home health care, social work, and counseling. The real issue is that many fast-growing occupations offer low pay and few (if any) benefits. For the past three hundred years or so the way we've distributed economic bounty is through jobs, with pay levels supplemented by union pressure, child labor laws, pensions, and other share-the-wealth strategies. The challenge of our increasingly high-tech economy is how to take a hefty slice of the economic bounty to offer ordinary workers—young and old alike—the reality of good jobs with decent compensation. In a sense, how do we expropriate the wealth created by robots to boost the pay of ordinary workers? Government, business, and educational institutions will have ample resources to tap for pursuing strategies that turn the dream of an inclusive, high-employment society into reality.

The grassroots unretirement movement is a major counterforce against the headwinds of aging, fiscal pressures, and educational letdowns highlighted by Robert Gordon and others. The drive to lead productive lives well into the latter stages of life can generate economic dynamism and social creativity and, at the same time, reduce the nation's fiscal burdens. Building incentives for unretirement into the American way of life will also open up opportunities for improving skills and education levels over a long work life, for some people even into their eighties.

In 2013, then Fed chairman Ben Bernanke addressed the new graduates at Bard College at Simon's Rock. "The history of technological innovation and economic development teaches us that change is the only constant," he said. "During your working lives, you will have to reinvent yourselves many times. Success and satisfaction will not come from mastering a fixed body of knowledge but from constant adaptation and creativity in a rapidly changing world."

Bernanke was talking to newly minted college graduates. He could have been addressing aging boomers, however. The baby boom generation is behind many changes in the workplace over the past four decades. Whether the gauge is minority, gender, or merit, organizations are more welcoming and more inclusive than in the '50s and '60s. Boomers have some years left in them to overhaul for the better society's vision of the last stage of life on the job. As I said toward the beginning of this book, the aging of the population is a wonderful moment to seize and to celebrate and to embrace. Time to get to work.

Afterword

MARY WHITE CAPTURES THE SPIRIT of unretirement. She works with
workers who have lost their jobs in St. Paul, Minnesota. When I interviewed her, she told me that she started working at age sixteen and
she continued working throughout college. When she graduated she
had a number of jobs, ending up in employee training at Control Data,
the once high-flying computer company. Sixteen years later she set up
her own employee-training consulting business in 2001. The venture
didn't survive the economic fallout from the bursting of the dot-com
bubble and the tragedy of 9/11. She quickly went to plan B, joining
HIRED, a dislocated-worker program. Her paycheck is less than what
she was making at Control Data and that's without adjusting for inflation. She had me laughing the whole time she was relaying her story.

I asked what "retirement" means for her. She qualifies for Medicare in
two years. At that point, she says, she will probably join one of her twelve
siblings, a school nurse in her late fifties, in Charlotte, North Carolina.
When it's time to move, "I would be working, but with the sister that
makes me laugh," White chuckles. "I would still do things, maybe career
counseling."

Adrian Dantley is another inspiring unretirement stalwart. He's a
fifty-eight-year-old former DeMatha High School, Notre Dame, and NBA
basketball star. The news broke in 2013 that Dantley is earning some
$14,000 a year as a part-time crossing guard at a middle school in Silver
Spring, Maryland, not far from where he lives. Ah, yet one more example
of a professional athlete who has fallen far, right? Hardly. Dantley lives
well. He's independently wealthy after fifteen years in the pros and

another seven years as a coach. "Nah, I just did it for the kids," he told the *Washington Post.* "I just didn't want to sit around the house all day."

That sentence could be the bumper sticker for the unretirement improv act.

DIY Research

Please, don't rush into this thing
—Percy Sledge

THE UNRETIREMENT INDUSTRY MAY BE in its infancy, but there are still plenty of resources to consult. I've compiled a somewhat idiosyncratic list to help you get started on your unretirement journey. The good news is that almost all the books and websites I mention offer additional resources to investigate. My focus is on places to learn more about encore careers and second acts, although I've included some books and research centers that are more about history, economics, and labor-market trends.

Websites such as LinkedIn, Manpower, and Monster are useful for senior workers, but I've skipped listing those and similar sites. They reach out to a much broader employment community and they're familiar since they show up on almost any job-hunt list.

Have fun with your exploration, and good luck with your unretirement transition.

Two web-based portals are worth highlighting up front. Encore.org is a pivotal organization and its website is at www.encore.org. The AARP at www.aarp.org is a behemoth in the senior industry. Other information-rich portals for further research include:

American Association of Community Colleges, Plus 50
(programs geared toward older students): plus50.aacc
.nche.edu

Life Planning Network (a community of professionals):
www.lifeplanningnetwork.org

Transition Network (resources for professional women
over fifty): www.thetransitionnetwork.org

Vital Aging Network (community discussions of aging):
www.vital-aging-network.org

The scholarship in the field of aging and work is diverse and fascinating.
You can gain insight into all kinds of senior trends from the research and
data sets at any of these centers:

AgingStats (federal interagency on aging-related statistics):
www.agingstats.gov

Brookings Institution: www.brookings.edu

Center for Retirement Research at Boston College: http://crr
.bc.edu/

Employee Benefit Research Institute: www.ebri.org

Ewing Marion Kauffman Foundation: www.kauffman.org

John J. Heldrich Center for Workforce Development at
Rutgers University: www.heldrich.rutgers.edu

Retirement Research Center at the University of Michigan:
www.mrrc.isr.umich.edu

Sloan Center on Aging and Work at Boston College: www
.bc.edu/agingandwork

Stanford Center on Longevity: http://longevity3.stanford.edu

Urban Institute: www.urban.org

Books for policy insights, personal inspiration, and practical guidance:

*Old Age in the New Land: The American Experience Since
1790* by W. Andrew Achenbaum

The Encore Career Handbook: How to Make a Living and a Difference in the Second Half of Life by Marci Alboher

Composing a Further Life: The Age of Active Wisdom by Mary Catherine Bateson

Risk Less and Prosper: Your Guide to Safer Investing by Zvi Bodi and Rachelle Taqqu

Closing the Deficit: How Much Can Later Retirement Help by Gary Burtless and Henry J. Aaron (editors)

Managing the Older Worker by Peter Cappelli and Bill Novelli

A Long Bright Future: Happiness, Health, and Financial Security in an Age of Increased Longevity by Laura L. Carstensen

Live Smart After 50! by Natalie Eldridge (editor)

The New Frugality: How to Consume Less, Save More, and Live Better by Chris Farrell

What Should I Do with the Rest of My Life? True Stories of Finding Success, Passion, and New Meaning in the Second Half of Life by Bruce Frankel

The Big Shift: Navigating the New Stage Beyond Midlife by Marc Freedman

Encore: Finding Work that Matters in the Second Half of Life by Marc Freedman

A History of Retirement by William Graebner

Great Jobs for Everyone 50+: Finding Work That Keeps You Happy and Healthy . . . And Pays the Bills by Kerry Hannon

What's Next? Follow Your Passion and Find Your Dream Job by Kerry Hannon

The Hard Times Guide to Retirement Security: Practical Strategies for Money, Work, and Living by Mark Miller

Working Longer by Alicia Munnell and Steven A. Sass

Aging and Old Age by Richard Posner

Old Age in English History by Pat Thane

Smart Women Don't Retire—They Break Free by Transition
Network and Gail Rentsch

Get a Life: You Don't Need a Million to Retire Well by Ralph
Warner

Some online resources focused on jobs for seniors, from temp work to
full-time employment:

Jobs Over 50: http://jobsover50.com

ReServe: www.reserveinc.org

Retired Brains: www.retiredbrains.com

Retirement Jobs: http://retirementjobs.com

Seniors4Hire: http://seniors4hire.org

What's Next: www.whatsnext.com

Workforce50: www.workforce50.com

There are a number of places for senior entrepreneurs to visit for guidance and help. Many of these websites offer a shortcut for finding local
organizations promoting entrepreneurship:

Babson College (top-ranked school for entrepreneurship):
www.babson.edu

Center for Productive Longevity: http://ctrpl.org

League of Extraordinary Coworking Spaces (a coworking
network): http://lexc.org

National Association of Business Incubators: www.nbia.org

Score (network of mentors and advice for entrepreneurs):
www.score.org

Senior Entrepreneurship Works: http://seniorentrepreneur
shipworks.org

Small Business Administration: www.sba.gov

There is no shortage of financial planning calculators online. But for the
DIY approach, I like two comprehensive sites in particular. Both are
good on Social Security. Henry "Bud" Hebeler is the force behind www

.analyzenow.com. It offers users the option of simple planners that are free to more complicated ones available for a modest charge. Hebeler's advice is conservative. He emphasizes savings. When things go wrong or you make a financial mistake he doesn't want the result to be catastrophic.

Another financial planning calculator I like is the brainchild of Boston University economics professor Laurence Kotlikoff. At www.esplanner .com, it has a basic planner for free. Give it a try to see how you like it. But you'll want the firm's centerpiece program if you decide to go with it. The program is time-consuming and requires lots of data. But it also spews out a lot of interesting analysis and suggestions.

Acknowledgments

NOT THAT LONG AGO, I had lunch with Ross Levin, a certified financial planner and head of Accredited Investors, Inc. in the Twin Cities. We get together for lunch periodically. At one point I ran some ideas by him. He convinced me to focus on writing a book about rethinking retirement. Thanks, Ross.

Later on I met with Marc Freedman, the visionary behind Encore.org, for coffee at the original Peet's Coffee & Tea store in Berkeley, California. We checked up on family, friends, and work. When we finished our drinks we took a walk into the Berkeley hills. It was a beautiful day, and we covered so many topics on that walk, finally catching our breath on the top of a hill with a stunning view of San Francisco Bay. (I wish I had taped our conversation, but I knew I'd mostly capture my labored breathing.) Freedman's enthusiasm for the project was infectious and he shared so many ideas during that walk. Thanks, Marc.

Looking back, a heartfelt thanks to the experts, older workers, senior entrepreneurs, and people in transition who took the time to share their stories and insights with me. I learned so much from their experiences and I enjoyed the conversations. Several people were remarkably generous with their time and helped shape the book. Art Rolnick, senior fellow and codirector of the Human Capital Research Collaborative at the Humphrey School of Public Affairs at the University of Minnesota, closely read an early draft, and I took his reactions to heart (well, most of them). Other invaluable readers were Stephen Smith, Peter Farrell, Ron Jepperson, and Richard Yankwich. I'm especially grateful to Alison McGhee, the highly accomplished author and editor. She did a terrific job going through a rough manuscript and offering sound guidance for thinking through what I was trying to say on the page (and she did it kindly). Colleague Laurie Stern conducted several interviews and reporter Frankie Barnhill helped out too. Tony, my music-loving, leading-edge baby boomer brother, eagerly took on the job of finding some of the lyrics that start each chapter.

You wouldn't be reading this book if Peter Ginna, former publisher and editorial director at Bloomsbury Press, hadn't believed in the project. Rob Galloway and George Gibson of Bloomsbury seamlessly picked up the task of shepherding it to publication when Peter left for a new adventure. I've known book agent Joelle Delbourgo for a long time now and she is always professional and warm throughout the process of bringing a project to fruition. Cathy Paper, the entrepreneur behind RockPaperStar, has been an enthusiastic supporter. My former boss and good friend Sarah Lutman let me test out the unretirement idea in one of her What's Up series of conversations about town. My work base is at American Public Media, the public radio programming behemoth. A special nod to the chief executive officer, Jon McTaggart, and the chief operating officer, Dave Kansas, for creating an environment where aspiring authors can take a chance.

I'd probably still be writing drafts of the manuscript—okay, I would still be at the keyboard—without Carolyn Wall's gin and tonics and wonderful company. Aren't you glad it's done? Time to get out the convertible!

A final note, which dog lovers will understand. Mollie Farrell, a Wheaten terrier, lived for more than seventeen years. Despite her advancing age, Mollie made it through a last harsh Minnesota winter and the final writing of this book. Yes, she slowed down and didn't bark at neighborhood dogs the way she once did. She had her brief moments of blankness. Still, Mollie hobbled around until *Unretirement* was done. She had a good, long life.

Notes

UNRETIREMENT OWES A DEBT TO the research of so many scholars, and acknowledgment of their work is critical. At the same time, *Unretirement* isn't an academic text, and I want it to appeal to a broad audience. The Internet has made it easy to look up references and attributions. In most cases, I tried to put credit in the text. So, if I mention a book or article in the text and it's easy to find the reference by putting the information in your search engine, I didn't include it in the endnotes.

Chapter 1

1   Robert Shackleton, *Baby Boomers' Retirement Prospects: An Overview*, Congressional Budget Office Study, November 2003.
2   Steve Utkus, "Too Gloomy a View," Vanguard blog, August 21, 2012.
3   Eugene Steuerle, "Comments by Eugene Steuerle," in *Closing the Deficit: How Much Can Later Retirement Help*, ed. Gary Burtless and Henry Aaron (Washington, D.C.: Brookings Institution, 2013).
4   Sara Rix, presentation at the Gerontological Society of America annual meeting, New Orleans, November 2013.

Chapter 3

1   Richard W. Johnson, Gordon B. T. Mermin, and Eric J. Toder, "Will Employers Want Aging Boomers?" Urban Institute, 2008.

Chapter 4

1   Dean Baker, "The Nonsense About a Demographic Crisis," Beat the Press blog at the Center for Economic and Policy Research, December 8, 2012.

2   Richard Johnson and Karen Smith, "Impact of Higher Retirement Ages on Public Budgets: Simulation Results from DYNASIM3," in *Closing the Deficit*, ed. Burtless and Aaron.

3   Henry J. Aaron, "Entitlements and Population Aging: Crisis, Problem, or Opportunity," Stanford Institute for Economic Policy Research, 2012.

4   David Cutler, Ezekiel Emanuel, and Topher Spiro, "How the Federal Government Can Save $100 Billion or More in Health-Care Costs: Alternatives to Blunt, Misguided Policies that Merely Shift Costs," Center for American Progress, October 2011.

5   Dean Baker, "Liberals Working for the Right," www.truth-out.org, June 18, 2012.

6   "Macroeconomics of Recessions," panel discussion on January 18, 2013. The rough transcript is housed at Professor Brad DeLong's Grasping Reality blog.

7   Rita Choula, Lynn Feinberg, Ari Houser, and Susan C. Reinhard, "Valuing the Invaluable: 2011 Update—The Growing Contributions and Costs of Family Caregiving," AARP Public Policy Institute, 2011.

8   Stephanie Coontz, "The Family Revolution," greatergood.berkeley. edu, September 2007.

Chapter 5

1   Kim Lee DeAngelis, "Reverse Mentoring at the Hartford: Cross-Generational Transfer of Knowledge About Social Media," Center on Aging and Work at Boston College, May 2013.

2   Giovanni Peri, "The Effect of Immigrants on U.S. Employment and Productivity," Federal Reserve Bank of San Francisco, August 30, 2010.

3 Pew Research, "When Baby Boomers Delay Retirement, Do Younger Workers Suffer?" issue brief, Economic Mobility Project, September 2012.

4 Benjamin F. Jones, "Age and Great Invention," *Review of Economics and Statistics* 92, no. 1 (2010): 1–14.

5 Sara Czaja, "Embracing Boomers: How Workplace Design for Maturing Knowledge Workers Benefits Everyone," Herman Miller, 2005.

6 Cindy Lustig and Patricia A. Reuter-Lorenz, "Brain Aging: Reorganizing Discoveries about the Aging Mind," *Current Opinion in Neurobiology* 15, no. 2 (2005): 245–251.

7 David Bank, "David Galenson: World Shouldn't Look Past 'the Wisdom of the Elders,'" Encore.org, November 7, 2007.

8 Richard Florida, *The Rise of the Creative Class*, 10th Anniversary Edition (New York: Basic Books, 2012).

9 Raj Aggarwal, Krisztina Holly, Alex Salkever, and Vivek Wadhwa, "Anatomy of an Entrepreneur: Family Background and Motivation," Kauffman Foundation Small Research Projects Research, July 7, 2007.

10 Karl Marx, *Capital: An Abridged Edition*, ed. David McClellan (New York: Oxford World's Classic, 2008).

11 Daniel Bell, *Work and Its Discontents: The Cult of Efficiency in America* (Boston: Beacon Press, 1956).

Chapter 6

1 Peter Cappelli, interview with Knowledge@Wharton, University of Pennsylvania, December 6, 2010.

2 U.S. Equal Employment Opportunity, Selected List of Pending and Resolved Cases Under the Age Discrimination in Employment Act (ADEA), August 2012.

Chapter 7

1 W. Andrew Achenbaum, *Old Age in the New Land* (Baltimore: Johns Hopkins University Press, 1978).

2 Social Security Administration, Age 65 Retirement, http://www.ssa.gov/history/age65.html.

3 Abraham Epstein, *Facing Old Age* (New York: Alfred A. Knopf, 1922).

4 William Graebner, in *History of Retirement: The Meaning and Function of an American Institution, 1885–1978* (New Haven: Yale University Press, 1980). Graebner a terrific discussion of Osler. You can also read a draft of Osler's talk online at profiles.nlm.nih.gov/ps/access/GFBBYH.pdf.

5 Epstein, *Facing Old Age.*

6 Carole Haber, *Beyond Sixty-Five: The Dilemma of Old Age in America's Past* (Cambridge: Cambridge University Press, 1983).

Chapter 8

1 Brian Gratton, "The Poverty of Impoverishment Theory: The Economic Well-Being of the Elderly, 1890–1950," *Journal of Economic History* 56, no. 1 (March 1996): 39–61.

2 Robert Whaples, "Pensions, Politics, and the Elderly: Historic Social Movements and Their Lessons for Our Aging Society," book review, www.EH.net.

Chapter 9

1 Jerry Jordan, "Money and Monetary Policy for the 21st Century," Fraser Institute, Critical Issues Bulletin, 2005.

2 Jack VanDerhei Statement for the Record, United States Senate hearing on *The Role of Social Security, Defined Benefits, and Private Retirement Accounts in the Face of the Retirement Crisis*, December 18, 2013.

3 Dean Baker, "Work-Sharing: An Effective Tool against Chronic Unemployment," testimony before the Congressional Black Caucus, at a hearing on "Out of Work but Not Out of Hope: Addressing the Crisis of the Chronically Unemployed," March 17, 2010.

Chapter 10

1 Neil Howe, Richard Jackson, and Tobias Peter, "The Global Aging Preparedness Index," Second Edition, Center for Strategic and International Studies, 2013.

Chapter 12

1 Richard W. Johnson, Gordon B. T. Mermin, and Eric J. Toder, "Will Employers Want Aging Boomers?" Urban Institute, July 2008.
2 Gary Burtless, "Who Is Delaying Retirement?" in *Closing the Deficit: How Much Can Later Retirement Help?* ed. Burtless and Aaron.

Chapter 14

1 Paul Romer, "Economic Growth and Investment in Children," *Daedalus* 123, no. 4 (1994): 141–154.

Index

Note on the Author

CHRIS FARRELL IS SENIOR ECONOMICS contributor at Marketplace, American Public Media's nationally syndicated public radio business and personal finance programs. He is also economics commentator for Minnesota Public Radio. An award-winning journalist, Chris is a contributing editor for *Bloomberg Businessweek*. He is also the author of *The New Frugality*. He lives in St. Paul, Minnesota.